142.7
C694e

Collins, James
Daniel.

The existentialists

DATE			
MAY 3 1982			

The Existentialists

THE

Existentialists

A Critical Study

BY

JAMES COLLINS

Associate Professor of
Philosophy at St. Louis University

GREENWOOD PRESS, PUBLISHERS
WESTPORT, CONNECTICUT

Library of Congress Cataloging in Publication Data

Collins, James Daniel.
   The existentialists.

   Reprint of the ed. published by Regnery, Chicago.
   Bibliography: p.
   Includes index.
   1. Existentialism. I. Title.
   [B819.C6 1977]   142'.7   77-2918
   ISBN 0-8371-9565-9

Copyright 1952

HENRY REGNERY COMPANY

Originally published in 1952 by Henry Regnery Company,
Chicago

Reprinted with the permission of Henry Regnery Company

Reprinted in 1977 by Greenwood Press, Inc.

Library of Congress catalog card number   77-2918

ISBN 0-8371-9565-9

Printed in the United States of America

To My Wife

PREFACE

My own acquaintance with the existentialists came about indirectly, as an extension of studies in Kierkegaard and phenomenology. It is always an interesting and profitable question in the history of philosophy to inquire about the consequences of given doctrines. Although the results of Kierkegaard and Husserl lead in many divergent directions, there is one point of convergence in existentialism. This doctrine is an aftermath of the joint impact of these two thinkers (along with Kant, Hegel, and Nietzsche) upon Western thought. It was from this perspective that I began to examine the writings of the leading existentialists.

From a study of the sources, existentialism is seen to be a challenging and instructive philosophy. It embodies a legitimate continuation of several important European traditions and addresses itself to vital problems of the greatest contemporary moment for both philosophy and life. Hence it comes as something of a shock to find, during the postwar years, that American and British philosophers tend to dismiss this current of thought without serious consideration. Perhaps the somewhat morbid popular interest in the personality of Sartre may be advanced as an excuse for not giving careful hearing to the arguments of the existentialists. Another reason, more intrinsically philosophical, is that the methods and viewpoints espoused by this school are very foreign and lacking in rigor. Something of the antipathy and even scorn displayed by European logical positivists during the 1930's toward existentialism has been transferred to our lands, with the growing popularity of logical empiricism. It seems as though there is no common ground between existentialism and a philosophical climate that is nourished upon pragmatism, scientific methodology, and semantics.

Yet in point of fact, the existentialists have had a good deal to say about the movements fashionable today in English-speaking countries. They are quite aware of what is passing for sound philosophical currency in other circles and have given these tendencies considerable attention. There is even an unsuspected measure of agreement upon certain issues between existentialism and the reigning attitudes in America and Britain, although the disagreements run more deeply. But to disagree intelligently with logical empiricism and naturalism is not the same as to dismiss them unheard or to be blissfully ignorant of their main contentions. Common courtesy, if not prudent openmindedness, recommends that we give the existentialists, in turn, a fair hearing.

It is at this point that even the well-disposed reader is apt to get discouraged, because of the vast ocean of existentialist literature. One cannot reasonably be expected to devote a lifetime to the study of this philosophy, and yet the heap of books would seem to demand just that. In this predicament, most people sensibly turn to some introductory work that can serve as a guide to existentialism, its major exponents, and its underlying theses. Unfortunately, consultation of popular guides must be listed as one of the deterrent causes preventing an intelligent appreciation of existentialism among English-speaking readers. There are some excellent accounts, but there is also an unconscionably large number of superficial and even inaccurate surveys. This is the price inevitably paid for achieving a certain amount of fame and literary success.

The present book does not pretend to open up an easy path to understanding existentialism, nor is it an exhaustive analysis; there are several different ways of approaching this matter, all of them rewarding. But the procedure followed here does attempt to meet certain needs that are not satisfied elsewhere. For one thing, it avoids a premature settlement about the meaning of existentialism. Too often, an arbitrary abstraction or a wholly one-sided definition is set up as the pattern by which to judge the entire movement. Yet nothing is clearer, from even a preliminary acquaintance with these thinkers, than that they admit the most radical differences of opinion among themselves. Consequently, I have thought it better to proceed at first upon a merely nominal definition and to postpone until the final chapter any extended attempt to draw general conclusions about the significance of existentialism as a whole. The picture that does emerge is drawn more in terms of methods and problems than of a common fund of doctrinal content. This gives sufficient latitude to domestic quarrels as well as to tenets they undoubtedly share.

In a word, emphasis has been placed upon the existential*ists* rather than upon existential*ism*. The latter conception is formulated only gradually and inductively, to the extent that the individual thinkers do exhibit some shared traits. But first of all, sufficient opportunity is given to each existentialist to present his own distinctive views. The four representatives chosen here— Sartre, Jaspers, Marcel, and Heidegger—are acknowledged to be the most original and comprehensive minds in this group. This is not to deny, of course, the valuable work done by less well-known existentialists, especially in France and Italy. But it is upon the shoulders of these four men that the main burden of existential inquiry squarely lies.

I have not followed the conventional division into French and German schools. Interpreters of existentialism often confine their main attention to, say, Sartre and Marcel, and then make a hurried comparison with Heidegger and Jaspers. Or the latter pair is taken as prototypal, thus forcing Sartre and Marcel to conform with a preconceived formula. It has seemed much more natural and in accord with the actual content of their thought to make another arrangement that cuts entirely across national lines. I have treated Sartre and Jaspers first, since they seem to me to remain closer to the historical background of existentialism as it extends from Kant to Husserl. In this sense, their positions are more traditional than those of Marcel and Heidegger. The two latter philosophers appear to be breaking loose from their immediate antecedents and to be venturing along paths that are both very new and very old. Many commentators prefer to culminate their investigation with the views of Gabriel Marcel. But I believe that at least the possibility of greater advances is present in Heidegger's thought, unsatisfactory though it be in some basic respects.

The critical standpoint from which I have tried to weigh existentialism is that of a philosophical theism and realism. The comparisons drawn between Augustine and Aquinas on the one hand, and the existentialists on the other, have not been, I hope, of too arbitrary or artificial a nature. All these men are occupied with the same generic sort of problems, the problems of existing men, despite the enormous differences in historical situation and technique. This abiding similarity of philosophical reflection has been recognized by most existentialists themselves, leading them to define their stands, either positively or negatively, by reference to Plato and Aristotle, Augustine and Aquinas. For their part, contemporary Thomists—notably, Gilson and Maritain—have spoken of their doctrine as the authentic existentialism or, at least, as the only philosophy of being in which existence receives its rightful place. But the details of this comparative study have never been worked out in a circumstantial way. Moreover, the patient, philosophical spadework has been brushed aside by some Christian and anti-Christian writers in favor of apologetic warfare. The latter tendency has met with a severe stricture in the encyclical letter *Humani generis*, issued in 1950 by Pope Pius XII. Significantly, the one existentialist in question, Gabriel Marcel, has explicitly repudiated the designation "Christian existentialism." The major problems still unsettled lie at the properly philosophical level of discussion. It is an added fact that the very success of a comparison between theistic realism and existentialism provides an added motive for many students for using rhetoric rather than reason in their dealings with existentialism.

I am grateful to Professor Charles W. Hendel of Yale University for giving me encouragement, at a crucial moment in the writing, concerning the general worthwhileness of making American philosophical studies on existentialism. He is in no way responsible, however, for the particular shape of the present approach. I am deeply indebted to Saint Louis University for providing me with the necessary research facilities and the services of a typist. The editor of *Thought* has kindly consented to the use of materials on Jaspers, Sartre, and Marcel which originally appeared in that journal. The publisher's readers have offered several valuable criticisms.

JAMES COLLINS

Saint Louis University
May 15, 1951

ACKNOWLEDGMENTS

Personal permission to quote from their books is very kindly given me by Professors Martin Heidegger and Karl Jaspers.

I am also grateful to the following publishers for permission to make quotations from their books: The Beacon Press (Marcel's *Being and Having*); A. Francke Ag. (Heidegger's *Platons Lehre von der Wahrheit*); Librairie Gallimard (Marcel's *Du Refus à l'invocation* and Sartre's *L'Etre et le néant*); Walter De Gruyter & Co. (Jaspers' *Descartes und die Philosophie* and *Existenzphilosophie*); Harper and Brothers (Wilder's *The Ides of March*); Alfred A. Knopf, Inc. (Sartre's *No Exit* and *The Flies*); Max Niemeyer Verlag (Heidegger's *Sein und Zeit*); Philosophical Library (Jaspers' *The Perennial Scope of Philosophy* and Sartre's *Existentialism*); R. Piper & Co. Verlag (Jaspers' *Von der Wahrheit*); Pontifical Institute of Mediaeval Studies (Gilson's *Being and Some Philosophers*); Springer-Verlag (Jaspers' *Philosophie*).

Table of Contents

TABLE OF CONTENTS—*Continued*

The Existentialists

Chapter I

Existential Backgrounds
Kierkegaard, Nietzsche, Husserl

Existentialism, perhaps more than other philosophical movements, is usually evaluated on cultural and social grounds. Both its supporters and its opponents point to the general conditions of society as an explanation of its appearance and rapid spread in Europe. To existentialists themselves, one of the strongest reasons for accepting this new standpoint is its honest attempt to meet the needs of the age. This way of thinking tries to be responsive to the predicament of contemporary man and to supply an interpretation of his anguish and aspirations. It pays heed to the moods, catastrophes, and projects which are usually passed over by academic philosophies. Instead of retreating to a realm of eternal verities or of scientific methodology, it hugs close to the terrain of ordinary living. Its modishness should not distract from the fact that it has given articulate form to the universal sense of catastrophe and of a need for radical reconstruction of intellectual and moral patterns.

This same close link between existentialism and the course of actual events is regarded by its critics as a sure sign of its transitory and nonphilosophical character. They view this movement as a concealed way of salvation rather than as a serious effort at rational analysis. Its fashionableness is often understood in the sense of a passing fancy, an esoteric cult, that will have its brief strut on the stage and then pass into oblivion. After the memory of wartime experiences with groups like the French *maquis* grows dim, a flood of rational sanity will sweep away this pathological stress on insecurity, sudden death, individual destiny, and risk. Existentialism is the formulation of Europe's present nightmare, and like all nightmare products it must eventually give way to daytime sobriety.

It is unreasonable to expect any definite issue from a debate of this sort. Pointing out the social context of existentialism is a legitimate procedure only so long as it does not usurp the primary task of careful examination of the evidence advanced in support of its doctrines. It is just as inconclusive to remain at the historico-cultural level of appraisal here as it is to recommend or reject Dewey's instrumentalism solely because of its close affinity with the scientific and technical triumphs of twentieth-century America. Verdicts drawn up on such a basis beg the question, one way or the other, about the significance of a relation between philosophical theory and social conditions. It is well to weigh this connection, but the outcome will not settle philosophical issues.

In studying existentialism, there is a danger of so foreshortening the historical perspective that its roots in the philosophical tradition are overlooked. The kind of approach favored by the existentialists is not entirely novel; it has striking parallels in St. Augustine, Pascal, and other respectable thinkers. The more immediate preparations for existentialism go back to the nineteenth century, and it is upon a solid groundwork that this philosophy seeks to build its structure. Whether existentialism has maintained genuine doctrinal solidarity with its past is not the main issue at present. What must be explored is the heritage of characteristic problems which it owes to a noteworthy group of forebears. The existentialist response to the challenges of our day could not have taken the form it did, were it not for the work of these predecessors. At least, this response becomes more intelligible to us when viewed against its background.

Many minds contributed to the current of thought from which existentialism stems, but the heaviest debt is owed to three men: Kierkegaard, Nietzsche, and Husserl. This can be affirmed without any implication that these three thinkers would give blanket approval to the use to which their views have been put. Husserl, indeed, lived long enough to repudiate Heidegger's appeal to his method. Nor is the importance of these men fully measured by their contribution to existential philosophy. They bear other and perhaps more significant relationships than that of being grand-fathers to existentialism; nevertheless, they can be fruitfully stud-ied from this angle. The existentialists went to school at their feet and worked out some of the consequences of what these sources taught. To have developed these possibilities may prove to be the permanent accomplishment of current philosophies of existence.

1. Sören Kierkegaard.

Both in his personal life and in his writings, Sören Kierkegaard (1813–55) supplies the prototype of the existential thinker. His own protest against the academic, social, and religious establish-ments of his day have set a pattern for the existential criticism of the accepted institutions and philosophies of our time. Kier-kegaard called himself a thoroughly polemical nature, meaning thereby not only that he possessed a naturally contentious spirit but also that his positive views could only be developed through sharp contrasts and oppositions. He is best understood when placed in the line of European moralists, men who have criticized their contemporaries in a satirical yet constructive way. Despite their attempts to provide metaphysical underpinnings, the ex-istentialists have retained this fundamentally moral orientation of philosophizing. An examination of Kierkegaard's major protests prefigures the lineaments of the existential outlook.

(a) THE INDIVIDUAL VERSUS THE CROWD. Although Kierke-gaard is not usually recognized as a social critic, he has offered some penetrating analyses of the social ills of the nineteenth cen-tury. His Works of Love,[1] composed at the same time as the Communist Manifesto, diagnoses the situation of 1848 in an in-cisive and radical way. Both Marx and Kierkegaard agree that contemporary industrial society has endangered the dignity of the human person. They point out that man counts for nothing in a society that is governed primarily by impersonal "laws" of production and consumption and by the ends of selfish gain. Both critics see that the primacy of human values must be championed against the reigning bourgeois interests. The sharp divergence between them comes when more concrete proposals are made for reconstructing society along humanistic lines. Marx identifies the "truly human man" with the social group which can integrate itself so closely with the processes of industrial production that the gap is closed between human desires and material possibilities of social control. Thoroughly socialized man, having no illusions about a transcendent goal, is the Marxian solution to the inhumane conditions of the modern world.

Kierkegaard moves in the opposite direction. He does not believe that we are under any necessity to work out the immanent logic of capitalism or that the remedy is to be found in an exclusively social direction. For it is a utopian hope to think that a humane society can be produced without a direct reformation of individual life. Social change within the state is more profound than political reorganization, but the ultimate success of both social and political revolution depends upon the basic transformation of individual existence. Kierkegaard's observation of his environment reveals that men are ridden by a total forgetfulness of what it means to be an individual. His analysis of this condition both harkens back to the Biblical warning against forgetting the manner of men we are and also foreshadows some characteristic existentialist themes.

Kierkegaard refers to man in industrial society as a cipher man or a fractional man, since as an individual he commands no respect and cannot have significance. This is due to the paramount devotion paid to the ideal of equality. Although equality is one of the abiding human goals, it cannot be pursued in isolation from other objectives, such as freedom and personal responsibility, without sacrificing the members of society to the collectivity. The modern individual is "lost" in the crowd and "at a loss" without the crowd. He finds it uncomfortable to stand out in any unusual way, since issues are decided on the basis of what everybody thinks. Anonymity is the saving virtue, numerical superiority the decisive consideration, and mass opinion the criterion of truth. No one cares to act in a distinctive way, since such conduct would count for nothing except as a sign of queerness. Here is a source of the existentialist antipathy toward the anonymous, featureless standards which prevail in our age.

There is need for a recall of the individual to himself, an awakening to the possibilities of self-determination that slumber within him. This is not a plea for economic or political individualism, since the ascendency of the crowd would also result from an individualistic appeal to unbridled self-seeking. Neither laissez faire nor collectivism can arrest the process of universal leveling, since neither policy is directed to an inward edification of the individual self. Kierkegaard looks for "uncommon men," who will take the first steps toward a renascence of personal integrity. These men are not to be found in a privileged class or nation, since it lies in the power of every member of the crowd to extricate himself and realize his own singular nature. This is an aristocratic ideal, to the extent of acknowledging that the best in a man is left untilled when his character is determined mainly by group pressure and catchwords. It is aristocratic in the Socratic sense of singling out each man from the irresponsible public and requiring him to render personal account for what he believes and acts upon. Yet this demand of self-scrutiny can be placed upon *everyone*—this is the personalist way of supporting, in nonquantitative terms, the movement toward equality.

The famous Kierkegaardian doctrine of the three spheres of existence—the esthetic, the ethical, and the religious—fits into this context.[2] It is a theory about stages in the growth of personality rather than a metaphysical scaffolding, after the manner of Hegel's triad of moments. Kierkegaard's dynamic conception of personality is of seminal importance for existential thought. Certain broad and fixed traits belong permanently to human nature. The common human condition is shared by all men and constitutes the given, necessary factor. But man is the one being endowed with conscious freedom and hence with possibilities for existing at various levels of adequacy. He can propose his own leading principles, organize his life around them, and thus transform the given reality into a freely orientated self. There is no place for philosophy of nature in Kierkegaard and the existentialists, because they are wholly absorbed in a study of the venture of human freedom and its pitfalls.

Kierkegaard's descriptions of various moods and attitudes characteristic of the different spheres of existence have inspired a good many later phenomenological analyses. His studies of boredom, despair, and dread have proved to be specially fertile sources. He draws attention more to the dark and turbulent moments than to the tranquil ones. But this is not a morbid preference made in order to institute a literature of gloom and frustration. The underlying argument (lost sight of by those existentialists who revel in such descriptions for their own sake) is that an internal law of growth impels the individual to venture beyond the cautious shores of esthetic satisfaction. If he resists the natural prompting to cultivate ethical and religious qualities, the result is disorder of soul and paralysis in practical affairs. The darker moods announce the consequences of failing to follow through to the full flowering of personal existence.

Boredom, for instance, is a warning that all the goods of life may turn to ashes in the mouth. When a man concentrates all his energies upon pursuit of momentary pleasures, no matter how refined and subtle, he exposes himself to surfeit and a state of tedium from which his esthetic principles cannot rescue him. Anguished dread is the state of spiritual growing pains of a man who stands poised at the brink of personal exercise of freedom, in the full awareness of its consequences for time and eternity. He is held fast in awful fascination at the stakes. Not this or that object but the entire range of objects of mature choice arouses dread in him. If he should then retreat within himself and shut out all aid from God, he is on the road to despair, the "sickness unto death." Kierkegaard's own interest in these states of soul is primarily religious and ethical, whereas his successors have exploited the psychological and metaphysical aspects of such concrete treatments of the human situation.

Yet even Kierkegaard is not innocent of drawing a speculative conclusion from his own choice of subject. He deplores the rationalist tendency to understate the role of the emotions and reduce will to a function of reason. The rationalist account of man is unbalanced for failing to give due weight to the affective side of our lives. An understanding of the whole man and his attitudes toward reality awaits an appreciation of the great resources of the passions, which are decisive in shaping individual outlooks. Without the passional factor, especially will, there is no way of advancing from the dreamy, esthetic state to the moral and religious phases of existence. It is not voluntarism but an honest attempt to see man steadily and in his actual dynamism which prompts this emphasis upon other powers than reason. The persuasiveness and originality of many existentialist arguments are due to this widening of the anthropological horizon to include all the relevant forces in man.

Will and practical reason are accorded more autonomy by Kant than by Kierkegaard. The latter conceives the ethical stage as standing in need of reinforcement from, and alliance with, either the esthetic or the religious principle. Either the ethically responsive person will imagine himself to be acting in accord with a secular moral law of his own making or, perhaps, one to which he is unconditionally related—and then he relapses into moralizing estheticism; or else he will trace the moral law itself to its source in a personal God—and then he completes the movement of existence to its culmination not in duty but in worship. This is an either/or which has continued to confront the existentialists and to differentiate one variety of existentialism from another.

The capstone of Kierkegaard's view of the individual is man's freely acknowledged bond with God. The entire drive of the dialectic of the stages of existence points at the conclusion that to be an individual in the plenary sense is to orientate one's life toward God. On this reckoning, every description of the human person which neglects or depreciates the tendency to transcendence is out of focus. All existentialists, whether admitting the religious solution or not, make allowance for some sort of movement of transcending or seeking beyond the immanent structure of human nature. Kierkegaard's own interpretation rests upon an examination of man's desire for an eternal happiness, a desire that cannot be satisfied by the finite goods and temporal situations of life. Yet he does not admit the naturalist reproach that the inclination to transcend our world is, in effect, a flight from our historical and concrete responsibilities. The individual in the pregnant sense is one who has faith in God's existence. For Kierkegaard, this means having faith in Christ as the God-Man. God is not found by leaving the world behind in a flight to the beyond but by discerning His presence in the temporal process itself.

Religious faith is the Archimedean lever whereby the "accentuated" individual can move the world. It is his foothold and secret strength for withstanding the pressure of the herd. The man of faith is a nonconformist, as far as human conventions and mass impulses are concerned. He can stand out as an exception, since he has accepted a call from God precisely in his own singular reality. Faith is not susceptible of mass techniques: each man believes in his own heart and on his own responsibility. Yet it is a paradoxical vindication of the ideal of equality among men, since it does not fall within the disposition of fortune or of privilege. Each individual can make the act of faith, provided only that he does so on the basis of his own freedom. This is the crucial opportunity for becoming an individual in the highest existential sense.

Ideally, Kierkegaard should have rounded out his teaching on the individual with a complementary study of the community. He does make several fugitive references to a new social mode of being which will correspond with his reconstruction of the person. But characteristically, he leaves the task of further social analysis to future laborers in the field, because of the greater urgency of the problem of the individual. His legacy to the existentialists is the problem of reconciling individual and society. His own religious statements underline the difficulties rather than suggest a way of integrating the two poles. Each individual is related to God as the alone to the Alone. Only in God is there a common intersection of the lines of individual destinies. Kierkegaard speaks about God as entering into every personal union among men as the third party, but he does not expand this hint into a thoroughgoing renovation of the basis for social relations. For all merely human associations seem to present threats to individual integrity and barriers between the individual and God. Above all, the Hegelian notion of a concrete universal tends to divinize the actual social institutions and rob the individual of his free, creaturely approach to a transcendent God.

(b) THE EXISTENT VERSUS THE SPECULATIVE SYSTEM. Kierkegaard's attack upon Hegel[3] has been widely reported as a repudiation of all philosophy and of all reason. This interpretation seems the more plausible, at least regarding philosophy, because Kierkegaard himself looked indulgently upon Hegel's claim to have elaborated the definitive philosophy. Hence he seemed to be faced with the alternative of accepting Hegel or of rejecting not only the Hegelian system but all philosophy along with it. Since he regarded this system as the major theoretical bulwark of the mass mind, Kierkegaard could not compromise on the issue as so formulated, despite the disastrous alternative. Although he saluted the Greek realism of Socrates and Aristotle from a distance, he saw no evidence of its survival in his own day. Since all contemporary philosophies were infected with idealism, a repudiation of absolute idealism seemed to Kierkegaard to entail a repudiation of philosophy itself in any concrete form.

Whatever the ambiguity surrounding his attitude towards philosophy, Kierkegaard's mind is clearly set forth in regard to the rationalism-irrationalism controversy. He accepts neither horn of the dilemma, but the popularity of rationalism among his own contemporaries led him to emphasize its shortcomings just as strongly as those of irrationalism. The Kierkegaardian critique of romanticism and the esthetic outlook is aimed at the latter doctrine, whereas his polemic against the Hegelian system is directed against excessive claims made for reason. Several of the existentialists, in turn, have waged battle on both fronts, despite the widespread charge that they tend to foster an irrational point of view.

Kierkegaard balances his stress on moods, passions, and will with an equally vigorous affirmation of the intelligibility of the real order. Things in the world and events in history are not absurd in themselves and their interrelations. They have a definite intelligible structure, which is not only intrinsically knowable but also actually comprehended by God. This is the meaning of Kierkegaard's neglected statement that existing reality *is* a system for God. It stands open to His vision, although it is only by Him that it can be known comprehensively and systematically. As far as creaturely intelligence is concerned, Kierkegaard distinguishes among abstract thought, existential thought, and pure thought. Abstract or objective thinking is the approach employed by the natural sciences, mathematics, and logic. These are valid disciplines and yield reliable knowledge about the essential aspects of things. But they have two limitations: they do not attain to actual existence and do not involve the personal relationship of the knowing individual to the things known. Disinterestedness and objectivity are the primary notes of abstract thinking. This is the proper way to treat things, as distinguished from personal selves. Even human nature, in so far as man is one natural thing along with others in the world, is accessible in a partial way to the objective method.

In order to gain some insight into existence or the disposition of man's freedom, another avenue is needed. Kierkegaard is more successful in describing what existential thinking is *not* than in specifying its positive features. It is not merely an extension of abstract thought, since it does not labor under the two limitations mentioned above. It does attain somehow by reflection to the existential act, and it does include the relationship of the knower to what he knows. In fact, existential knowledge is constituted precisely by the manner in which the meditative individual relates himself to the aims of existence. Existence is not predicated of things but of persons in their moral dispositions. Existential truth, for Kierkegaard, is a moral and religious state of being rather than a purely cognitive perfection. It rests on the attempt to shape one's conduct in accord with what one knows about the purposes of freedom. At its maximum, it is the true or upright state of being fully committed to search for eternal happiness.

Kierkegaard places strict limitations upon the finite understanding of existence and existential truth. In the natural order, an individual can have reflective, existential knowledge only of his own existence and of other selves only in so far as they bear upon his own freedom. Religiously, the power of Christian charity affords direct acquaintance with the existential conditions of other persons through a sort of empathy. On only one point—a negative one—is Kierkegaard emphatic. The existential situation cannot be transcribed within an idealist system of pure thought. For the latter is based upon dialectical necessities and a presumption of the basic completeness of the historical process, whereas existence has freedom and genuine novelty as its proper medium.

Thus Kierkegaard's opposition is to "pure" thought, or the systematic identification of thought and being, rather than to the "abstract" thought of the sciences. His position is nonidealist rather than irrationalist, although he does not see that systematic explanations can be made on a nonidealist basis. The existentialists have followed him in setting off the type of knowledge which deals with *things* in the world scientifically and objectively from that sort which is adapted to the special task of studying the human *person* and the realm of existence. But they have not found in Kierkegaard sufficient indications about the cognitive aspects of existential reflection or subjective thinking. It is not a form of subjectivism and arbitrary creation of fantasies. But directions are lacking about how to discern the natural cognitive factor in the midst of affective sympathy and religious faith. The philosophical status of existential understanding is left in doubt by Kierkegaard.

For Kierkegaard's philosophical descendants, the value of the philosophical life itself cannot be taken for granted. Having been called in question by the sceptical Dane, philosophizing enters again into the category of problems at issue. The venerable axiom: "First live, then philosophize" takes on new relevance from Kierkegaard's suggestion that philosophy may be antivital rather than in continuous harmony with the ends of human life. Above all, metaphysics has been subjected to critical examination, following Kierkegaard's observation that it does not figure as one of the three stages of existence. The unavoidable question arises as to whether there is any legitimate place for metaphysics in an existentially-centered viewpoint. Most existentialists agree that an affirmative answer cannot be made until the history and the methodology of metaphysics have been subjected to a thorough revision.

Another acute problem raised by Kierkegaard is the relation between metaphysics and ethics. In attacking Hegel's ethical theories, he is careful to trace out the metaphysical roots of the position he opposes. This has left the existentialists with the choice of either tackling ethical matters independently or making their investigation contingent upon a previous settlement of the metaphysical foundations of moral theory. Kierkegaard has made it impossible for these philosophers to undertake ethical studies without first declaring their mind, one way or another, about metaphysics and its bearing upon a philosophy of conduct.

Kierkegaard's actual practice often belies his profession of eschewing metaphysical speculation. His criticism of Hegel is carried out in a thoroughly speculative spirit. In order to have a self-sufficient system, Hegel would have to make a "presuppositionless" start in his thinking. When it is a question of human cognition, Kierkegaard believes that such a beginning can be made only at the price of wiping out the distinction between God and the finite mind. There is an implicit realistic metaphysics of creator and creature behind this objection. Kierkegaard withstood any dialectical merging of these two modes of being. Man is genuinely and radically finite, so that at no time in his development does he discover himself to be a phase in the self-explication of the absolute. Hence he cannot draw upon some creative idea implanted in his mind as its a priori structure, on the strength of which an entire philosophical system can be developed from the internal resources of the central idea. Kierkegaard requires a real rather than a dissimulated dependence of human intelligence upon the data of the physical world gained through the senses. In the existentialist tradition, he tends to counterbalance Husserl's claim to make a presuppositionless beginning.

Apart from this polemical appeal to the senses, however, Kierkegaard fails to specify the exact contribution of sensation to human knowledge. He is satisfied with having drawn a distinction between logical motion, with which alone the Hegelian system is equipped to deal, and the real motion of physical processes which is grasped through the senses. Having used this empirical argument of Hegel's chief foes, Trendelenburg and Schelling, he does not follow up its consequences. The senses might be expected to contribute toward knowledge of physical things in their existential character. But Kierkegaard does not follow this lead, since he has associated existence too exclusively with the exercise of human freedom in the formation of self. For the same reason, he is prevented from applying existence to God. He is the fountainhead of the existential commonplace that God *is*, but does not *exist*. Existence cannot be predicated of the eternal, immutable being, since to exist means to be engaged in becoming, time, freedom, and history. This has given rise to the existentialist quandary of how to relate existential thinking to the divine Being, who is by definition placed beyond the existential order. Man is not only central in existence: he is the only truly existential being.

(c) THE ILLUMINATION OF EXISTENCE BY CHRISTIAN FAITH. Kierkegaard was not unaware of the dangers in this conception of existence, since it would seem to cut off man from both God and the non-human world. His own answer to the problem of man's relationship to God was formulated in terms of faith in the Incarnation. In the person of Christ, God Himself enters into the zone of the existential. The immutable becomes a changing being, the eternal puts on temporal process, the suprahistorical enters into history. This is the paradoxical nature of faith. Rather than mediate these extremes of reality in Hegelian fashion, Kierkegaard spoke of faith as a crucifixion of the understanding. He rejected as a rationalistic compromise the customary apologetics of the Hegelian divines. If their explanations were valid, then there would be no room for faith as a free venture.

Kierkegaard injected the problem of Christianity into the heart of existential discussion.[4] He was highly critical of the actual condition of the Established Danish-Lutheran Church as well as of the very notion of "Christendom." To him, these settlements came dangerously close to sanctioning a comprise between Christian faith and the spirit of worldliness. On the other hand, he maintained that the attitude of faith is indispensable for synthesizing the many aspects of existence. The full meaning of living a life under trial, of suffering and sacrifice, of communication and joy, can only be plumbed with the aid of the Christian teaching. Christian faith, as the supremely existential attitude, is the central standpoint from which to develop the implications of these personal situations. For it provides a way in which to reconcile the immanent tendency to remain loyal to our earthly condition and the equally importunate drive toward transcendence. Both movements are strengthened through the gracious initiative of the transcendent being in becoming present as an existent person in history. Whether the *instant*, the act whereby believers are made contemporaneous with Christ through faith in the Incarnation, cancels out secular history or gives it orientation and significance is part of the ensemble of Kierkegaardian problems.

Most existentialists agree that existence is a historical reality and that some sort of faith is a motive force in human history. There is no unanimity, however, on the relevance of Christian faith for the hermeneutic of existence. Several possibilities are opened by Kierkegaard's own wrestling with the problem of faith. His torments of soul can be taken as an involuntary confession of antagonism between his existential insights and the tenets of Christianity. Atheistic existentialists regard as axiomatic the groundlessness of belief in God and Christ, even though this absurdity must be included among the given elements in the historical condition of Western men. Another interpretation is that

Kierkegaard misunderstood the relation between Christianity and a philosophy of existence. Instead of patterning a theory of existence after the deliverances of revelation as an independent standard, it might be better to submit these religious deliverances to philosophical analysis and thus to uncover their underlying secular import. Finally, Kierkegaard's reluctance to speak of himself as "being" a Christian can be construed in a strict way as meaning that the Christian life is one of constant "becoming," in which there is no room for complacent assertions of having realized the Christian requirements. It is then possible to accept literally his designation of Christ as "*the* historical, *the* existential" individual, without making this truth the major premise of existential investigation. The culmination of personal life in communion with God would then be intimated rather than laid down as a first principle. Kierkegaard himself leaves his readers free to make their own reading of existence, since such freedom is the condition of acquiring individual selfhood.

2. *Friedrich Nietzsche.*

Although the Danish literary critic, Georg Brandes, tried to introduce Friedrich Nietzsche (1844–1900) to the writings of Kierkegaard, this direct literary contact was never made. Nevertheless, there is a definite intellectual affinity between the two. This is due, in part, to the common cultural and religious situation in which they were reared and against which they both rebelled. Chronologically and by foresight, they span the nineteenth century. The trends which Kierkegaard dealt with in their nascent phase came to maturity during Nietzsche's lifetime. The latter's reaction to the completed movement is in continuity at many points with Kierkegaard's earlier appraisal. Similar traits of character and sensibility also drew them on the same side of many arguments. Both men flourished more in combat and disturbed solitude than in peaceful society. They were proud, sensitive, and intense individuals, given much to introspection and gifted with a superb command over language. Each left as indelible a mark upon his national literature as upon the European mind as a whole.

The differences between Kierkegaard and Nietzsche are no less striking and instructive. As might be expected in the case of such subtle and dialectical thinkers, their antagonisms spring paradoxically from the very likenesses they display. Perhaps this is the reason why the existentialists of our century have found them so attractive and stimulating, when studied together. Evaluating these thinkers is not an operation of balancing together two rows of complementary items, but one of confronting agreement and contradiction with respect to the same problems. It is an established practice among existentialists to give equal hearing to both forerunners and then to develop an original theory with the aid of this dialectical tension.

(a) NEW MORALS FOR OLD. Nietzsche's phenomenology of modern culture and morality is a variation on the familiar Kierkegaardian and Schopenhauerian theme.[5] He deplores the predominance of the impersonal public in determining our conduct and our institutions. There has been a deliberate campaign to suppress outstanding individuals and exceptional courses of action in favor of standardized men and safe mediocrity of aim. Like Kierkegaard, Nietzsche regards mass journalism as the most potent instrument of the leveling process, since it promotes anonymous thinking and irresponsible action. The tendency in social life is towards "one flock and no shepherd," one amorphous mass in the midst of which no original person dare speak his mind, assume creative leadership, or go his own way in the face of numerical opposition. What Kierkegaard calls the apotheosis of the crowd is termed by Nietzsche the rule of flock morality. In place of individual intrepidity, the drift of the totality sets the goals of human aspiration.

Inevitably, the collective sights are aimed too low. Instead of goading the individual on to further peaks of adventure and experiment, the approved middle-class norms stifle innovations and the works of genius. The assured result is frustration and stagnation, since the major lesson of history is ignored: that man is *a still unfixed animal.* Nietzsche's humanism is based upon the indefinite capacity of man to surpass himself and to leave behind the previous outposts of achievement. The charge of being antivital is laid against the existing moral code and social structure for suppressing life's urge to posit ends never before obtained. Since Christianity is identified as the bulwark of this debilitating conservatism, Nietzsche calls revealed religion an enemy of life and a traitor to mankind. It encourages conformity, routine, and complacency, at the expense of the daring unrest which alone has justified human existence by its creative fruits.

Nietzsche's criticism of accepted standards is not made in the spirit of anarchy and destructiveness. His ultimate intent is to remove the disabilities placed upon unusual individuals, without eliminating the mores which govern the herd. He states explicitly his opposition to both collectivism and individualism, in so far as both views rest upon a conviction of the fundamental equality among men. Unlike Kierkegaard, he is unwilling to admit an acceptable sense in which equality can be reconciled with self-development toward maximal ideals. He establishes a complete antithesis between humanism and egalitarianism. Instead of acknowledging the Christian paradox that the highest perfection is accessible to all—on condition that each man detach himself from the crowd and pass singly through the wicket of responsible living and response to grace—Nietzsche places a gulf between the flock and the true philosophers. He is therefore willing to tolerate the conventions regulating the lives of ordinary mortals, as long as no claim to absolute validity is advanced. For if this claim were enforced through the use of social power, the norm of mediocrity would be extended to the fortunate few. They would be prevented from laying down their own tables of the law and so from producing a breed of supermen.

Kierkegaard and Nietzsche present existentialists with conflicting inferences from the principle that human nature is no mere given substance subject to quantitative mass regulation. In one way, Kierkegaard's is the more radical mind. For he has sufficient faith in the capacities of human freedom and the workings of divine providence to hold that, despite the evident inequalities in things temporal, an essential equality obtains in matters involving the highest good of eternity. Nietzsche, on the contrary, has a strictly deterministic and atheistic outlook. Hence the physical, intellectual, and social gradations among men are taken as absolutely decisive. Only the gifted few have a destiny for the furthest reaches of existence. The new morality of creating one's own ends and procedures is intended only for the liberation of these exceptions from mass tyranny. It is to their interest that the crowd should retain its own restricted perspective, which serves as a support and foil for the splendid ways of genius. Hence Nietzsche is ready to retain flock morality on condition that it provide a subsoil for such noble fruit.

Kierkegaard himself admits that ethico-religious equality rests on a proportionate obligation, which takes realistic account of actual differences. Furthermore, he allows for a restitution of inequalities even in the perspective of eternity, but inequalities based now on the actual exercise of freedom rather than on the distributions of fate and a hierarchy of opportunity. Where he differs most emphatically from Nietzsche is in maintaining the accessibility of the highest good to everyone and the correlative duty of everyone to seek a direct relationship with the absolute. Nietzsche's aristocratic transvaluation of values is radical on one level, whereas Kierkegaard suggests that the categories of the crowd are essentially evil and never to be tolerated. He would have the crowd dispersed by bringing every individual in it to self-awareness as a free capacity for God's eternity.

Existentialist ethical doctrine has been worked out with an eye to these conflicting interpretations. Few of the existentialists profess an ethics of the elite founded on a rigid separation among grades of men. But neither is there unqualified support of Kierkegaard's stand. For one possible alternative is to generalize Nietzsche's theory of creative morality, extending it from privileged geniuses to all men. All men may be regarded as having the power to reject given values and to fashion their own norms. Nietzsche's stylized morality would then be the prerogative and obligation of everyone, and to fail to develop a distinctive way of acting would incur censure in every case. This approach depends, however, on the exclusion of God and of any permanent standards of good and evil. Here again, Nietzsche proves to be a guide down a dark path.

(b) NEW GODS FOR OLD. Nietzsche reported that he was an atheist by instinct and that what kindled his heart on first reading Schopenhauer's philosophy was its unashamed atheism. The denial of God suited his temperament and his systematic aims. He resembled Marx in refusing to submit arguments for God's existence to rational analysis and in resting his own criticism on broad cultural judgments. Although both Marx and Nietzsche disclaimed any ultimate reliance upon the genetic method of disqualifying a belief by assigning subjective origins to it, nevertheless this type of reasoning became their mainstay in undermining belief in God. Nietzsche's postulatory atheism furnished a model for those existentialists who wish to describe an existence lived entirely apart from God. His philosophy encouraged them to maintain that both belief and disbelief in God are optional attitudes and that it is worth experimenting with the assumption that God does not exist.

The revolution in values, Nietzsche teaches, can never be carried out in all thoroughness until loyalty to a transcendent order is suppressed.[6] Platonism in the ancient world and Christianity in the modern era have been the great champions of the supranatural order of values. It is God in the traditional Christian sense whom Nietzsche seeks to destroy with the hammer blows of his dialectic. If a transcendent, immutable entity is admitted, there results a devaluation of the temporal sphere and a dichotomy between what "merely appears" and what "truly is." The practice is to identify "true being" with the systems and interests of the dominant group in a society. Instead of open admission of the shifting power-basis of moral distinctions, the dominant class places its moral values on a divine foundation, congeals them in their present form, and imposes them universally.

Once again, the comparison with Kierkegaard is fruitful for understanding the domestic debates among contemporary existentialist philosophers. Nietzsche's rejection of the Christian God rests on the assumption that, since Christianity is a total system, it includes in an essential way the public standards of culture and morality promulgated under Christian auspices in the nineteenth century. Consequently, an attack upon the latter entails the annihilation of Christianity, especially of its central tenet: the existence of God. Here Kierkegaard's distinction between Christian religiousness and "Christendom" becomes relevant. In Kierkegaard's estimation, the real malaise of the age lies in the confusion (due sometimes to hypocrisy and sometimes to woolly thinking) between the eternal God and the traditions of men, between Christianity and the various establishments which water down the Christian requirements to the vanishing point. To Nietzsche's training in anti-Christianity, Kierkegaard opposes the desperate need for training in genuine Christianity in an age when everyone takes for granted the fact that he is a good Christian.

The one critic takes his contemporaries at their own word when they appeal to religious motives and sanctions in support of the status quo, whereas the other regards this appeal as blasphemous. Nietzsche holds that Christianity and belief in God must stand or fall with the present social order; Kierkegaard warns that Christianity and theism cannot survive unless they are detached from the abuses and distortions of "Christendom." Has God proved to be like the murderous Greek deity, a devourer of his own offspring, or has He been betrayed and forgotten by a so-called believing generation? The existentialists are divided among themselves over this issue.

A further matter of dispute between Nietzsche and Kierkegaard concerns the relation between being and becoming. Nietzsche regards it as axiomatic that a transcendent, immutable being is incompatible with our world of becoming. His counsel that we remain true to the earth means, in effect, that we must sweep out all traces of piety toward such a being. The situation is complicated, however, by Kierkegaard's remark that freedom enters even into the way in which we regard our own finitude and gifts. From his standpoint, loyalty to our human condition involves the possibility of deliberately misreading the nature of that condition. Although it is evident that certain theories about the transcendent being do depreciate the finite order, this is not a necessary consequence. Kierkegaard understands the precept of fidelity to our own state to mean that individual existents must refuse to pretend to be other than they are: temporal, finite, subject to becoming, dependent upon God. His usual advice to the Hegelians is that we should be content with being men and cease imagining ourselves as gods.

Only God is; only finite existents become. Neither being nor becoming is endangered when the relationship is one of free creator and creature. The creature remains loyal to himself by existing in the presence of God and as oriented toward participation in eternal happiness, without any reduction of the one mode of being to the other. Kierkegaard resists both a pantheistic amalgamation of God and man and a phenomenalist attempt to make the world an independent, divinized flow of appearances. In the social sphere, Kierkegaard concludes that any deification of a particular set of historical circumstances runs counter to the law of becoming. The proper mode of being of finite things is to continue in forward advancement: this is dynamite set off under every premature declaration of the possession of beatitude upon earth.

Nietzsche declares the death of God but retains a succedaneum of divinity. He admits a sense in which being maintains its primacy over becoming. In the dynamic and eschatological order, "I will" is ordained to "I am," heroes are en route to becoming gods, rebel geniuses of every age are anticipations of the supermen to come. But the kind of being which belongs to the higher breed, the gods of the Nietzschean dispensation, is that derived from a will to absolutize temporal process. Becoming itself is apotheosized by being rendered absolute and eternal. It is an eternity of complete immanence, a passionate restriction of all one's interests and valuations to the things of time. The new meta-physical doctrine of the eternal recurrence of the same realities is not a literal cyclic theory, like that of the Greeks. It has been infected by Christian influences and is a moral call to man's free-dom. Zarathustra proclaims his faith in this earthly life as all in all. He summons us to consecrate all our energies and aspirations to the finite world of becoming as an end sufficient unto itself. This is Nietzsche's substitute for eternity and being. What he hails as the highest act of the will to power—installing oneself within a closed rather than an open universe—is the exact equiva-lent of Kierkegaard's description of the despair from which there is no issue. The highest hope of life and the final sickness unto death: this is the heart of the Nietzsche-Kierkegaard dialogue on self-inclosed finitude.

Kierkegaard looks for no lasting city on earth, since man is a pilgrim of the absolute. Nietzsche declares that the whole of hu-man history is the lasting city, so that no particular moment in the recurrent cycle can claim this title. Kierkegaard vindicates the integrity of that which appears and becomes in history by regarding historical existence as the loving handiwork of the eternal God; Nietzsche makes a smiliar vindication by denying the real transcendence of eternal being. Kierkegaard tarries on metaphysical territory only long enough to expose the errors of pantheism and phenomenalism; Nietzsche proclaims an end to all metaphysics, only to make this proclamation the prologue to a new theory of being. These contradictions have been height-ened rather than lessened by the existentialists, who keep the question of God and man at the center of discussion. They hesi-tate in their own turn about whether to eliminate or to recon-struct metaphysics, whether to view transcendence as a relation to the transcendent God or as a restless search after a foundation within the world.

Nietzsche's criticism of the sciences has had a more pronounced influence than his ontology of the eternal return of the same. His remarks on the valuational motives behind the scientific enter-prise have been incorporated into most existentialist philosophies.[7] He shows that the ideal of seeking truth for its own sake cannot be taken for granted but rests upon a judgment that such an attitude is worthwhile and, indeed, preferable to other approaches to objects. In making this observation, Nietzsche is recalling a forgotten aspect of the older doctrine on the transcendentals, which points out that the true and the good impenetrate each other. Truth is a good for the intellect, just as the good can be subjected to intellectual analysis. Nietzsche would like to conclude from this impenetration that the scientific search after objective truth is always perspectival and regulated by some project of the will to power. He fears that if the appetitive relationship is overlooked, the scientific ideal will supply the last refuge for the absolutist doctrine on being.

The existentialists agree with Nietzsche that science is not "value-free," in the sense of escaping social and moral regulation in view of human needs and purposes. Yet they do not reduce its competence within its own area, for in this respect Kierkegaard provides a counterbalance to Nietzsche. The Kierkegaardian view of abstract modes of knowledge has been combined with Kant's theory of science by Jaspers as a defense of the peculiar values of the objective sciences. Despite their stress upon concrete approaches, most existentialists recognize the indispensable contribution of abstractness, generalization, and disinterestedness in the study of nature and of man in his objective side. The distinction is accepted between the intrinsic requirements of the natural sciences and the ordination both of scientific knowledge and of the scientists themselves, *qua* men, to the embracing ends of human existence. Subjective or existential considerations become primary in the region of freedom and personal formation. The bearing of scientific findings upon personal happiness cannot be determined solely on the basis of the objective scientific method. Existentialists try to secure the distinctiveness and primacy of existential thinking by limiting rather than by disparaging the abstract, objective techniques of scientific control. This limitation runs counter to the philosophical program of positivism, which is pledged to universalize a single method for its own extrascientific purpose.

When Kierkegaard refers to "science," he has in mind not only the special sciences but also Hegel's claim that scientific truth culminates in his own system. This same association is present in lesser degree even in Nietzsche's mind, since he seldom treats the question without repudiating absolutist theories of being and knowing. Only a century's removal from Hegel has enabled contemporary existentialists to examine the problem of scientific inquiry without special reference to his philosophy.

Thus Kierkegaard's distinction between abstract and pure or absolute thought is now widened to apply to all illegitimate efforts to harness the activities of the sciences to the cause of a particular philosophy. For instance, existentialists are critical of the naturalists' contention that their special conception of the world is so intimately bound up with the scientific outlook and method that either naturalism must be accepted or scientific progress must be repudiated. A similar detachment is made of Nietzsche's insight into the valuational basis of the scientific approach from his special preoccupation with establishing an immanent metaphysics of unconditional relativity and perspectivity of truths. There is no need to make a completely pragmatic explanation of scientific activity, out of fear lest the objectivity of science be bound up with an invidious distinction between the realms of reality and appearance. Existentialists are inclined either to accept forthwith Nietzsche's identification of the real with finite phenomena (without casting suspicion on the probity of scientists) or to reopen the entire question of the relation between a transcendent being and a world of becoming (without the prejudice of having to choose between them).

3. *Edmund Husserl.*

The impact of Edmund Husserl (1859–1938) upon existentialism has not been as uniformly felt as that of Kierkegaard and Nietzsche, but it is nonetheless of the first magnitude. Phenomenology provides the indispensable method for Sartre and at least a major strain in Heidegger's procedure. The relationship is less intimate in the case of Jaspers and Marcel, although the Kantian background of the former and the descriptive practices of the latter draw them close to the spirit of Husserl's philosophy. All existentialists would endorse Sartre's statement that the publication of Husserl's *Ideas pertaining to a Pure Phenomenology* (1913) was the outstanding philosophical event of the years just preceding World War I.[8]

Mention of this book rather than Husserl's earlier writings in mathematics and logic is significant. The great issue which has divided both his followers and his critics turns around the nature of the connection between method and transcendental idealism in the development of phenomenology. In his *Ideas*, Husserl suggests that a pure phenomenological philosophy of an idealistic sort grows directly from his earlier achievements in methodology and logic. Whether or not they accept this claim, existentialists are inclined to pay considerable attention to Husserl's later publications, in which the theory of a transcendental constitution of the world is central. Their interest in (and, in some instances, quarrel with) phenomenology is ontological as well as methodological. As with their approach to Kierkegaard and Nietzsche, they find in Husserl relevant problems and adumbrations of a solution rather than finished doctrines which can be adopted as they stand.

(a) PHILOSOPHY AS A RIGOROUS SCIENCE. Husserl's methodological plea for a return to the "things themselves" does not involve any commitment on the controversy between idealism and realism. It is primarily a resolve to place philosophy on a sound footing by clearing out unclarified notions, unexamined assumptions, and loose argumentation. The philosopher should strive for a direct presentation of what he is concerned with, guiding his systematic constructions by the way things appear in his conscious experience. The guiding axiom is that things are as they appear, as they are seen to be. A discriminating report on the phenomena rather than an illusory chase after a hidden substratum is the rule for making philosophy a rigorous discipline.[9]

Husserl gives comfort neither to sheer empiricism nor to subjective idealism. His famous attack on psychologism is intended to clear up the empiricist confusion between the psychological and the logical orders. The need for psychological studies of mental life is undeniable but cannot be made a substitute for logical inquiry into meanings. There is a clear-cut distinction between the variable psychic operations by which a truth is grasped or expressed and that which is meant through these functions. The latter will remain the same, whatever the changes in psychic life. Logical truth has no sufficient foundation in empirical conditions but requires an a priori basis. Furthermore, the empiricists fail to attend to an important aspect of experience: the invariant factor of identity, the form or essence, which alone permits the appearance to be what it is and to be recallable as the same meaning. Scientific generality, however, is built upon this public and permanent factor in the object. Phenomenology attempts to determine certain of these stable, general structures in our experience, employing what Husserl calls an intuition of essence or eidetic intuition.

Lest this misleading terminology seem to favor certain traditional positions, Husserl rules out several possible misinterpretations of his method. He does not posit a separate realm of essences, since he studies objects precisely as they present themselves immanently in consciousness for purposes of knowledge. Nevertheless, consciousness does not exercise an arbitrary formative power over the formal structures. They have a fixed, a priori nature as constituted in experience. Essences are grasped through a distinctive act of cognition, the intentional act. It is characteristic of consciousness to be *of* something, and that to which it refers is the field of intentional objects. The knowing act *(noesis)* and the known object *(noema)* are distinct and correlative factors in scientific knowledge. There can be no arbitrary reduction of the noema to the noetic act.

The mind intends its object, and the office of phenomenology is to bring this objective intention to fulfillment. When the object itself is exhibited in perceptual intuition, the search for evidence and truth is fulfilled. Yet intuition is not contrasted with reasoning and reflective analysis. It is not facile insight or esoteric revelation but a hard-won seeing of the phenomenon as it is in itself and for our view. Only when the mind's intention is satisfied by the self-presentation of the object, is indubitable, necessary truth acquired. Philosophical certainty is of this type. Descartes was right in excluding the contingent and the probable from the body of wisdom. Systematic acquisitions of a necessary sort give content to phenomenology in matters concerning the foundation of all science and method.

Existentialism does not regard mathematical certainty as the model for all philosophical thinking, and neither does it seek to provide the logical foundation of the sciences. Yet it is attracted by certain congenial features of phenomenological method, especially its epistemological neutrality. Although such neutrality is not an end in itself, it serves two important purposes. By recalling us to a fresh, unprejudiced scrutiny of the face of things, it brings to a halt the sterile quarrel of idealism versus realism, a controversy which has made itself stranger to the only region in which a solution is likely to be found. The existentialists agree that, whatever the eventual settlement of the problem of knowledge, it cannot be reached through an extension of the older epistemological positions but only through an unfettered reinspection of the given factors in knowledge. Secondly, this neutral stand suggests that in the original cognitive situation the distinction between subject and object has not yet been drawn. Existentialism hopes to bypass a good many of the modern epistemological difficulties by criticizing the dichotomy between subject and object. It furnishes more careful descriptions of the cognitive union between mind and being, as it appears before our later reflection establishes distinctions and lends support to the primacy of one principle over the other.

The quest after essential knowledge, in the sense assigned by Husserl, is a fundamental preoccupation of the existentialists. It enables them to overcome one of the dangerous tendencies of Kierkegaard's thought: the retreat to a sphere of ineffable, individual privacy. Existentialists have attempted to effect a strategic union between Kierkegaard and Husserl at this point.[10] From the former, they derive their orientation toward the richness and uniqueness of individual existence. Kierkegaard supplies the material content of the existential dialectic by stressing the importance of the concrete person and his interior life. But this emphasis is maintained by Kierkegaard at the expense of confidence in the philosophical enterprise. Lest they be locked up in private revelations, the existentialists have appealed to Husserl for methodological justification of philosophy. He gives them confidence that, even with a starting point in the individual, generalization can be validly made in terms of generic, essential traits. The great problem confronting the existentialist movement is whether a synthesis is really possible between Kierkegaardian content and Husserlian form, between individual existence and purified universal essence. Many critics contend that such a marriage results in the destruction of both partners. Even the existentialist leaders grant that these streams of thought must be modified considerably, before one is permitted to claim both the concreteness of the individual existent and the generality of philosophical reasoning.

Precisely here, in the relation between the individual thinker and the work of studying essential objects, there is a clash of outlooks between Kierkegaard and Husserl. For Kierkegaard's recurrent charge against Hegel was that the latter leaves unclarified the relation between the empirical and the absolute ego. So wary is Kierkegaard of the systematic transformation of the empirical self into the absolute mind, that he allows no legitimate sense in which the individual finite being is transcendental. At most, the individual can direct himself toward a transcendent being, but he can do so only because of his own utter distinctness from such an order of reality. The individual carries out his essential thinking precisely as an empirical, contingent existent who retains his actual bonds with other beings and reflects within and upon these existential conditions.

The individual holds a paradoxical position in Husserl's phenomenology. His Cartesian notion of indubitability requires him to retain the individual self and its reflective experience. But it is a condition for the attainment of essential knowledge that belief in the given, actual world of nature be suspended, placed in brackets. The content of the natural attitude of positing an existent world is indeed retained, but no use is made of the belief itself. It is put out of play by the *epoché*, the suspension of existential assent. This step is dictated by the Cartesian-Leibnizian principle that in a rigorous science only apodictic truths are admissable, that is, those truths the contradictory of which in unthinkable.

Since the natural attitude is imbedded in the contingent world of space and time, it must be reduced before philosophy can be given scientific form. The *epoché* includes the self as one bodily and psychic entity in the natural world of contingent existents. In this sense, phenomenology has to do with essences and only with essences: it admits no existence as relevant which has not been found within purified consciousness itself or validated by this consciousness. Still, essences are treated precisely in so far as they present themselves in individual conscious experience. The individual ego somehow survives the eidetic reduction of all naturally posited matters of fact.

Unfortunately, Kierkegaard did not justify his own position through a further consideration of the canons of philosophical knowledge of existents. He abandoned the area of philosophical discussion too rapidly, leaving latter-day existentialists with an apparent choice between Husserl's theory of scientific rigor and a flight from the terrain of philosophical science in matters of existence. Some existentialists attempt to carry out the analysis of human existence within the phenomenologically prescribed brackets, whereas others have taken the more difficult road of criticizing the Husserlian claim to a unique and universal scientific method. In doing so, however, they have had to reckon with the later phases in Husserl's own view of an adequate philosophy.

(b) RADICAL TRANSCENDENTAL IDEALISM. Husserl proposes to push the examination of truth and evidence back to its roots, back to the beginning of being in the sense of truth.[11] This radicalization is required, if phenomenology is to be a truly presuppositionless science. In suspending our conviction in the world as existing

independently of purified consciousness, phenomenology is critical of the assumptions of the physico-mathematical sciences, psychology and metaphysics. The latter science is restricted to the
area of reality, that is, of being as realized in a spatio-temporal
universe subject to causal conditions and contingency. All the
traditional sciences depend for their validity upon an original
positing of a real world, within which the scientific objects and
laws are exemplified. Phenomenology is a foundational science,
because it inquires about the origin of this widest framework of
scientific understanding.

Phenomenology is also a historical science in its role of working back from the present attitudes in the sciences to their original outlooks, which have become sedimented through long fa-
miliarity and technical usage. If, for instance, the root meanings
of modern mathematical conceptions are reactivated, one comes
to appreciate the modern world-view in its originary lineaments.
One discovers that the totality of objective beings in nature—
which constitutes the presupposition of both commonsense and
scientific outlooks—is itself posited by the mind. The suspension
of belief must be widened to include not only the empirical self
and other natural existents but the entire theoretical attitude,
which is oriented to the objective being of the world. The
phenomenological reduction is not consummated until reflection
is centered immanently upon a transcendentally purified consciousness, upon that which alone remains immediately valid after
the entire belief in a world has been placed within brackets. The
totality of objects or noemata remains within the immanent possession of this radical reflection, but there is no unexamined presumption about the origin and givenness of this system.

The pregiven world underlying our historical standpoint presents a challenge to phenomenology. Husserl regards this datum
as a clue, leading him to discover an equally primary act of constituting on the part of the transcendental ego. Our passiveness
before this pregiven world is due to the obscuring of the constitutive act, for it has been covered over by sedimented layers of
secondary meanings. Phenomenological reflection takes as its goal

the firm presentation of an absolute founding act of pure consciousness. Husserl makes an imperceptible transition from the constitutive act of the ego, regarded as bringing something to meaningful determination in *knowledge* alone, to this same act as a literal founding of the *being* of the object (although never an arbitrary, "subjectivistic" production). He unites these two senses of "constitution" in virtue of his conception of being as that which is given validity as an object (actual or possible) for intentional acts within the unity of consciousness. Even the traits of contingent existence can in principle receive their foundation from the purified ego. In his final phase, Husserl allied phenomenology with the high tradition of German idealism.

Perhaps the most serious difficulty encountered by Husserl is that of escaping from solipsism or isolation within the self alone.[12] In the transcendental reduction, the bare surviving minimum is still an individual ego, although little indication is given of the community of meaning between individuality in this perspective and in the natural viewpoint. The world appears as a totality for this individual ego: the self still has its being as in the world. From an analysis of what appears in the intuitive self-presence of the world in consciousness at this level, Husserl attempts to work out a public zone of being. In successive order, he describes the constitutive acts whereby the transcendental, individual ego secures its own psycho-physical nature, the co-presence in the corporeal universe of other bodies presumably belonging to other selves, and the community or intersubjectivity among these monadic selves. The constituted presence of one's own body is fundamental to the entire argument. Intersubjective communication is upheld because of the possibility of intending the same world of objects and because of sharing in the common type of universal consciousness. The constitutive source of the world of validated experience is the intersubjective community of selves.

In face of this thoroughgoing constructive idealism, the existentialists have been obliged to clarify what they mean by a search after origins. An original situation is either one which confronts man with limits and presuppositions that cannot be over-

come without destroying his proper manner of being as an existent individual or one which indicates the source in consciousness
from which the world and man are derivable. A choice between
these conflicting interpretations is made more imperative by Kierkegaard's assault on the presuppositionless character of idealist
systems. If understanding operates after the fact or in dependence
upon the initiative of being, then one can never entirely forget or
do away with this relation to what is other than consciousness.
Kierkegaard points out the comical aspect of an enterprise which
places huge parentheses around man's actual need of an originary
irruption of existence into consciousness and then proceeds to
sublate or explain away our dependence on a given factor. This
argument can be applied to Husserl in the degree that he describes the world of men and things as ontologically dependent
upon a constitutive act, whereas the entire descriptive operation
continues to rest upon a given, finite, existential basis.

All existentialists are sympathetic towards the project of a renewal of the basic meanings of being by means of a critique of the
sciences and the attitude of objective, theoretical thinking. Most
of them also express dissatisfaction with the present state of metaphysics and seek a reformation in terms of some sort of distinction between ontology and metaphysics. Husserl's universal ontology has met with a wide measure of acceptance only from
Sartre, who nevertheless gives it a radical revision. The rationalistic postulate upon which Husserl's essay in ontology rests has
been subjected to a thorough criticism by the existentialists, who
prefer to insist with Kierkegaard upon the independence of being
from our ways of determining the experience of being. There is
an equivocation at the heart of Husserl's theory of the transformation of pre-given factors. Because these factors come to be
known, and given standing, in scientific systems, they do not drop
their given character in the order of being. Most existentialists
restrict the constituting activity to noetic and moral functions.
Data are transformed cognitively in being recognized for what
they are. The founding of being itself means an acknowledgment of its presence and irrevocable givenness rather than a revo-

cation of this givenness. Especially in the transformation of the human self, reference is made to a moral passage from a mere thing of nature to a responsible, free agent, rather than to an ontological passage from individual self as empirical to this same self as transcendental and originative of being.

These differences come to a head in the divergent approaches to existence. Husserl's technique of suspension of belief in the naturally existent world leads him back, as it led Descartes, to the individual self as the existential foundation. The Husserlian self is immanently present to itself and hence is the self-founded beginning of philosophy without any assumptions, logical or ontological. Unlike the Cartesian self, however, it is endowed with many of the functions of deity, since the order of knowing is also the order of the foundation of being. This transcendental beginning is required to confer meaning and hence phenomenologically validated existence upon objects in the world. Sartre's inquiry about the absolute priority of transcendental existence over essence and the relative priority of essential meaning over mundane existence takes its rise from this metaphysical doctrine. It has the advantage of furnishing a strict explanation of the correlation between human existence and being-in-the-world, which is one of the common premises of existentialism.

From Kierkegaard's standpoint, however, the conferral of scientific validity and objectivity is quite different from a conferral of existence. The two kinds of endowment can only be taken as synonymous in a Hegelian context, wherein a logic of implication supplants causality and hence wherein the conditions of the possibility of human experience are also the sufficient conditions of being, in any philosophically relevant sense. Kierkegaard's thought challenges Husserl's unnoticed assumption that what cannot be understood by the transcendental ego cannot be. The human mind is measured by being and does not supply the absolute measure of being, even for purposes of scientific strictness. To exist, in the Kierkegaardian sense, is to emphasize separation rather than immanent identity between the finite individual and any absolute source of being and truth, as well as between thought and being. Existential certainty is founded on a recognition of this unyielding distinction, rather than on its reduction to a higher synthesis. For being is more than being-in-the-sense-of-truth, the "more" being measured by the difference between logical consequences and physical causality. Furthermore, being in the sense of existential truth is precisely an affirmation of the dependence of our way of existing and knowing upon that which is other than our self and constitutive of our reality as a free creature. Existent reality carries its validity within itself as it stands in contingent, temporal situations. It is philosophically relevant precisely in its natural condition. There is no need to wait for a transcendental deduction before discovering the philosophical status and implications of human existence.

Finally, the existentialist doctrine on reflection contains elements drawn from both Husserl and Kierkegaard. To the former it owes its preoccupation with basic meanings; to the latter it owes its primarily moral accent as a qualification of personal inwardness and freedom. Both thinkers respect some sort of individual reflection, although Kierkegaard locates the decisive factor of reflectiveness in an act of will measuring one's projects by the norm of the eternal being. He recognizes a distinctive contribution of will and man's passional side to the state of reflection. From both sources, the existentialists inherit the difficulty about how the reflective individual can communicate with other selves. How to steer clear of solipsism, whether moral or epistemic, is one of the major problems. Kierkegaard's appeal to a common bond in God and Husserl's reference to the body and the public world of science provide clues to the social ties that unite men. For a satisfactory answer, however, the existentialists find it necessary to incorporate these hints into a new view of things.

The existentialist philosophies are not mere mosaic works pieced together out of fragments taken from Kierkegaard, Nietzsche, Husserl, and other predecessors. However enlightening a study of existential backgrounds may prove to be, this approach must be kept in a strictly subordinate role. Historical explanations are apt to overlook the original features in contemporary efforts and to evade the task of theoretical evaluation of arguments. Existentialism must also be examined and appraised in terms of the actual ways it has developed. Serious attempts at independent thinking have been made, and the final result in each case bears an original stamp and presents a challenge to other philosophical viewpoints.

Chapter II

Sartre's Postulatory Atheism

Jean-Paul Sartre (1905——) occupies a paradoxical place in the existential movement. In the popular mind, he represents the typical existential thinker and man. This reputation is his reward for taking care to communicate his views through the literary medium: his short stories, novels, and plays are often the only point of contact between the lay reader and contemporary philosophy. Hence he is responsible both for the notoriety of existentialism and for the suspicion with which conservative people regard this entire current of thought. As he himself has remarked, the present literary furor over his existentialism is a repetition of the cult of dadaism, which sprang up after World War I.

Precisely this literary success and popular audience have caused many academic philosophers to dismiss Sartre without serious study on the ground that his doctrine is only a passing sensation. Moreover, they are apt to extend this judgment to include all the existentialists and thus let the passage of time and fashion take care of all the problems. This disdainful policy is convenient but is not likely to achieve the intended result. For whatever his literary ventures, Sartre rests his case ultimately upon something philosophically more substantial than propaganda and pornography. He has not belied his own good training in philosophy at the École Normale Supérieure or his years of teaching philosophy in Le Havre and Paris. Alongside of his journalism must be ranged his technical phenomenological studies on the imaginary, imagination, and the theory of emotions, which won him professional recognition on the eve of World War II. These investigations demonstrated his ability to handle the technique of Husserl and Heidegger, the writers whom he studied most carefully during an academic stay in Germany.

In 1943, Sartre issued his first major philosophical work, *Being and Nothingness* (the word *le néant*, in this title, means literally: *non-ens, nothing*, but with the connotation of an active *naughting*). It is intended as the ontological foundation for an entire philosophy, culminating in a theory of man and morality. But like Heidegger, Sartre has been unable, so far, to carry out his ambitious project. This is due partly to the multifarious literary and political activities in which he has become involved. A more intrinsic obstacle to the completion of his plan is the amount of serious criticism directed against *Being and Nothingness* by other philosophers. Perhaps the most frequent objection has been that the outlook advocated here is antihumanistic and amoral in import. If this charge were true, it would be difficult to develop a practical theory of human conduct on such an unpromising basis. Consequently, Sartre has been trying to show, during the past few years, that the proposed extension of his viewpoint is theoretically feasible. His address on *Existentialism is a Humanism* (1946) is a minor contribution in this direction which has, however, convinced none except his own followers. He has announced a treatise concerning man and morals, but so far it has not been completed.

What makes Sartre's position the more unusual is that it runs counter to the other forms of existentialism on important issues. He is not regarded by other existentialists as the spokesman for their common attitude. Sartre and Gabriel Marcel have both warned French readers that they represent antithetic positions, and Marcel explicitly denies that Sartre's fundamental descriptions apply to his theistic existentialism. Heidegger himself, despite his strong influence over Sartre's mind, does not acknowledge his French admirer as making a legitimate continuation of his own views. One reason for Heidegger's vigorous repudiation of an atheistic interpretation of his philosophy is his desire to separate himself from Sartre. Jaspers has also made it clear, through his recent statements about the philosophical attitude towards God, that existential thinking is under no internal compulsion to arrive at a godless outlook. The problem of God is central both to Sartre's philosophy and to his quarrel with the other existentialists.

At the same time, there is an unexpected convergence between these domestic criticisms and those passed by theists in the Scholastic tradition. Sartre has invited critical examination by the latter group by taking explicit issue with realistic theism, as he understands this position. He has indicated his divergence on such characteristic questions as the relation between essence and existence, moral law and human freedom, consciousness and being. The challenge has been accepted by a number of thinkers in the Aristotelian-Thomistic line of philosophy, thus furnishing a good example of philosophical dialogue in actual operation.

1. *Phenomenology, Ontology, and Metaphysics*

In their eagerness to reach the more concrete and practical issues involved in the Sartrean world view, many students have neglected the fundamental questions on method and theory of the sciences which underlie this outlook. Sartre himself has never encouraged this narrow concern with practical applications but has consistently stressed the importance of his general methodology. Indeed, the key to his way of reasoning is provided in the subtitle to *Being and Nothingness*: "An Essay in Phenomenological Ontology." This juxtaposition of phenomenology and ontology suggests the historical background of Sartre's speculation. It is located in the tendency to work out an ontology on phenomenological grounds, a project to which Husserl, Scheler, and Heidegger devoted themselves. Sartre agrees with this program and claims that, where his illustrious German predecessors failed, he can succeed.[1]

The trouble with these forerunners was that they did not adhere with sufficient fidelity and singlemindedness to the phenomenological standpoint itself. They did not base ontology squarely upon their methodological premises but smuggled some doctrinal content in from alien sources. The privileged place of the ego as a transcendental sphere of reflection in Husserl's philosophy is evidence of his dependence upon the Cartesian and Kantian theories of being. He introduced a special zone of reality so that phenomenological studies could be made to yield results relevant for a theory of being. But this supposes that the inquiry into essential structures and the conditions of intentionality is not adequate by itself to found an ontology. Sartre calls this assumption into question.

The Sartrean "radicalization" of phenomenology develops in this perspective. It is unnecessary to make covert borrowings from extraphenomenological sources in order to constitute an ontology. In the strict sense, it is even improper to speak about the ontological *consequences* of phenomenology. The findings of this method are, as such, significant for determining the meaning of being. In settling the general structures of the meaning of being for man, it already accomplishes the work of ontology. Ontology is not a further deduction and hence does not require the introduction of further principles. Reflection upon the situation within which intentional meanings are founded, supplies the required starting point for a phenomenological ontology. Hence Sartre regards his own procedure as remaining more faithful to the possibilities and exigencies of the Husserlian approach than the ways followed by Husserl himself and Heidegger.

Readers of *Being and Nothingness* are often bewildered by the abruptness of the Introduction and its apparent lack of connection with the seven hundred pages of analysis which follow. The actual background is prepared by Sartre in his earlier phenomenological studies. In these preparatory essays, he makes it clear that there is no adequate distinction between a science of phenomena and a science of being. The latter discipline cannot hope to do more than comprehend the general structure of human reality as present to the world, and this insight can be acquired by phenomenology from its own resources. It presumes only that man is capable of interrogating and assuming responsibility for himself through self-comprehension and that in his self-clarification and self-determination consists his "true reality." Consciousness displays itself, moreover, as a reference to things in the world. The sum of meaningful intentional acts and structures and the sum of meaningful realities coincide. In grasping the sense of essential projects, one thereby illuminates the face of being.

In the opening lines of his investigation on imagination, Sartre describes the ordinary perceptual situation.[2] The individual is looking at a white sheet of paper on his writing desk. He distinguishes between this paper as a thing, having its own reality, and as it is for him. This distinction can be drawn legitimately because the qualities of the paper seem to be ascertained by me without being produced by the spontaneity of my consciousness. What the thing is in itself is a sort of inert being. The only way in which it can retain some autonomy and reality of its own is to be an inert *existence in-itself*. Yet it is present to me, the perceiving individual, and hence has a reality for me. Consciousness does not exist after the manner of a thing but is an active form of *existence for-itself*. Thus the conditions of perceptual existence appear to be: thing and consciousness, a realm of inactive being in-itself and another realm of spontaneous being for-itself, *l'en-soi* and *le pour-soi*.

Sartre regards this report as a naïve ontology. Although it lacks the refinement and especially the essential orientation provided by phenomenology, it does have an ontological bearing. Within the context of the intentional activity of consciousness, as determining significant objects in the world, such an analysis can be given a properly ontological formulation. This generalization is made in the Introduction to *Being and Nothingness*, where the theory of being in-itself and being for-itself is proposed. The description is highly compressed, striking one like a prologue delivered in heaven. As an outline of the regions of being, it is unavoidably dogmatic and simplistic; the rest of the book is an attempt to dispel these defects by showing that the attitudes of men do indeed require this interpretative pattern. Sartre holds that ontology must begin with a few postulates, which express the conditions for the description of intentional phenomena, that is, acts of the mind which are essentially directed to some object of knowledge or desire in its otherness from the conscious subject. The purpose of the subsequent chapters in the treatise is to establish the presence of these factors in all the basic situations involving human reality.

There is an admittedly circular relationship obtaining between the introductory framework and the more particular studies. The latter are guided by the general commitments about the broadest contours of being and, in turn, are supposed to confirm these primary assumptions. Actually, the later detailed descriptions are predetermined both in the type of evidence admitted and in the outcome for ontology. They are carefully controlled applications and illustrations of a thesis rather than fresh and unbiased inspections, since their ontological significance is already decided by restricting the meaning of being to the field of phenomenology. The only aspects of being that are admitted into court are precisely those features which tend to corroborate the thesis that the sum of reality is contained in being in-itself and being for-itself.

Sartre does more than maintain that his analysis reveals these two modes of being. He claims that these are the *only* basic components of reality and that they furnish the nearest substitute for a comprehensive notion of being as such. He denies that we can obtain a unified concept of being or go beyond the finite and immanent modes of being. He is close to Nietzsche in repudiating any transcendent being and in substituting endurance of the dichotomy of consciousness and substance for a grasp of being as such. By restricting his attention to human meanings and their foundation in finite existence, he reinforces his view that the phenomenological report is final in every respect. He thereby defends not only the rightful autonomy of this science but also its claim to be coextensive with the science of being and ontological meaning.

Hence Sartre's ontology rests on a twofold option that precedes all his philosophizing. He starts by accepting Nietzsche's atheistic postulate and Husserl's postulate of a self-sufficient phenomenology. On these two underpinnings rests his entire system of thought. They are indispensable and mutually strengthening foundations. Without the support of a postulatory atheism, he could not confidently restrict ontology to a reflection upon the conditions prevailing within the phenomenological reduction. And without the latter, he could not gain entrance to a self-contained region wherein rigorous, generalized findings can be made without reference to God or an actual, causal order. Sartre's descriptive essays are elaborate attempts to remove the arbitrary character from these radical postulates and to confirm them by demonstrating their competence in interpreting our human plight.

A similar purpose is served by the distinction made between ontology and metaphysics, a distinction which is traceable eventually to Husserl's attitude toward empirical existence.[3] True to its phenomenological constitution, Sartrean ontology focuses upon the universal essential structures entering into the organization of the world. Metaphysics is possible only as a subsequent discipline incorporated into the wider context of ontology. Its stated purpose is to investigate particular events, contingent processes, actual beings, in order to determine their origin in a hypothetical way. It can never reach apodictic certainty, since it deals with contingent particular instances and physical causes. At most, it makes surmises about the actual causal origins of *this* particular world, leaving the assured analysis of world-in-general to ontology. Thus Sartre makes metaphysics a hypothetical, particularist, and causal discipline, in contradistinction to the certitude, universality, and non-causal character of ontology. Actual existents cannot be dealt with philosophically apart from the phenomenological reduction, and to deal with these aspects within the phenomenological context is to admit the impossibility of achieving scientific rigor in their regard. One should place little confidence in the deductive explanations of metaphysics and should remain satisfied with ontological descriptions.

The contrast between these two sciences plays an important role in Sartre's philosophy, since it enables him to offer a description of human existence without becoming entangled in embarrassing questions about God and the soul. The latter entities are problems for philosophy only under the heading of metaphysics, not of ontology. For the mind is not led to ask about God and the human soul except in terms of an adequate cause needed to explain this or that particular set of contingent facts. According to the phenomenological principle that scientific certitude refers only to what sustains universal, necessary, and essential relations, metaphysical inquiries about contingent, particular modes of being and their actual causes can never attain scientific standing. This principle is applied by both Max Scheler (the German phenomenologist and philosopher of religion) and Sartre to discredit the Aristotelian-Scholastic demonstrations of the existence of God and an immaterial soul.

Both thinkers make the conditions governing phenomenological investigations universal standards of scientific inquiry. It is, indeed, legitimate for this discipline to prescind from questions of actual causal origin, since it operates within parentheses drawn around the actual world. But once the study of essential forms in their apparential presence in consciousness is identified with ontology, the principle of causality is excluded from the real order as well as from the intentional order. An ontology so conceived will not be required to make inference to an immaterial principle of life in man or to a transcendent God. But it is absolved from this requirement only because it is also cut loose from actual existents in their own reality. The *aperçus métaphysiques* with which Sartre concludes his major work are guesses about a phantom world which even he does not take too seriously. Sartrean metaphysics is an attenuated extension of the same myth-making function which produces his ontological first principles of being in-itself and being for-itself.

2. *The Myth of Being In-Itself*

In one of his summary definitions of existentialism, Sartre describes it as the doctrine which maintains the primacy of existence over essence and which takes its start from man's subjectivity.[4] Although his claim to have identified the common core of exis-

tential doctrine is repudiated by the other existentialists, this definition does capture the essential features of his own position. Its
precise meaning can be appreciated, however, only in the light of
his general ontology. This doctrine has three main traits: it is a
realism based upon the nature of consciousness and its phenomenal object; it defines *being* in terms of opaque, inert stuff; it regards *consciousness* as a powerful principle of lack and existence,
whence stem the essential structures of our human world. Each
of these aspects must be examined in order to grasp the sense of
Sartre's definition of existentialism and locate the soft spots where
criticism must be directed. The first two points will be considered
in the present section; the meaning of consciousness as *le néant*,
or the naughting function, requires separate treatment in the following section.

(*a*) PHENOMENAL REALISM. One characteristic habit of the
existentialist mind is to carry on its inspection of things within a
given historical framework, which not only provides a concrete
setting but also determines the questions and evidences to be admitted. Thus Sartre prefaces his analysis of cognition with the historical remark that the major achievement of modern philosophy
has been the reduction of being to the series of its manifesting appearances.[5] It is unnecessary to consider the problem of knowledge except in terms of the Kantian distinction between phenomenon and noumenon. And within this perspective, it is only possible to see the matter as Nietzsche portrayed it.

Nietzsche tried to shock his readers by making unqualified
declarations about the end of the reign of truth. He proclaimed
that "truth" is dead and all is "falsity." By this he meant that our
world can no longer give credence to the idealistic theory of an
absolute truth about a realm of things-in-themselves. There is no
infinite mind encompassing within itself all the dialectical conflicts and partial insights of finite minds. This follows because in
the order of being there is no absolute reality existing behind
the appearances. The appearances are all in all; conflicting occur-
rences stand as they are, without receiving support or justification from elsewhere. Because there is no behind and no beyond,

man must learn to find his absolute and his truth solely in the process of finite events. In Kantian terms, there is no noumenal order except the order of the phenomena themselves. If there is any true knowledge of being, it must be knowledge of being as wholly phenomenal and constituted by the phenomena.

To Sartre, Nietzsche's aphorisms are like flames spurting from the sword of the angel of Eden. They warn us against returning to a naïvely paradisaical state of mind, which would search for a transcendent or noumenal source of our experience. Sartre is ready enough to admit that Nietzsche himself could not endure his own doctrine in all its literalness and that he restored the absolute in the guise of an immanent law of cyclic return. But it is part of the economy and strategy of the Sartrean method not to inquire whether the reality of an absolute, transcendent being can be rehabilitated without having recourse either to Kant's noumenal ideal or Hegel's absolute dialectical mind. He permits criticism of Nietzsche only on those points where the latter ceases to be the prophet of atheistic existentialism. It requires a more radical criticism of the Kant-Hegel-Nietzsche span in the history of philosophy to enable the mind to make that return "to the things themselves" demanded by Husserl and Sartre. Some other aspects of this criticism are brought out by Marcel and Heidegger.

Sartre seeks to combine his theory of self-sufficient phenomenal being with realism rather than with subjective idealism. Granted that being is nothing more than the totality of appearances which are linked together according to an essential law; granted that being does not stand behind the appearances but is constituted in and by them. Nevertheless, the being of the phenomenon does not exist only in as much as it reveals itself to the mind. Like Berkeley, Husserl is wrong in concluding that the being of the phenomenon is merely that of being perceived.[6] In opposition to this view, Sartre maintains the "transphenomenality of being." This means that the intentional relationship of perceiving and being perceived does not exhaust the real. The act of perceiving is also to be regarded precisely as a mode of being proceeding from and revealing a real principle: human subjectivity. Similarly, the appearance or the perceived object stands in relation to other appearances as well as to the conscious perceiver. Thus there is a twofold transphenomenality: that of the knowing subject and that of the known object.

It is imperative for Sartre to prove first of all the transphenomenal reality of the conscious subjectivity and, later on, the being-character of the object. This is the force of his remark that his existentialism begins with human subjectivity or the Cogito. "Cogito" means "I am thinking," and it stresses the existing "I" or self just as much as its act of thinking. It is the same thing to make a beginning here and to assert the primacy of existence over essence. What is most valuable about Descartes' account of the Cogito is the affirmation of its existence as an indubitable datum. Historically, however, this starting point has always led to subjectivism and idealism. In order to circumvent such an outcome in his case, Sartre corrects Descartes' description of the primary situation.[7] The Cartesian thinking self is attained as a unity of states and acts of reflective knowledge, in which consciousness intends itself as an object. But this reflective Cogito is a secondary and derivative condition of consciousness, one that is built up by pure acts of consciousness. It is necessary to probe farther back until the prereflective Cogito is reached. This radical regression can be made by observing the difference between two ways of having self-awareness. The self as described by Descartes is formally posited through a reflective act; it has become itself the object of an intentional meaning and process of unification. But there is a more primitive situation in which consciousness is concomitantly aware of itself in the very act of knowing some object in the world. In knowing something, there is also at least an implicit awareness of doing the knowing. This suggests that the fundamental reality of human subjectivity is not a personal self but a non-posited, non-objectified, prereflective consciousness. At the source of all objects, including the ego, is the pure act of consciousness, the prereflective Cogito. In this sense alone is the Cogito the point of departure for Sartre.

In thus revising Descartes, Sartre is also criticizing Husserl. The ultimate phenomenological reduction is not to a special ego-sphere of reflective consciousness, for this in turn has its presuppositions. The most radical bracketing and suspension of belief extend to the ego itself, reducing it to one among the objects intended by consciousness. The bedrock zone of autonomy is only reached when consciousness in the second degree (the reflective, personal self) is brought back to its presuppositions in consciousness in the first degree (pure impersonal spontaneity of consciousness). The ego and the world are principles of unification posited by unreflective consciousness: they are noetic and noematic correlates within which it is possible to have personal selves and objects. But in becoming conscious of an object, there is also consciousness of consciousness. The formula for the Sartrean Cogito is not: "I am conscious of this chair," but rather: "There is consciousness of this chair." And in this consciousness of the object, there is an interior awareness of consciousness by itself. Consciousness grasps itself in an absolute way as a pure spontaneity, an act of positing and intending, rather than as something posited and intended. All is clear and limpid here, since consciousness attains its own phenomenal reality in an immediate certitude. This is the perfect existential certitude, an absolute interiority that needs no completion or further reduction and that is the absolute source of all existences, personal and objective. It determines itself to existence and is a first condition for all particular existents. The primacy of existence and subjectivity is assured without admitting the prejudice of a self or subject in a privileged position.

Husserl did not make a sufficiently radical reduction to be able to ask himself why consciousness ever posits the ego as well as the world. But the problem confronts Sartre, once he describes radical consciousness as an impersonal spontaneity. He thinks that consciousness produces the ego, as an ideal unity of its own actions, states, and qualities, in order to mask its own impersonality and sheer spontaneity. It is unable to bear this sense of absolute interiority and lucidity, in which there is no distinction between being and appearance, the possible and the real, the willed and the inflicted. Hence consciousness deceives itself by projecting the self as a unified personal center, which can make these distinctions. Acquiescence in this self-deception is the basic, non-moral meaning of "living in bad faith." It generates the natural attitude of accepting the world and the personal self as given substances and accepting hard-and-fast distinctions between possibility and actuality, being and appearance, what one wills and what one suffers from the action of another, independent agent. Fortunately, however, this deception is never carried out completely. Consciousness can make return to its own pure spontaneity. Consequently, there is both a motive and a means for breaking with the natural attitude. Contrary to Husserl, Sartre does not regard the phenomenological reduction as a highly specialized technique, limited to a few experts and based mainly on intellectual discipline. It is a matter of having the courage to face what lies behind the self, and such courage is within the grasp of us all.[8]

Unlike Jaspers and Marcel, Sartre insists upon the impersonal character of primary existential subjectivity. He runs counter to the Kierkegaardian trend of equating the existential and the personal individual. In this respect, he comes closer to the neutral description of consciousness offered by William James. But it is not so much the findings of empirical psychology as the difficulties of Husserl's transcendental idealism which force him to make primal consciousness an impersonal condition, constitutive of the personal self. For there is an opaque aspect of the personal self that is unattainable by others and that may lock up the self in its own stronghold. Sartre tries to bypass the problem of the existence and knowledge of other selves at the outset of his analysis by declaring the primary nature of consciousness to be wholly lucid, impersonal, and hence shared by all. Semantically, however, he shares the same difficulty with Hume of referring to "consciousness of consciousness" as consciousness of it*self*. Even when he speaks of "consciousnesses" in the plural, he implies some self-identity in the particular phases of the feeling of pure interiority. He dissipates the unified self, only to find a kind of selfhood in the moments in the stream of pure spontaneity. Sartre administers the rules of method firmly in his own favor. When it is a question of establishing its *non*reflective, *im*personal and *non*-posited character, he is ready to admit the distinction between actuality and possibility, being and appearance. But these distinctions are not permitted to apply when the appearances would seem to show the actual presence of personal selfhood at the heart of interior consciousness and spontaneity.

The primacy and privilege of the reflective self are attacked in another way by Sartre. From the prereflective subjectivity, he claims to show the transphenomenal reality of the object. There is a mode of being in the direction of the object which is also incapable of assimilation to the intentional relation of meaningful being and hence incapable of reduction to the reflective ego. He terms his proof of this reality a new ontological argument.[9] It passes from consciousness to being, but not from idea to object. It concludes to that which is not merely objective and whose mode of being is the least perfect.

The conscious act is an absolute event and a condition of knowledge, but it is not the only absolute or the sole condition of knowledge. This becomes evident from a further analysis of consciousness. To be conscious of something is to be in the presence of that which is not consciousness itself. The intentional character of consciousness means that it is directed not only towards an object but also towards that in the object which is more than a noematic correlate of the intentional act. This implies the presence of a reality that is unassimilable to the status of an intuited essence, even though it has no meaning apart from such intuition. Furthermore, the Cogito is related to the non-self by other acts that are not cognitive and that cannot be reduced to variations of reflective consciousness. Although the object does appear in consciousness, it is not in every respect defined by this relation or produced in a transcendental way. It is an object of consciousness only because it is also a mode of being in-itself. This is the second absolute pole of being and the second indispensable condition of knowledge.

(b) Description of the In-Itself. Sartre summarizes his phenomenist realism in the statement that the "being of that which *appears* does not exist *only* in so far as it does appear. The trans-

phenomenal being of that which is *for consciousness* is itself *in-itself (en soi)*."[10] This balanced formula expresses his resolve to retain the starting point in the (prereflective) Cogito and the argument from consciousness to being and at the same time wring from these premises a realistic conclusion that resists productive idealism. Consciousness terminates in being in-itself only in its phenomenal aspect. Our knowledge is of the phenomenal essence or binding pattern among appearance. The transphenomenal being of the object is literally transcognitive; it goes beyond the possible scope of human intelligence. Analysis of consciousness only indicates the direction in which such a reality lies. There is no cognitive grasp of the existing act of the In-itself, even though the fact of its existence is established through the new ontological argument from the exigencies of consciousness. If an understanding of the existential act of things is a measure of the existential character of a philosophy, then in this respect Sartre's philosophy falls short of the measure.

Sartre seeks to avoid the obvious criticism that he is reinstating the Kantian noumenon as a counterweight to constitutive idealism. His reply is that the In-itself is not a distinct reality from the phenomenon: that which appears is the same being which is also in-itself. This is not an adequate principle of difference, however, since Kant did not intend the things-in-themselves to occupy another region of being distinct from that of the phenomena. In both philosophies, the dualism between the knowable and the unknowable aspects of being remains a sharp one, and the difficulty must be faced as to the grounds on which the unknowable can be asserted. Kant remained more consistent with his principles by refusing to make any theoretical commitment about the noumenal order, whereas Sartre does offer a theoretical deduction of the existence of the In-itself in general.

As far as determining something about the nature of being in-itself is concerned, Sartre admits the necessity of relying upon an emotional experience for the first clues. This experience is not sufficient by itself to indicate the nature of the In-itself, but careful reflection upon the emotional encounter does yield an indirect understanding. Phenomenological description of certain unique emotional attitudes takes the place of direct eidetic intuition of the transphenomenal being of the object. For this reason, there is an intimate fusion, even in his technical treatises, of Sartre's talents as a novelist and his philosophical intelligence. Imagination not only supports and enlivens analytic understanding but supplies it with the required data at critical stages in the argument.

The background for Sartre's theory of the In-self is found in his novel, *Nausea* (1938).[11] The hero, Roquentin, is present one day in the city park. He is seated on a bench near an ancient chestnut tree whose thick, black, formless roots sink deep into the earth. He has a sudden illumination which seems to reveal to him the true face of objective reality. Individual items of experience are swept away as so much surface froth. Beyond the familiar relations which things sustain with us as our tools and as catering to our practical needs, the hero of the novel (Sartre's spokesman) is brought in contact with the amorphous, bloated reality of being in-itself. Like the roots of the chestnut tree, the transphenomenal being of each object is simply there, one portion crowding out the other through its equal and equally senseless hold upon existence. In the face of this sea of vagueness and sodden passivity, Roquentin is overwhelmed with a sense of the superfluity of all things, including his own self. He experiences a great disgust before the radical absurdity and unintelligibility that remain when the trappings of human convention are removed.

Later on, Roquentin is able to formulate his experiences in more precise terms. The key to his nausea is the discovery of the complete contingency of everything, the total absence of any reason for transphenomenal being. No existent thing is explainable by, or reducible to, another. They all share in an absurdity which is the senseless meaning of the being of the phenomenon. To exist, in this sense, is simply to be there as an obtruding presence, an obscenely resistant fact. Existence of this sort cannot be deduced but only submitted to in its utter gratuity and senselessness. Every being that shares in the In-itself is *de trop,* too much of a dead weight for itself and others. The In-itself surrounds and penetrates us as a stifling fullness, an absolute that gives no response, no shelter, no hope. In all its disgusting ultimacy, it simply *is.*

Nausea or what William James refers to as "a nameless *Unheim-lichkeit*" steals over the mind that honestly faces this fact.

Being and Nothingness merely recasts this account in philosophical language, without adding to its theoretical justification. The weak point remains the nature of the link between the original emotional experience and the ontological reflection. No matter how genuine and compelling a mood of this sort may be, it cannot be transformed into a philosophical first principle without passing certain tests. No reason is advanced by Sartre for making an unconditional ontological generalization out of this experience. He admits that the mood could not by itself establish his principle, but the relevant issue is whether it has any formally ontological significance whatever. Sartre's extrapolation is accomplished more after the manner of a creative novel than an essay on ontology. Imagination remains his major tool in discerning the traits of being.

To realists, the main fault in Sartre's theory is its overstatement of certain features in order to avoid creative idealism.[12] For instance, Sartre recognizes that the known object is not fully known by man and not even fully intelligible to him under present conditions. This indisputable fact is exaggerated to the point of confusing that which is not fully intelligible to man and that which is unintelligible and unthinkable in itself. It would be sufficient to observe that the mind uncovers rather than creates this mode of being and that what it does uncover fails to exhaust the being of the thing. This is not the same as claiming that being in-itself is absurd and beyond the standards of reason. The latter assertion has no essential connection with a realism of knowing but depends upon a reduction of the being of the In-itself to a sort of chaotic prime matter. Like dialectical materialism, Sartrean existentialism defends cognitional realism at the expense of the graded reality and intelligibility of the things known. Only an arbitrary limitation of knowledge to the material phenomenon enables this philosophy to equate the transphenomenal with the transintelligible.

There is a further motive impelling Sartre to declare the absurdity of the being of the world: he seeks to defend the integrity of existence. He accepts the common realistic premise that the unique existence of this individual finite thing cannot be deduced by mere logical implication from a prior principle. An existent being must be respected in all its contingent givenness and concrete uniqueness. But this provides no warrant for Sartre's further inference that therefore the In-itself character of beings is absurd and underived. The nondeducible character of the existent does not entail its unintelligibility and imperviousness to *every* sort of rational justification. Existence has meaning when taken along with the essential nature, even though there is no way available for our determining this meaning beforehand.

Sartre is right in defending the contingency of existent things, but he offers no proof that the best or only defense is by allying contingency with absurdity. He has simply assumed that the contingent means the underived and unintelligible, whereas contingency by itself excludes only a certain type of derivation and meaningfulness. It is incompatible with a necessary deduction or emanation from an absolute mind and with an a priori determination of meaning on the basis of ideal, dialectical necessities alone. But contingent being is precisely that mode of being which owes its origin to a free, creative production and which realizes an irreplaceable meaning or individual essential structure.

What impels Sartre to identify the contingency of the In-itself with its absurdity and lack of causal origin is his plan of subverting the traditional proofs for God's existence. Once it is established that the being of the In-itself is unamenable to intelligible explanation, then it escapes the force of the principle of causality. And if this same transphenomenal reality is by nature underived, then it would be piling absurdity on absurdity to assign a cause for it. Only when God is explained in terms of the Hegelian mind is there plausible ground for invoking such desperate means of saving the integrity of the existent order. Within the climate of absolute idealism, a Kierkegaard was obliged to stress the opposition between existence and systematic reason. But he was not impelled by a Sartrean will to atheism to maintain, in addition, the utter unintelligibility and underived nature of the existentially real.

3. *Consciousness, the Power of Negativity.*

Although the myth of the In-itself serves Sartre's atheistic ends, it also leads him to the verge of irrationalism. His interpretation of the being of the In-itself would seem to give the primacy to that which is meaningless and amorphous. If an existence of this sort were given unconditional primacy, then existentialism would certainly be an enemy to the rational and to the humane. Furthermore, the description of a bloated, oppressive mass of ontological seaweed bears little resemblance to the world of human experience and leaves a gap to be filled. By itself, it affords no basis for objectively founded meanings, controlled generalizations, or reasonable planning and hope. Pertinent discussion of the In-itself is really forbidden, once it is placed beyond our intelligence.

Sartre is aware that no philosophical theory of the world can be developed from the standpoint of the In-itself. Hence, once he has placed it beyond the constitutive power of reflective consciousness, he turns back to consciousness as the source of recognizable structures and relations in the world. He declares that his ontology transcends both sides of the dispute over idealism and realism. But instead of getting genuinely beyond these alternatives, he is rather in the position of playing off the one against the other, as the turn of speculation seems to require.

Despite a good deal of harsh criticism of Hegel, Husserl, and Heidegger, he has appropriated their doctrines on the negating and creating power of consciousness.[13] He could not remain within the bounds of an empirical and realistic examination of knowledge, since then he would have to admit that in large measure our perceptual and intellectual meanings are drawn from a natural sphere of being in-itself that possesses its own essential intelligibility and determinations. Instead, he must account for all such meanings and patterns in terms of the intentional activity of consciousness itself. Consciousness, as so regarded, is erected into the second mythical entity, the For-itself. Without the ordering activity of this demiurge, there would be no verisimilitude in Sartre's account of the world about us.

The significance and structure which we find in our humanly familiar universe are wholly the products of the For-itself. This statement goes far beyond the common-sense recognition that human practical activity accounts for many new meanings and determinations. Whereas Dewey's pragmatic naturalism does not entirely rule out the intrinsic structure of nature, this exclusion is systematically required by Sartre's doctrine of the invertebrate nature of the In-itself. Hence these determinate traits are due exclusively to the work of consciousness. The world of significant being is the world of intentional acts and objects. The transphenomenal being of the object owes its multiple differentiations, meanings, and essential structures entirely to the projects of subjectivity. Hence it is to an analysis of the intentional activity and structure of consciousness that Sartre turns for the content of his ontology.

From idealism, he appropriates the view that consciousness is productive in so far as it is a power of negativity. Hegel's hymn to the omnipotent richness of negativity in *The Phenomenology of the Mind* is repeated in a minor key by Sartre. It is only by *not being* the being of the In-itself that consciousness can give rise to the world we experience. This process of "nothing-ing" is required because of the nature of being in-itself. The latter is a dense, viscous, cohesive mass which enjoys the self-identity of opaque and sunless matter. There is no room in being in-itself for the activity and self-lucidity of knowledge. To "make room" for the cognitive activity means to carve out a hollow region in the womb of the In-itself, a lack of being in-itself and a perspective of distance and distinctness. Consciousness is a gnawing worm in the heart of being, but one whose activity stirs up human reality to produce rich works.[14] Thus the naughting-function of consciousness is not nihilistic in intent but supremely creative. It permits the light of meaning and structured order to shine through the dark chaos of being in-itself. Consciousness not only assists at the birth of the world of human meaning but is its generative source, in virtue of a temporary victory over unintelligible being.

That the conquest of cognitive, emotional, and practical meaning is only a transient one is the point of difference between Sartre and Hegel. Instead of being the agent and expression of absolute mind, human subjectivity is a precarious growth at the heart of being in-itself, a fragile creation that is constantly threatened by the inroads of the In-itself. The past events of consciousness, as well as one's own body, tend to relapse again into the static realm of transphenomenal being and thus to bring an end to the splendid reign of creative consciousness. Whereas Hegel was assured beforehand of the synthesis of being in-itself and being for-itself in absolute mind, Sartre looks forward to no such happy outcome. Consciousness and substance, negativity and stolid self-identity, are pitted against each other in an unequal struggle. Sartre's viewpoint marks a return to the pre-Socratic feeling that our human cosmos, born of conflict, is always on the verge of being engulfed in the primal abyss of dark night.

In his treatise *On the Soul*, Aristotle outlined the realistic sense in which the mind is a sort of naughting power.[15] His predecessors had disputed with each other about whether the soul knows things by being like them or by being unlike them. Aristotle agreed with the latter view to the extent that the soul can know material things only because it is not itself material. Mind is other than the being to be known, and it knows the thing precisely as that which is other than itself. Yet the difference and distance between mind and material being are not retained for their own sake but only as a condition for making the knowable object like the mind, so that the union can be effected from which knowledge results. The cognitive act itself is a positive realization of being in a new mode. Being and mind are related as the full and the void only in the initial moment of knowing, since the cognitive act achieves a new fullness of being. There is thus no incompatibility, in the Aristotelian explanation, between fullness of being and intelligibility, although it requires a distinctive immaterial power on the part of the soul to attain the fullness of becoming all things in a noetic way. The Sartrean consciousness never becomes the being of the In-itself through a noetic union: it affirms not the being of the other as other but its own otherness from being.

The basic difference between these two theories of knowledge arises from diverse theories of being. According to Aristotle, the "nothingness" or potential character of the intellect is due to its need to receive an intelligible determination in the first instance from the sensible existent. The existent thing has its own essential nature, an embodied structure, which is the foundation of its intelligibility. The activity of consciousness is a kind of naughting, in the sense that it must remove the material conditions which prevent a grasp of this structure. Consciousness is also active in affirming the intelligible content of the real existent, which it recognizes as other than itself and as the ultimate referent for its own intellectual constructions. But the Sartrean In-itself cannot furnish any such intelligible determinations, manifesting an intrinsic essential structure to consciousness. Hence for Sartre, consciousness is differentiated from being not as the knower is distinct from the known but as a region of objects and essences not founded by the In-itself. Consciousness does not make itself a lack so that it may receive from being in-itself intelligible determinations in a nonmaterial way. It makes itself a lack of chaotic indetermination so that it can become the originative source of a definite, structured universe.

There is a surprising consequence for Sartre's ontology. He has shown that the two aboriginal poles of being—the In-itself and the For-itself—have an existence of their own, although not an existence which is contained within the reflective self-immediacy of the ego. To this extent, existence enjoys a primacy over essence. Essences are intentional projects of consciousness in the direction of being in-itself: hence they are included within an existential context "at both ends." But a further question arises in regard to the proper object of ontology: meaningful being. The ordinary existents of our experience depend for their significance upon the establishment of human intentional activity at various levels. Until intentional projects have been instituted by consciousness, distinct and significant objects are not present in being. From this standpoint, existence as a factor in the familiar world depends upon the essential structures specified by consciousness. Thus within the sphere of the meaningful being of the world, essence asserts its primacy over existence. Because consciousness intends definite essences or patterned sequences of appearances, the existent world is rendered present as a significant whole. Sartre remains faithful to his phenomenological method in placing empirical existence within the framework of intentional essences, as far as the sense of being is concerned.

A good deal is made of the problem of the priority obtaining between essence and existence. Sartre regards it as a mark of a theistic outlook that it must assign first place to essence over existence, and likewise a mark of his existentialism that it maintains the opposite order.[16] The historical question is not settled in this simple fashion. If, for instance, St. Thomas's philosophy be regarded as a typical theistic position, then Sartre's statement cannot be accepted as it stands. It is true that a divine exemplar idea is held by Aquinas to be present in God's mind, even before the production of a particular creature. This exemplar notion is not, however, a sort of master die in accord with which finite individuals are struck off, in assembly-line fashion. It represents the entire being of the creature in its unique existential act and individual traits, as well as in its essential nature. In the case of the individual existent itself, there is no question of the priority of either essence or existence, although the act of existing enjoys the primacy within the being. The one cannot be prior to the other in any temporal or spatial sense, since neither essence nor existence is a thing that can have being by itself. They are *co-principles* in finite being and hence require each other simultaneously in order to constitute the actual being, which has a composite reality. Furthermore, these principles of being are mutually proportioned, so that in the real thing the existential act partakes of the determinateness and intelligibility of the individual essence, whereas the essence receives its definitive act of being through the existential principle. There can be no independently enjoyed being on the part of one principle alone, by the very nature of their relation and mutual reference.

Actually, Sartre's thesis refers rather to the moral order than to the metaphysical. As Marcel explained, a decade before Sartre began writing, there are two senses in which the term "essence" can be taken. It can mean the nature or kind of the being, and in this sense there is simply a simultaneous relation between the real, individual essence and its act of existing. Or it can be understood as the freely developed moral character of a human person. In the latter sense, it is true that the existent agent precedes the essential traits of character which result from the exercise of his freedom. Sartre himself admits that the general conditions specifying the human kind of being and its limits are present at the outset: this is equivalent to admitting the initial co-presence of essence, in the first use of that term.[17] And theistic morality is insistent upon the individual's responsibility for determining his own character throughout a lifetime of free decisions. But the metaphysical and moral meanings of "essence" need to be distinguished; when they are distinguished, Sartre's special mark of existentialism is exposed as resting upon ambiguity.

Because consciousness is the source of essences, Sartre also regards it as the explanation of manyness in the world. The In-itself is a shapeless, homogeneous mass, which is insufficient to account for the distinctions and multiplicity encountered among beings. These traits are the consequence of the different essential lines of human activity which constitute the world. As a solution to the problem of the One and the Many, this theory gives only a proximate answer. It assumes that the conscious mode of being is already fundamentally distinguished from the unconscious. This or that product of intentional subjectivity can be differentiated only on condition that subjectivity itself has already been set off somehow from being in-itself. Sartre does not account for this first and most radical differentiation, upon which all manyness (in his theory) depends. The function of naughting is simply posited as an ontological characteristic already there. The question of the actual origin of consciousness is relegated to "metaphysics" and hence to a discipline which can only make guesses that deserve no scientific consideration.[18]

From his own standpoint, there is no reason why the dense,

opaque, absurd being of the phenomenon should ever give rise to a principle that is eminently agile, reasonable, and illuminative. The In-itself does not contain the qualities required to constitute consciousness. And since it is by nature inert and purposeless, it could not serve as a causal, purposive agent in the production of a zone of subjectivity. Yet everything happens *as if* being did give rise to *le néant* as its fundamental project. For Sartre to banish this difficulty to the nether region of metaphysics is to confess his inability to face one of the most pressing issues of philosophy. It also reveals that his distinction between ontology and metaphysics provides him with a handy repository for storing away from critical inspection the difficulties to which his theory of being inevitably leads.

There are two avenues whereby Sartre can make reply to this objection. He can say that a sufficient reason need not be expected in the case of that which lies beyond the bounds of rationality; he can also invoke the primacy of existence in order to dispense with a proportionate cause for existent consciousness. The first escape hatch can be used only if Sartre is willing to apply the principle consistently and rigorously. If no rational demands can be made upon the In-itself, then it must cease to perform any intelligible function in his system. In that case, it cannot serve as the sufficient reason for the doctrine of a fundamentally absurd universe, and neither can it provide a reasonable ground for retaining a minimal phenomenist realism. But if the In-itself can be grasped somehow indirectly in an emotional experience, containing a sufficiently determinate (even though negative) content to guide a reflective analysis, then it does come indirectly within the region of determinateness, intelligibility, and the claims of causality. It cannot have a definite status in a theory of being at one moment and no such status at the next.

If Sartre chooses to invoke the thesis of the underived nature of existence, then other difficulties crop up. He consistently merges the view that our knowledge of a contingent existent cannot be derived from knowledge of a prior principle with the quite different contention that the existence of the primal modes of being requires no cause. The first thesis is a noetic one, referring to our manner of gaining knowledge; the second is an ontological one, referring to the origin of a being. The first is a hallmark of realism, the second is peculiar to atheistic existentialism. It is one thing for a being to have an adequate cause and quite another thing for us to be able to ascertain the existence of this being merely by an inspection of its purported cause or ideal principle. The realistic denial of the latter claim does not entail a denial of the former.

The only reasonable basis on which Sartre could forbid our asking about the sufficient cause of conscious subjectivity would be if such an inference were the same thing as deducing existence from a purported cause. By using the terms "deduction" and "inference" interchangeably in this instance, he blurs the difference between two modes of reasoning. We cannot proceed by a priori reasoning from a cause or ideal principle to an existent as its necessary effect. But this does not settle the problem of whether the contingent character of a mode of being, whose existence is given, does not permit and even require us to reason in an a posteriori way to the existence of an actual cause of this contingent existent. In respect to Sartre's two existential poles of being, no attempt is made to deduce or otherwise derive our knowledge of the actual presence of consciousness or the In-itself from a supposed higher source. The givenness and contingency of existence are respected by being taken as the starting point rather than the terminus of the inference. Hence the existential character of the For-itself is not a bar to inquiring about its cause. At least, Sartre admits that his ontological principles cannot supply the answer.

4. The Will to Atheism.

The vital consistency and persuasiveness of Sartre's philosophy are due to a passionate conviction that remains inaccessible to direct philosophical criticism. He lives in the wake of Hegel and Nietzsche or, rather, of that side of Hegel's mind which was developed by Nietzsche. There is an irrational depth in Hegel that escaped the notice of the confident rationalists who propagated the optimistic implications of his dialectic. Hegel wrote prophetically that he and his nineteenth century were overcast by a speculative Good Friday, the loss of belief in God. Despite his heroic efforts at reconciliation of opposites, Hegel never achieved the Easter morning of a systematic rational whole of speculation. His heritage to Nietzsche was the sense of living in a world without the religious God. Nietzsche tried to present the death of God as the good news of human liberation, the latter-day humanistic evangel rather than the message of Calvary. He spent himself in the attempt to make a godless world a human and hopeful one, in which man would regain rank and value.

Sartre's own "lucid atheism" is in the Nietzschean tradition of combining a denial of God with a reinstatement of human values on a consciously mythical basis. His experience of disgust-with-being is a "primitivized" emotion, one that is already laden down with a resolve to eliminate God. He regards God's nonexistence as a postulate, a freely taken attitude that is not necessarily forced upon him by the actual situation of man. Atheism is the emotional a priori corresponding to the theoretical absolutizing of the phenomenological reduction. Like Nicolai Hartmann, the German philosopher who worked out a theory of values and conduct in a world where God is nonexistent, Sartre embraces a postulatory atheism as one of the regulative ideas of his entire philosophy.[19]

He is not unaware of the thetic character of his atheism. But he considers himself justified in proceeding in this way as a countermeasure to theism. In Sartre's estimate, atheism is only a contrary postulate to the equally gratuitous assumption of theists that God does exist. He does not sustain this charge, however, by a direct examination of the procedures of theistic philosophers in the realistic tradition. Hence he does not offer criticism of the claim that knowledge of God is a consequence of a previous analysis of finite existents. Instead, he points to the ontological argument employed by Descartes and the dialectical proofs offered by Hegel, methods which are admittedly a priori and postulatory.

Once he has advanced his postulate, however, Sartre does seek to make a reasonable defense of the atheistic principle. He takes his cue again from Nicolai Hartmann, who contends that the idea of God is contradictory in itself and traceable to man's wishful thinking. Sartre's indirect justification is based upon three arguments: the intrinsic contradiction in the notion of God, the impossibility of creation, and the genetic explanation of the idea of God.[20] The first two arguments will be considered here, postponing the third one for the section on freedom. In each case, the problem of God discloses itself as the problem of human nature as well.

The intending function of consciousness can also be understood as a tendency to transcendence. Moreover, this transcendence is in a vertical direction as well as towards the constitution of a world. As Hegel perceived in his doctrine on unhappy consciousness, human subjectivity is essentially restless and dissatisfied with its mundane condition. Taken by itself, the For-itself is a lacuna and an interrogative activity. But it is always seeking completion and a satisfactory answer. It hopes to found itself, to give itself a firm, substantial mode of being. It attempts to flee from its own intrinsic emptiness and contingency by acquiring a stable plenum of reality. At the same time, consciousness does not want to lose its own integrity and distinctive existence; it tries to protect its self-presence and activity. Contradiction surrounds the movement to transcendence from the fact that the only stable foundation for the For-itself is the In-itself, that is, that mode of being which excludes consciousness, self-presence, and agility of spirit.

Man cannot avoid trying to combine being in-itself and being for-itself in a superior synthesis: this is the most essential drive of his nature. What he could avoid doing, but usually does, is to project this synthesis into another world and endow it with actuality. The illusory union of the In-itself and the For-itself is the same as the God of religious belief.[21] God is not a real transcendent being but only the directional limit of man's self-transcending activity. It would be impossible to have an actual God, because of the contradictory notes comprising the notion of deity.

God would be both necessary and contingent, underived and derived, eternally immobile and temporally active. Above all, He would have both a close compression of being and the distance produced by consciousness. He is the hypothetical reconciliation of two modes of being that can never be reconciled. There is a radical cleavage at the center of being which cannot be healed by positing a unifying God. Just as there can never be a unified notion of being—combining in itself the properties of consciousness and substance—so there can never be a really existent God.

It is apparent that this reasoning is just as strong and just as weak as Sartre's general ontology. The contradiction lies not in God or in the religious conception of God but in the Sartrean theory of the modes of being. He defines being in-itself in a univocal and material way and then shows that being, as so defined, excludes consciousness and the other attributes usually applied to God. Clearly enough, the trouble lies in the doctrine of the In-itself and not in the concept of a purely actual being. This doctrine overlooks the gradual convergence of consciousness and being in the higher forms of living things. Far from being in contrast with every sort of self-identity, consciousness is the means whereby animals and men secure a more perfect self-identity than is possible for material things deprived of consciousness. At these higher levels of existence, self-identity is not equated with limp immobility but displays itself as conscious self-presence.

Similarly, Sartre has given a one-level account of consciousness. He assumes that the human mode of being for-itself is the only way in which conscious life can be realized. Because of this prejudgment, he feels no obligation to discriminate between what belongs to the nature of consciousness as a perfection of being and what attaches to consciousness in virtue of special human conditions. It is true that our human way of being-conscious always involves a real distinction between the knower and the known and that our cognition is directed to an object other than itself. Even in self-consciousness, some such distinction remains, although here the gap begins to be closed, indicating that its presence is not due to the intrinsic requirements of consciousness.

The more perfect the type of cognitive act, the more intimate is the union between consciousness and the object known. Man possesses the world more closely and comprehensively than do beings with a less adequate conscious life. The increasing immanence of the cognitive union suggests that the factors of otherness and distance are due to the finite conditions under which consciousness operates in the world. There is no intrinsic barrier against supposing both self-identity and self-consciousness in an infinite being. This is, indeed, no proof of the existence of such a being but only a clearance of one alleged hindrance to making such a proof. Just as there is no reason for stipulating that self-identity always implies the unreflective compression of material parts, so there is no reason for reading the characters of decompression, lack, and distance into the constant nature of consciousness. In an infinitely actual being, self-identity would be achieved precisely by self-presence as a conscious act of being. The conscious life of an infinite being would be necessary and self-founded, just as its being would be both self-conscious and actively creative.

Sartre's antinomy shows only that prime matter and intelligence cannot be the same, not that being and intelligence cannot coincide in an infinitely actual being. Moreover, his analysis of finite consciousness is a warning that modifications must be introduced, when a perfection is attributed to an entity realizing the traits of existence more fully than man. Since the starting point of such a comparative study must be the finite instances within our immediate range, it is unlikely that we can gain a perfectly adequate notion of divine consciousness, even though we can see that there are no intrinsic obstacles to the presence of consciousness in God. Yet the main issue is left untouched throughout this discussion, since theism does not try to establish directly the presence of consciousness in God but to demonstrate that a conscious mode of being is required for a being of infinite actuality. Sartre fails to join issue on whether or not an infinitely actual being is demanded by the structure of finite existence.

A similar ignoring of the central problem weakens the second argument against God, based on the nature of creation. If being were present in the divine subjectivity, it would be a purely intrasubjective mode of being. As such, it could never represent an objective world and could never rouse in the divine subjectivity a will to create the objective order of things. The point of this objection is lost unless it be recalled that, for Sartre, consciousness is defined precisely as a lack of being, in the sense of the In-itself. Hence it would seem to follow that every aspect of subjectivity is permeated by this absence of being and impotence to account for the existence of the In-itself. This would militate against a creation of being *ex nihilo*, that is, without drawing upon some previous stuff.

What Sartre has done is to translate the realistic proposition that our finite minds cannot give rise to the beings of nature into the altogether different proposition that no mind whatever can give rise to natural being. Because his ontology makes human consciousness epiphenomenal in respect to the In-itself, he universalizes this relation for every case of mind and being. Since human subjectivity is pictured as a fortunate accident clinging to the surface of being and forever dependent upon this morass, it is concluded that the origin of natural being cannot be ascribed to a creative act of a divine consciousness. Even if the Sartrean schema were verified for human consciousness, no inference could be made from the noncreative character of our minds to the impotence of a purely actual being with respect to the production of being in-itself. Moreover, the noncreative status of our minds does not prevent human subjectivity from having a conception of objective reality and even some acquaintance with the In-itself. To the extent that being of a sort can be attributed to the In-itself, it bears some faint likeness to the infinite being of God and hence can be known by Him. Although the infinite actuality of God would prevent Him from having the same mode of being as the In-itself, it does not follow that He could not know the possible structure of this other mode of being and therefore be able to will its creation. Such representation would be impossible only if consciousness were limited to a knowledge of its own modes and projects.

Sartre senses the weakness of his attack on creation and hence bolsters it with two further remarks. Recalling Leibniz's description of creation as a continuous fulguration from a central dynamic source, he proposes a dilemma. Either this continuous creation robs beings of their *Selbstständigkeit* as distinctive entities or else it poses them in contradistinction to God and hence removes from them the least trace of having been created. Both horns of this dilemma call for critical comment. Sartre, like Spinoza and Hegel, plays fast and loose with the German word *Selbstständigkeit*, which can mean both substantiality and independence.[22] In the traditional terminology, a substance enjoys a superior mode of being, since it does not require a further subject in which to inhere. But inherence in a subject and dependence upon an efficient cause were clearly distinguished, so that a finite substance was regarded as free from inherence and yet constituted in being by a causal influx. Sartre considers mainly the Cartesian and Leibnizian theories of divine creation and, indeed, gives no hearing to the earlier Scholastic theories on God.

The other half of the dilemma brings out Sartre's own implicit identification of distinctness and absolute independence. Only on this condition would the exercise of a distinct act of existing constitute a breaking of the bond of creature with creator. The only way in which things could be other than God would be by becoming utterly cut off from Him. This view is in obvious reaction to the Spinozistic theorem that finite things are modes of the divine substance and hence have *this sort* of dependence; it is also moving away from Hegel's judgment that finite, particular phases in the dialectic of the absolute are *unselbstständig* by themselves. But it takes no account of the theistic position, which defines a creature both by its substantial distinctness from God and by its creaturely dependence upon God. Beings with which we are familiar retain their own peculiar character at the same moment as they display their dependent nature. Dependence upon some causal source is the condition for, rather than the destruction of, the distinctive reality of finite things, as long as they are not regarded as modes or moments of the divine being.

Finally, Sartre adds that, if creation by a deity is no explanation, we should not conclude that being creates itself. If this were so, then being would be *causa sui*, self-caused, with the attendant impossibility of existing before it produces itself. Actually, the drive of human nature to be God is equivalent to a drive to be a self-creative *causa sui*. This criticism may have some telling force against the Cartesian and Leibnizian theories of God. But even Descartes, who popularized the application of the name "cause of itself" to God, readily admitted that "cause" is used here in a formal rather than efficient way. He was reminded by critics of his *Meditations* that for God to be an independent being *(ens a se)* is not the same as to be a self-caused being *(ens causa sui)*. This observation also applies to Sartre's argument, with the added note that his real difficulty centers about joining being and causality in the same subject. The contrast between inert being in-itself and agile being for-itself prevents Sartre from noticing the proportion between the kind and degree of being and the kind and degree of causal power among things in nature. Here, he can conceive of causality in no other way than as an injection of essential meaning, just as in the previous argument he could not conceive of knowledge otherwise than as a projection of intentions. It would be a scandal for him to regard causal activity as communication of being, and hence he never succeeds in analyzing the pre-Cartesian notion of creation. But the full import of Sartre's positive intent is not manifest at this point, since he is gradually preparing the way for his special doctrine on human freedom.

5. *Human Freedom.*

When viewed in its proper perspective, Sartre's provocative theory of human nature is a consequence of his general ontology. Or rather, it is a more concrete way of expressing ontological theses, which were concerned from the start with man's manner of being. This immediate relationship between ontology and philosophical anthropology must be kept in mind, especially when attempts are made to extend Sartre's principles into the moral field. In working out an ethics on the basis of atheistic existentialism, Sartre's former colleague at the *lycée*, Simone de Beauvoir, declares that the main reason for opposition to Sartre is the repugnance many people feel toward his teaching on man.[23] Hence she bids us have the fortitude to follow the facts, no matter where they lead. Nevertheless, this way of stating the case is misleading, since it constitutes an exact inversion of the true state of affairs among philosophers. It is because of reservations about his general description of being that Sartre's brand of humanism has been sceptically received. The main weight of critical opinion concentrates upon the "facts" about being in general. If criticism extends to Sartre's view of man and Beauvoir's ethics, it is in continuity with the more fundamental discussion of the In-itself and the For-itself.

Sartre characterizes man as a useless passion.[24] In his system, man cannot be regarded in any other way, since human nature is constituted by a futile and yet unquenchable thirst to be God. Thus the dynamic ideal of all human striving is to realize a state of being that is intrinsically contradictory and incapable of realization. Like Hegel, Sartre teaches that man is an unhappy consciousness; but there is no longer an absolute being to assuage the sorrow and redeem the striving. To be a man is to try to be God: man is nothing other than this vain desire for self-divinization.[25] Transcendence towards the divine is the radical project of human nature, one that by definition cannot be consummated.

There need be no criticism of this doctrine on the ground of its being pessimistic or optimistic. This alternative is relatively insignificant. The main question is not that of a fitting emotional response but of the soundness of Sartre's notions on being and consciousness. They are systematically incapable of supplying an accurate description of man's religious aspirations. This can be seen from the failure to distinguish between the attitude of seeking to *be* God and that of seeking to *become like* God, through participation in His holiness. Because he has defined God as the hypothetical juncture of human subjectivity and being in-itself, Sartre cannot define religious transcendence otherwise than as a search after self-realization of deity. This conclusion is also required by his view that either a creature is completely isolated from God or is merged with the divine being. Hence it is a systematic necessity which regulates this misrepresentation of man's religious bond with God. Sartre's ontological scaffolding cannot stand the weight of an intentional activity, the entire meaning of which is to try to realize in a finite way some likeness of the infinite perfection of God and to have a creaturely sharing in eternal life. There is no way to preserve the difference between being a partaker of the divine nature and being the divine nature, between becoming perfect like our heavenly Father and becoming the heavenly Father. Kierkegaard's description of man as existing before and striving in the presence of God stands in sharp contrast with Sartre's a priori deduction of what man's religious passion ought to be.

Sartre claims to be accepting Dostoyevsky's challenge that if there be no God, then all things are permitted. For Sartre, the denial of God is the beginning of man's self-development. The test case, upon which he is willing to rest his claims concerning the liberating effect of atheism, is the question of human freedom itself. He contends that only after God has been banished as a living belief, does man really become free and conduct himself as befits his nature.

One way to show this is to reduce the whole problem of God to insignificance.[26] Even if the existence of God were proven, it would make no difference for mankind. The meaning of this obscure remark is that creation of a free being would relieve that being of all responsibility toward, and bond of dependence upon, its creator. As Marcel has noted, this antithesis between being dependent and being free is based upon the assumption that "to receive is incompatible with being free." This dialetic of heteronomy versus autonomy is not unlike the naturalistic pathos popular in America today. Sartre's defiant Orestes is blood brother to Thornton Wilder's Julius Caesar. Wilder has Caesar exclaim: "How terrifying and glorious the role of man if, indeed, without guidance and without consolation he must create from his own vitals the meaning for his existence and write the rules whereby he lives."[27] Sartre adds as a polemical footnote that only a hypocrite, acting in bad faith, or an ignoramus can believe in given standards of conduct and moral values.

The Sartrean self is bound by no prescribed rules, for the simple reason that all rules are the product of this self. Human subjectivity is a spontaneous, autarchic center of freedom, since it underlies all its essential projects and need be under bondage to none of them. Every act of this self is free; every act proposes an intentional project and hence sets a value for itself. There are no laws set for man, because there is no transcendent being to legislate for him. He makes his own values and his own morality.[28] All human courses of action are good in so far as they seek a self-proposed end. The only condition is that one should act in good faith and should share freedom with others. A man does act in good faith when he acknowledges that there are no given standards and hence assumes unlimited responsibility for what he does. The man of bad faith is he who deceives himself into believing that he acts in conformity with a decalogue carrying some suprahuman sanction or at least deriving from a source beyond the individual himself.

Apparently, the only necessity man need admit is that of being free. He is "condemned" to freedom: he cannot *not* be free.[29] And the only ideal recognized by his freedom is that of making choices in an authentic spirit, that is, with full lucidity about his total responsibility for the ends he proposes and the means he takes. Added to that is the recognition that in choosing for oneself, one must also choose for all other selves. The authentic individual, the only genuinely free man, is the one who can bear to look at life from the perspective of an atheistic ontology. All other men are incapable of bearing the burden of this vision and hence seek various escape devices. They try to divest themselves of their freedom, and hence their actions have inhumane consequences both for the individual and for other men. Cowardice and courageous freedom are thus the great alternatives open to human subjectivity; the gaining of authentic freedom is the sole prize of life. A man is no more than the sum of his free acts, and his character will be good or bad in proportion to his approach to or flight from the practical consequences of Sartre's heroic atheism.

Confronted with this theory of freedom, the student's main difficulty is to decide how literally to take its various propositions. Either Sartre's aim of eliminating God at all costs and his custom of expressing ethical matters in ontological terms stand in the way of a precise statement of his meaning, or else they lead him to a position at variance with our experience. Human subjectivity is not an unbounded mode of freedom, since man is subject at least to the limitations of his kind and the possibilities afforded by nonhuman nature. In our previous discussion of the various uses of the term "essence," it was pointed out that Sartre allows the initial presence of universal, fundamental conditions that specify the human mode of being. It is surely within the framework of his nature or essence in this sense that man exercises freedom. Sartre does not inquire too closely into the origin of these limiting conditions or their influence upon the operation of subjectivity. The question of their origin is avoided as a metaphysical subtlety, that is, as a line of investigation that might lead straightway to an adequate cause of the contingent being of man. Moreover, reflection upon the relation between these fundamental conditions and liberty would destroy the prejudice that to receive is incompatible with being free. Even within a completely finite context, this statement is not verified. The recognition of one's limitations and the receipt of aid from others are normal conditions for personal development. While it is true that one must take an attitude toward what he receives, this is a psychological and moral act which does not wipe out the finite and conditioned character of the power to assume various attitudes. Moreover, it does not settle the question of conforming to objective conditions, once the choice is made. Sartre is paying the price for making a direct equivalence between phenomenological description of such intentional acts and their ontological explanation.

Sartre states explicitly that free choice, *liberum arbitrium* in the classical sense, is only an act of announcing projects and decisions already made by pure consciousness. More precisely, conscious subjectivity *is* nothing else than a series of acts, each of which is a free act in so far as it embodies this primal dynamism.[30] Freedom is here reduced to spontaneity, with the result that it loses all distinctive meaning. The distinction is wiped out between the acts of man in the wide and indifferent sense of whatever man does, and truly human acts that bear the stamp of his deliberate, reasonable choice. If this doctrine is followed through consequentially, it reduces the problem of choice to the sterile tautology that man desires what he desires and does what he does. Freedom in this vague and unavoidable sense is no peculiar perfection of man and no peculiar perfection of any qualitative group of human acts. Condemnation to freedom would then mean not only that one cannot alienate responsibility from himself but also that one cannot avoid acting freely and well by the very fact of initiating any project with resoluteness aforethought.

Sartre realizes that an unqualified acceptance of this view will lead to a glorification of power displayed for its own sake. Hence under cover of the new existentialist terminology, he is obliged to restore some common, objective standards. He says that one "ought" to act authentically and "ought" to respect the liberty of others.[31] He castigates ordinary men, persons living and acting in bad faith, for making "unauthentic" choices and lauds his own philosophy as a basis for making "authentic" choices. This contrast enables him to escape, at least verbally, from the charge of nihilism and amoralism. Whether more is involved here than a laudatory way of referring to his own preferences is the point at issue.

What authenticates an individual's act of choice, so that it becomes a humane act? Sartre offers two criteria: that it be done with perfect lucidity, and that it involve an acceptance of responsibility for other men as well. If these conditions are fulfilled, then the act is unconditionally free, value-creative, and authentic or good. Most moralists would grant that a clear understanding of the situation is a requirement of moral behavior, not in the specific sense of good behavior but merely responsible behavior. Freedom has its roots in an intellectual judgment, based upon a calm appraisal of the situation. But this is no guarantee that the choice will be a good one or in conformity with human nature. Sartre's hero, Baudelaire, testified that self-recuperation through lucidity is a condition of acting in a human way, but not a sufficient condition of good action. Malicious action may also be performed on the basis of unblinking honesty about oneself. As Marcel remarked, apropos of André Gide's similar celebration of lucid disillusionment as the distinguishing mark of humane conduct, there is a diabolical lucidity which can pierce the deepest shadows of the self without removing one bit of the gloom or one degree of the perversion.[32]

Taken by itself, an awareness of how man stands in existence is too formal a rule to prove useful in resolving particular problems of conduct. It is so hospitable that it is ready to authenticate any act, just as long as the self takes full responsibility for performing the act. Since diametrically opposed plans of action can be espoused by individuals who are equally convinced that no other moral law than their own intention exists, this criterion does not prove adequate for determining concrete choices or settling conflicts. Nor does it gain sufficient concreteness by an alliance with the social criterion. For the latter rests upon a quite neutral conception of responsibility. The attitude of choosing for other men as well as for oneself is compatible with the most diverse courses of action. There is a sense of social destiny dignifying the policies of dictators and petty tyrants as well as those of liberators and benefactors of humanity. The most ruthless use of power is often exercised by men who have a keen sense of its effect upon the lives of others. A man's sensitivity to the needs of others is no guarantee that he will appraise the situation correctly or will eventually act in accord with his better judgment. There is no evasion from the obligation to rectify one's personal intention according to a rule of the good.

Moreover, Sartre gives a quite special meaning to his dictum that, in authentic choice, the individual is also choosing for other people. It is not merely a reformulation of the ethical common-place that man is a political animal. Its primary basis is ontological. If the fundamental project of the self is to constitute its world, then it cannot choose for itself without determining the relative positions of other selves within its own world. Having care for other men is the same as having care for the integrity and order-liness of one's perspective, in so far as it involves other selves as constituent factors. They must be ordered as objects gathered about the primary subject or free self. Significantly, Sartre ad-mits that every concrete application of his social criterion is bound to end in failure. For another self is bound to rebel against being included as an object in my world. It has its own counter-world, within which I am to be fitted as an objective component. Hence social action is basically a form of mutual conflict and hatred, although this stark truth may be disguised and softened in various ways. Sartre confesses that mindfulness of others can-not result in the promotion of the common good of society on the basis of his own ontology.

This breakdown of the criteria of authenticity in choice paves the way for appreciating the final argument directed by Sartre against the existence of God. He seeks to undermine religious conviction by offering a genetic, psychological explanation of the idea of God. It is generated as one last, desperate attempt to rescue the values of social life in an objective direction. The only way to insure the existence of other selves is to examine the meaning of coming beneath the stare of another and feeling shame at the glance. But if the other is merely another finite self, a duel will go on between my attempt to stare him down and his attempt to overcome my project of transcendence. Although I may ex-change positions with others, becoming the stared-at rather than the starer, the object rather than the subject of the transcending process, still the distance is never overcome. Might not human community be rendered possible by including myself and all other finite selves as common objects for a transcendent starer, an absolute third party, which can itself never come under our

glance as an object? This Great Eye would include all men together in a common objective field, so that all would have the
same mode of being. Thus, Sartre concludes, God is the limiting
concept in our endeavor to establish the human totality as a *"we-
object,"* a social ideal that cannot be given embodiment.

What this argument proves is that social and political modes of
being cannot develop within the perspective of the prereflective
Cogito and its objects. The relation of starer and stared-at, subject and object, cannot lead to a tolerable form of society, unless
the squirrel cage is to be the prototype of communal existence.
This is actually the case in Sartre's play, *No Exit*, where the characters are unaware of any difference between the hell where they
are placed and our terrestrial existence. The author is thus afforded the opportunity to pronounce his favorite *mot: L'Enfer,
c'est l'Autrui.*[33] But this situation is amusing to the audience in
another, disconcerting way, for they perceive the discrepancy
between Sartre's hell-on-earth-in-society theme and the tested
possibilities of personal relationships. As a genetic argument
against God's existence, it traces the genesis of a fantastic, but
systematically dictated, caricature of the idea of God. The consequence is to make one sceptical of a philosophy which is forced
to give birth to such a parody. Speaking for man's religious outlook, Kierkegaard once protested pointedly against the view that
God is a *tertium quid*, an aloof observer who can never be
caught in the act and who never enters into communal relation
with us as a personal subject. But a protest of this sort is drowned
out by the systematic commitments about the general structure
of being which oblige Sartre to dismiss or distort the constant
testimony of the religious mind. His final word on the nature of
reality is an expression of the same despair and despairing fic-
tionalism which he accuses believers in God of perpetuating.
"The real is an abortive effort to attain to the dignity of *causa
sui*. Everything transpires as if the world, man and man-in-the-
world succeed in realizing only *un Dieu manqué.*"[34]

Sartre makes a brave appearance when he observes that if the
world is absurd, then man ought to face this truth openly rather

than allow his wishes to dictate his philosophy. But this is a hypothetical statement, not a rhetorical way of stating a truism. It proposes a hypothesis, which must be tested by its consequences. An intelligible notion of freedom, oughtness, and society is not permitted by this denial of God, despite its acceptance of Dostoyevsky's challenge. Sartre has shown what the consequences of God's nonexistence would be, not that this denial must be accepted by philosophy as its first principle. In his system, atheism is not part of the evidence but a presupposition deliberately laid down as a determinant of evidence. It is this wishful atheism that calls for a critical overhauling. Absurdity is not in the nature of being but is a conclusion following upon an aboriginal and systematically developed atheism, integrated with an autonomous phenomenological method.

It is unfortunate that Sartre's humanism *manqué* overshadows his genuine contributions to the analysis of human action. Sartre and Beauvoir have a firm grasp on the half-truth that man is not a clod and cannot become perfect after the manner of a mere thing. He must learn to affirm his own selfhood, assume his own attitudes, and take responsibility for what he does. This growth in freedom is not incompatible with recognition of the moral law. The moral law must be appropriated and made one's own, as Kant insisted. The work of human freedom is to interiorize the law, embrace it as one's own and, in doing so, give it an incommunicably personal import. Moreover, the circumstances and situations in which a man finds himself placed are often morally indifferent or ambiguous, until a personal stand is taken toward them. This does not argue to the absence of a universal moral law but to the office of human freedom in making it function in the context of concrete action. That is why man is required not only to be aware of his human condition but also to cultivate the virtues. They are principles whereby the moral law is appropriated by the individual and made relevant for particular lines of conduct.

Chapter III

Jaspers' Quest of Transcendence

Of all the existentialists, Karl Jaspers (1883——) is most likely to receive a sympathetic hearing among philosophers in America. His scientific training and achievements run counter to the prejudice that existentialism is an antiscientific movement, which can never appeal to the scientific mind. He acquired a thorough laboratory training under well-known pathologists and psychiatrists. For a number of years before World War I, Jaspers served as assistant in the psychiatric clinic at Heidelberg. From this experience, he wrote his first major work, *General Psychopathology* (1913), which was a pioneer text in this field. Six years later, he issued his second important scientific contribution, an acute *Psychology of World Outlooks*. Already in this book, his growing concern with philosophical problems and methods was apparent. This shift of interest was reflected in his academic work, since he transferred from the professorship of psychiatry to that of philosophy at Heidelberg.

Jaspers' academic associations have left their impress upon his writing. The development of his philosophy is more abstract and systematic than that of most other existentialists. He is less involved in philological byways than Heidegger, more restrained and balanced in his psychological analyses than Sartre, and more inclined to systematic constructions than Marcel. He is not a man of one book and not a writer of journals and aphorisms. His respect for the rigorous standards of philosophical exposition and for the history of philosophy makes his thought more congenial and accessible to nonexistentialists. Jaspers has taken explicit issue with the view that existentialism is a sectarian affair. For him, philosophy of existence is but a particular, contemporary determination of perennial philosophy.[1] In all his books, Jaspers stresses the need for striking a balance between tradition and original advance in the development of a truly perennial philosophy. It is mainly in Jaspers' books that the attachment of existentialism to the mainstream in philosophy is made evident.

In 1932, Jaspers published his three-volume work on *Philosophy*, in which he gave the first general explanation of his viewpoint. Many critics deemed this to be his major work, but this was a hasty judgment. Jaspers' *Philosophy* summed up his reflections on philosophical problems made during the previous decades and also provided a springboard for new advances. His academic connections were cut off by the Nazis because of his sharp criticism of racism and excessive nationalism. Nevertheless, he was able to deliver two sets of lectures during this period, on *Reason and Existence* and on *Philosophy of Existence*, which gave succinct expression to his ideas. Since the end of the War, Jaspers has been extremely active. His sense of responsibility in the current situation has led him to redefine the meaning of the university, examine the question of war guilt, issue a set of theses on political liberty, and affirm his belief in the European spirit. His is a brand of existentialism that does more than talk about engagement or the need to take one's actual predicament as the point of departure for speculation.

Under Allied occupation of Germany, Jaspers returned to the University of Heidelberg. His address delivered at the opening of the medical school was a moving recommendation of the humanistic values which should motivate university work and a sober appraisal of the difficulties under which Germans today must labor.[2] Another matter of concern for him was the relation between his existentialism and religion. Despite a number of hints in previous writings, Jaspers did not clarify his position on this question until he engaged in a series of postwar discussions with Protestant theologians. The results were summarized in his book on *Philosophical Faith* (which has been translated into English under the title *The Perennial Scope of Philosophy*).

More recently, Jaspers has accepted the professorship in philosophy at the University of Basel in Switzerland. At present, he is working on a four-volume *Philosophical Logic*, the first volume of which has appeared as a treatise *Concerning Truth*. In this *Logic*, he is attempting to restate his entire philosophy from the standpoint of the common relation which all modes of being and understanding bear to an all-inclusive reason. When it is completed, this work is likely to contain a definitive synthesis of his philosophy of existence.

1. *The Present Situation.*

Like the other existentialists, Karl Jaspers recognizes the importance of the philosophical notion of "situation."[3] It has certain connotations which permit its use in dealing with problems that are not adequately covered by the traditional Kantian notion of "world." The latter concept is associated with the most general formal conditions constituting the unity of our experience of being as phenomenal. But man's imbeddedness in the world is always achieved in terms of particular and concrete sets of circumstances, which emphasize the material aspect as well as the formal. Moreover, there are predicaments in which man finds himself that are not limited to the phenomenal order but address and condition him precisely in his use of freedom and his attitude toward transcendence. Thus to be placed in a situation has a wider meaning than to be placed in the world, although real situations are not found apart from a mundane context. Finally, situation does not convey the same rounded completeness as is suggested by world. It is a readier tool for a philosophy of transcendence that seeks to break through the sphere of total immanence.

Everyday, empirical being *(Dasein)* is being-in-a-situation. This is seen from the finite and conditioned nature of the things of our acquaintance. What they are and come to be depends in large measure upon the relations they sustain with each other.

What a being is capable of doing is specified by the particular field of action available to him and also by the mutual actions of other agents sharing this field. Hence Jaspers gives an initial description of situation as the field of interest for an empirical agent, the zone within which its activities can be displayed and its welfare promoted or assailed. There is nothing peculiarly existential about this preliminary definition, since man in his given reality does not yet display distinctive awareness of being implicated in existential predicaments. At the empirical level, he is involved in countless aspects of the milieu, some of them affecting him without his awareness and others coming within his conscious concern. In taking stock of his condition, capacities, and opportunities, a man becomes aware of some of his situations. This knowledge enables him to start a deliberate line of conduct for modifying these situations and hence controlling in some degree their influence upon himself.

There is some affinity between Jaspers' initial description of situation and the theory of the problematic situation proposed in John Dewey's *Logic*. They both make the problematic situation the starting point of all inquiry.[4] In Jaspers' hands, however, this key notion is developed neither according to a fundamentally biological analogy nor on the presupposition that a single logical formulation can be provided for resolving situational problems. Unlike some of the existentialists, Jaspers admits many levels of situations. We must scrutinize the economic and political structures of a society, the conditioning power of prevailing scientific outlooks and techniques, and the potentialities generated by the cultural relations between persons. Such an examination cannot be dispensed with in one's existential eagerness to study the states of soul of the human individual. The situations arising in interior life cannot be divorced from their material and social context.

Jaspers' *Man in the Modern Age*, written on the eve of the Nazi accession to power, is reminiscent of the biting social criticism made a century before by Kierkegaard. Just as Kierkegaard's social stand has been left in obscurity, so the existentialist critique of modern society is usually left in the shade. This unbalanced presentation lends plausibility to the charge of Marxists like Georg Lukács that existentialism is congenitally incapable of making social evaluations. This accusation is belied by Sartre's socio-political analyses, Marcel's descriptions of prevalent attitudes, and Jaspers' own appraisal of our times. He is not content to give a formal definition of situation or to begin straightway with the situations which he designates as being properly existential. A start must be made with the situations that condition our empirical life as given entities, operating in a particular historical field.

Our modern mood is one of uprootedness and insecurity, giving way at times to illusory hopes of achieving stability. We have developed a technical order which enables us to master nature and so to initiate vast changes in our material and cultural manner of living. Despite this control of environment and even of human relations, we are acutely aware of the vacuity of an existence lived without spiritual purpose or belief. We are in the biblical predicament of having gained the whole world and lost our immortal souls. A sign of this loss is the devaluation of the individual person. Despite a good deal of rhetoric about the dignity of man, he has been reduced to a low status. Both Jaspers and Marcel protest against taking a man's social function as the prime measure of his true worth. The modern individual is only "one of a number," a replaceable unit subject to technical manipulation and the leveling force of quantitative standards. As Marcel would say, he belongs to "a broken world," one that has fractured the dignity of the single-minded person.

Corresponding to the depersonalization of the individual is the loss of genuine community. Jaspers distinguishes incisively between human communities, in which personality is given the opportunity to grow, and the mass organizations encouraged by the modern state. With the educational and propaganda instruments at its disposal, the state has produced a standardized man who has willingly exchanged civic liberty and humanist culture for the pottage of class security or national pride. Jaspers counsels neither flight from the social scene nor supine acceptance of current political programs. The responsible individual should strive to dissociate the tradition of freedom from individualism and the values of political authority from totalitarian oppression. Since the outcome would be a new socio-political form, it would be acceptable to neither Western capitalism nor communism. A new synthesis of freedom and authority would result in the overturning of the capitalist-communist ideal of the mass man,[5] who can think only in terms of "all of us" and whose decisions are made on the impersonal basis of what "one says" (to employ language similar to that of Heidegger).

Jaspers' purpose is not to pronounce a cultural jeremiad. The philosophical implication is that the tragic conflicts of our age are due to its exclusive dedication to the ends of merely empirical being, without regard for the ultimate problems of human existence. When the value of men and things is restricted to their sheer factual status as "being-there" in our experience, all problems tend to get solved by mechanical means and by the deliberate cultivation of a mass-humanity. There results a deordination or rather a disappearance of all order among the sciences.[6] Each of the particular disciplines attempts today to provide a final answer concerning the nature of man. The newer sciences of sociology, genetics, psychoanalysis, and anthropology vie with each other for the honor of providing the central focus for our understanding of man. There is no recognized way of settling these disputes, because there is no universally acceptable principle of order. This is no accident but follows from the formal standpoint of these sciences. They treat of man exclusively in his empirical being, at which level, the unity and hierarchy among the aspects of his nature are not apparent. The consequence is a reduction of man to the status of a class member, a libido, a superbred animal, a cultural unit. These aspects of human existence tend to fly apart, making an integrated personality impossible. The fault lies, however, not with these sciences in their own line but in the imperialistic attempt to make one or another particular discipline supreme. In America, this imperialistic tendency is found especially among cultural anthropologists, who would like to erect anthropology into *the* science of man. Jaspers maintains that no claim to being the chief humane discipline can be substantiated as long as the question of being has not been raised in its existential amplitude.

It is, perhaps, too pat an answer to say that the social and scientific anarchy is due to the displacement of philosophy. Even the modern varieties of philosophy have been unable to cope with the problem of man. Jaspers expresses his dissatisfaction with the two leading philosophical schools, naturalism and idealism. They draw their method and categories too immediately from the empirical sciences. In fact, the philosophical situation is so aggravated today because the univocal tools of the special sciences are being taken as sufficient instruments for philosophical research.

Jaspers is not convinced by the disavowals of "reductionism" made by most naturalists.[7] Granted that naturalism does not *wish* to level down all human values to a materialistic plane, the problem is whether this philosophy can avoid doing so in accord with its own principles. A one-method naturalism is bound to impoverish the human spirit and to disregard the distinctive values that are disclosed, since it regards man only in his objective side. It is legitimate but not sufficient to study man in so far as he is one more product in nature's amazingly fecund and varied development. The unique importance and freedom of each human individual cannot be investigated without making such vast adaptations in one's approach and concepts that the bounds of naturalism are overpassed. Naturalism is occupied with only the objective correlates of such crucial human situations as decision, guilt, and death. A way must be found, however, to examine these experiences in their distinctive structure and presence in human existence. This cannot be done by remaining within the domain of the natural sciences, where man is treated according to the general categories of objective or empirical being. The nature of man as a personal subject requires a special procedure that can be called scientific only in an accommodated sense, the peculiar character of which has not been specified by naturalists.

The criticism of idealism is not nearly so trenchant as that of naturalism. In fact, Jaspers has in mind mainly the idealism of

Edmund Husserl. Jaspers is less indebted to Husserl than are any of the other existentialists.[8] He relies more upon psychological and psychiatric analysis than upon phenomenology for the material content of his philosophy. In an indirect way, he has brought out the difference between phenomenology and his philosophy of existence. In his study, *Descartes and Philosophy*, Jaspers goes over the same ground covered by Husserl in his *Cartesian Meditations*. The differences between the two reports are striking. They show that there is not an essential connection in every case between existentialism and phenomenology, especially that side of phenomenology which ministers to an absolute idealism.

Husserl espouses the Cartesian ideal of a universal science, objecting only to Descartes' hesitancy before the final reduction of essences to mind. Hence he places himself firmly in the tradition of Cartesian rationalism and considers his own transcendental idealism as the logical culmination of the Cartesian standpoint.[9] But for Jaspers, an existential philosopher is something more than a good Cartesian who has learned his lesson better than his master taught it. He is, in fact, a philosopher who does not permit to go uncriticized the primal dogmatism common to Descartes and Husserl. These latter thinkers initially lay down that the notes of clarity and distinctness belong to the fundamental intuition of the self. Only on this assumption can they conclude that a single rational method is capable of treating all philosophical problems and that a universal science can be constructed by this means.[10] The failure of naturalism and idealism to work out the problem of the internal differentiation of scientific method has a Cartesian source. From his critical standpoint, Jaspers holds that there is no univocal approach to the totality of being; a number of special methods are adapted to the special nature of the entities or aspects under consideration.

Jaspers admits with Husserl that Descartes did not philosophize with the desired rigor. But Descartes fell short not by failing to secure the ultimate identity between mind and its intentional objects but by failing to carry out his program of universal doubt.

He ceased to doubt just this side of where radical doubt should begin: with the existing self. Although it is evident that this self exists when it doubts, this is no sufficient reason for inferring that we have a clear and completely distinct knowledge of the self in its depth of being.[11] Descartes thought that all is clear and certain about the self simply because he ceased to investigate the problem of the origins of thinking and being. His doubt stopped, and the inward direction of his inquiry shifted, just at the point where being begins to grow obscure and objective reason to lose its bearings. The clear and distinct Cartesian universe is gained at the expense of a comprehensive study of the modes of being. The methodic doubt should have been applied with special strictness to the propositions that thought is coextensive with being, rather than included within it, and that this self which philosophizes here and now is sufficiently characterized as a thinking thing. Instead of probing the existential act of man, Descartes stopped short with a property and activity of this self. His criterion of clarity and distinctness is not proved to be valid universally for being.

Another area into which Descartes might have pushed his method of doubt is that of man's customs, morality, and religious belief.[12] His so-called provisional morality was never treated in a merely provisional way and never subjected to critical examination. Hence there is an ambiguity about Descartes' significance for modern philosophy. Both extreme rationalism and fideism can find support in him. He did not squarely face the difficulty about faith and reason, and this evasion has been his heritage to the modern world. Jaspers poses the problem in the following way. Either the Cartesian universal science will make relevant pronouncements about matters of faith or else faith will remain forever a stranger to natural reason. In the former case, religion loses its dogmatic independence; in the latter case, philosophy ceases to contain an unconditioned truth. This antithesis is kept concealed by Descartes' device of reserving his methodic doubt for purely speculative issues and for propositions in the natural order alone.

Through this description of the contemporary situation in culture and philosophy, Jaspers makes a twofold gain. First, the description helps to illustrate the meaning of his general theory of situation. For contemporary men will have to reckon with these trends as conditioning their activity and defining the possibilities for a new humanism. An abstract discussion of situation is no substitute for concrete analyses of the historical situations that actually prevail. Second, the philosophical problematic of our time has been determined. Neither an unreflective allegiance to the established order nor total reliance upon the natural sciences can bring men through the present crisis of dehumanized civilization. The sciences must be provided with a principle of order and integration. This can only be done by extending the matter of critical inquiry from the objective things of empirical being to the being of the human subject. Naturalism and idealism are inadequate to this further task. They must make room for a philosophical approach that is fitted for the study of man's peculiar mode of being. In a word, Jaspers concludes from his analysis of the present situation that there is urgent need for philosophy of existence.

2. Becoming Aware of Existence.

Jaspers does not pretend that he is starting entirely *de novo* in his existential enterprise. In all his books, he acknowledges the original note introduced into philosophical thinking by two forerunners, Kierkegaard and Nietzsche.[13] These two men were most sensitive to the contradictions in the modern mind. They called in question the ideal of an anonymous herd of men governed by external and unthinkingly accepted norms. They voiced the protest of the "underground man," the human individual who has been submerged and despised in an impersonal, quantitatively regulated society. With them, the special nature of the human existent first became a crucial question for philosophers. Jaspers asks, not that we follow their lead slavishly, but that we accept their challenge. Kierkegaard and Nietzsche are "exceptions," and hence their doctrines cannot simply be repeated by later philosophers. Our task is to realize in terms of our own philosophizing that to which they bore witness as intrepid and trail-blazing individuals.

The work of Kierkegaard and Nietzsche was both negative and positive. In a destructive way, they tried to wipe the slate clean of all remaining prejudices. Thus they extended the activity of doubt to reason itself and to the notion of a universal, objective, perfectly lucid science. This was illustrated by Kierkegaard's attack upon the Hegelian System and by Nietzsche's rejection of the idol of "objective truth."[14] Neither criticism was made in the interests of scepticism or nebulous emotionalism. The aim was to arouse a more thoughtful attitude in people who had been deluded by the superficial clarity of the Enlightenment or by the unquestioning dogmatism of religious faith. Man was now revealed as a being engaged in an endless reflection, which respects no particular authority or theory. His existence was vindicated in all its undomiciled elusiveness and independence, foiling every attempt to contain it within an objective science of empirical being or a conventional schema.

More positively, Kierkegaard and Nietzsche agree that our acquaintance with man's existential mode of being is interpretative and obscure rather than immediate and pellucid. What Heidegger calls the hermeneutic of existence yields infinitely diverse readings, which cannot be reduced to one single outlook or embraced within a single system. Because of the multifariousness of the real and its unsuspected novelties, being remains hidden and ambiguous. It discloses itself under various masks and surrogates. Its inmost secret can only be uncovered through a decisive leap, and even then the mystery is not removed.

Jaspers gives symbolic importance to the antithesis of faith and atheism presented by Kierkegaard and Nietzsche. Kierkegaard's leap leads him to an affirmation of existence through faith in Christ. Nietzsche's leap leads him to deny God and assert the will to power within the total immanence of the world. In face of this conflict, Jaspers feels justified in refusing to accept either solution as literal and unambiguous truth. Each remains for him a mere sign that does not surely reveal its signatum, a pointer that is in turn susceptible of receiving many interpretations.[15] Kierkegaard and Nietzsche are Heroes of the Negative, and yet they see the need for a renewed tradition and an ultimate affirmation. They oppose nihilism (with which Jaspers identifies Heidegger's philosophy) by agreeing not to will the naught, but to will the substance of being and the rank and value of man. Nietzsche's godlessness and Kierkegaard's Christianity are attempts to "tie the thread of reflection" by grounding thought in a freely affirmed existence, which is only reached by a leap into transcendence.

Jaspers comes closest to his nineteenth-century predecessors at this point and also finds here his principle of opposition to them. Their great contribution is to reinstate the *attitude* of transcendence; their shortcoming is to specify the nature of the *being* of transcendence, the transcendent being. Until his more recent books appeared, it was impossible to discover the exact import of Jaspers' criticism. It seems clear now, however, that what attracts him to Kierkegaard and Nietzsche is their recognition of the possibility of transcending the mundane and human modes of being. This is a welcome challenge to the immanent monism of both naturalism and idealism. But Jaspers does not want to overstep this cautious affirmation of the possibility of transcendence. All that is warranted by this proposition is the right to admit into human existence the attitude of transcendence or the act of transcending. It does not entail the right to determine in a definite way the nature of the transcendent being toward which the transcending act is directed. At least, it does not support so precise a doctrine as Kierkegaard's Christian faith or Nietzsche's faith in the coming of the superman. Jaspers is gradually preparing the ground for his own non-Christian theism. He goes farther than Nietzsche in asserting the reality of God, and stops short of Kierkegaard's acceptance of Christ's divinity.[16]

In order to appreciate the intermediate position of Jaspers, the third major source of his intellectual formation must be noted. It is not inaccurate to regard Jaspers' philosophical activity as an attempt to chart the course of Kantian reason in the encircling sea of Kierkegaardian existence. It is with Kant's help that he establishes his threefold division of philosophy into orientation in the world, clarification of existence, and metaphysics.[17] The Kantian influence is responsible for Jaspers' manner of distinguishing between empirical being and existence and his refusal to allow the human mind any access to the being of transcendence. These philosophical positions determine, in turn, Jaspers' attitude towards positive religion. His greatest historical debt is to Kant: Jaspers offers a Kantian interpretation of the findings of Kierkegaard and Nietzsche.

Jaspers makes a good deal of the distinction between empirical being *(Dasein)* and existence *(Existenz)*.[18] He regards it as a way of setting off his own philosophy from that of Heidegger, although this claim is not convincingly sustained. For Heidegger also makes a contrast between unauthentic and authentic *Dasein*, and distinguishes between them through a difference in their relation to transcendence. Jaspers' *Existenz* and Heidegger's authentic *Dasein* have a definite kinship. In any case, Jaspers maintains that any mode of being which fails to develop an attitude of transcending cannot be properly included within *Existenz*. It is precisely the relation to transcendence that endows the existential mode of being with its distinctive structure. The crucial issue in an existential philosophy is to make the transition from purely empirical being to being as existence-directed-to-transcendence.

Empirical being is the reality of the given, objective world. Jaspers regards as unassailable Kant's doctrine that the objective world is a purely phenomenal world, more the appearance of being than being. What is disclosed in the empirical world is not being in its absolute meaning but "object-being," which is found in the object of consciousness. The phenomenal or objective being includes the empirical subject, which is correlated with the object. The self which is restricted to empirical being regards as real only that which is an object for itself, a determination of consciousness. Hence a study of the forms and structure of consciousness yields knowledge of the objective appearances of being. This examination is made by the various particular sciences and by philosophical logic. Their report is a valid one, but it can lead to error precisely in the degree that it seems to sustain the claims of ontology.

Whereas Heidegger and Sartre admit the validity of at least a phenomenological ontology, Jaspers proposes to overturn every sort of ontology.[19] An ontology is an attempt to formulate a single, comprehensive theory of being on the basis of empirical being alone. It proceeds on the premise that being is identified with whatever is objective and *wissbar* (objectively knowable). The categories and method of ontology are limited to the traits of the objects of consciousness and yet pretend to give knowledge of being in general. This science derives the various kinds of beings from a First Being through a deductive construction. The result is supposed to be a systematic knowledge of all beings and the meaning of being as such.

Jaspers opposes this conception on both Kantian and existential grounds. The antinomies which Kant enumerated and which were extended to other spheres by Kierkegaard are taken as proof of the impossibility of elaborating a consistent and comprehensive system in terms of objective entities. Furthermore, the Kantian limitation of knowledge to objective reality is not the same as a limitation of all reality to what is objective. Jaspers is in full agreement with Kant that knowledge in the strict sense *(Erkenntnis* or *Wissen)* is confined to the world of phenomenal objects. But being is not thereby given a similar restriction: it surpasses the realm of appearance and objectivity. This is the same as saying that being surpasses ontology or the science constructed along objective, phenomenal lines. In addition, Jaspers appropriates the usual existential objections against any deduction of the existential modes of being.

Some critical remarks are necessary here. Because of Jaspers' penchant for describing pure types of outlooks rather than particular instances, it is difficult to identify the historical theories which would fall under the classification of ontology, as he understands it. But certain remarks in his *Concerning Truth* confirm the impression that he has in mind mainly the Aristotelian-Thomistic metaphysics.[20] For polemical reasons, connected with his criticism of religious claims to authority and revelation, Jaspers wishes to characterize Thomistic metaphysics as a major component of the "anti-philosophical" mentality, which his existentialism would like to uproot.

If this accurately expresses his mind on the matter, then the attack on ontology is not a convincing one. First of all, the given description of ontology does fit the procedure of Wolff and many Scholastic manuals, but it is only a parody of the thought of Aquinas himself.[21] The latter does not make a beginning with the first being, since he explicitly rejects the identification of being in general with God, the first being. Furthermore, his realistic metaphysics does not develop along purely deductive lines and does not admit the possibility of attaining utter systematic completeness. The two fundamental doctrines of God's freedom and man's limited, existentially orientated intelligence stand in the way of a total, systematic deduction within a Thomistic context.

Another weakness in Jaspers' refutation of ontology is his integral acceptance of Kant's theory of knowledge. What modifications he does introduce into this epistemology are intended to make room for the existentialist stress on the individual and transient aspects of reality rather than to provoke a thorough reconsideration of the main issues. He calls in question neither the limitation of strict knowledge to phenomenal, objective aspects nor the theory of the constitutive function of consciousness in general with respect to the world of phenomenal objects. Now these are precisely the doctrines which are challenged by a realist metaphysics; they are matter for critical discussion rather than first principles beyond all discussion.

Jaspers claims that, apart from Kant, there is no method available for saving existential insights. One of the most noteworthy instances of how a traditional philosophy is affected by contemporary problems is afforded at this point. Thomistic realists have been forced by just such predicaments as that presented by Jas-

pers to recover certain relevant aspects of the Thomistic philosophy which were for a long time obscured and even contradicted by the ordinary Thomistic handbooks. One of the major
causes of the rediscovery of Thomism as an existential philosophy
of being is the need to take account of Kierkegaard, without sur-
rendering to Kant. Jaspers does not give serious attention to this
alternative explanation.

A case in point—where Thomism and Jaspers' Kantianism find
different ways of preserving existentialist convictions—is the
question of the existing self and objective knowledge. Because of
his fear lest the uniqueness of human selfhood be slighted, Jaspers
establishes a gulf between knowledge and the self as existent.[22]
Knowledge is never permitted to reach to selfhood and existence:
conversely, the objective world of empirical being (to which
knowledge can attain) is emptied of definite existential content.
A dualism of empirical and existential being, object and self, is
the consequence. This leads Jaspers not only to remove the idealistic and naturalistic monisms of being but also to go to the other
extreme of advocating a purely equivocal notion of being.

This dichotomy is not required in the Thomistic explanation.
There is no preliminary "Copernican" assumption that consciousness constitutes the empirical thing in specifying the epistemic
object. Hence there is no tendency to think that objective knowledge of beings is comprehensive knowledge of these things or
that the categories found in some modes of being are the transcendental perfections found in all beings. If our finite minds
discover rather than legislate for the intelligible structure of the
beings of the world, it is possible to hold that our knowledge of
these things is incomplete and yet existential. Objects are not pure
products of our consciousness, working on some chaotic matter,
but are grounded in the existing beings of the world themselves,
taken in their cognitive relation to our knowing minds. The establishment of a cognitive relationship enables the mind to grasp
something about real things, including something about their ultimate act of being or existence (esse), without any pretence at
grasping everything about them. Nor is there any implication

that the traits of being, including the existential act, are realized in all domains of being in exactly the same way in which they are found in the sensible world.

There is no need to accept the Kantian reversal of the relation between mind and thing as the only way to safeguard the integrity of existence, because there is no necessary connection between realism and a rationalistic ontology which Jaspers rightly accuses of emptying out all existential meaning. The realism of Aristotle and Aquinas agrees that finite, contingent existence cannot be derived solely by deduction, but it also maintains that the perfection of existence is realized in different ways in different kinds of beings. This permits realism to recognize a definite existential aspect of the objective, empirical world which Jaspers' principles prevent him from acknowledging. This realistic recognition has two major consequences: the proper perfections of being are genuinely present in the "phenomenal" world of sense experience, and the existential act can fall somehow within the scope of our ordinary knowledge. The first conclusion is the foundation for a metaphysical approach to the transcendent being and will be analyzed at length in the following section. At present, it is the second consequence that must be examined by comparison with Jaspers' teaching.

Jaspers develops his theory of our grasp on existence in a rigorously logical way from his Kantian premises. Since there is a strict correlation between knowledge and objectivity, existence cannot be known. It belongs on the side of the free subject or active self rather than on the side of the knowable object. It is that which can never be objectified, and hence it is that which can never be known. But although there can be no existential knowledge, we can gain an awareness (*Innewerden*) of existence as it characterizes our own free activity.[23] This closely parallels Kant's distinction between knowledge of phenomenal objects and faith in noumenal realities. Jaspers adds that this awareness of existence is always of possible existence, never of the actual state of existence. A man can *be* an actual existent, but he can think about or become aware of only the *possibility* of existence. Our awareness represents existence in retrospect or prospect but not in its actual presence. Philosophizing takes its rise from existence and is directed toward existence, without ever coming into cognitive possession of the existential act itself, even through awareness.

A realistic philosophy also affirms that the human mode of being is an existential one and that each existent individual is unique and ineffable. But to exist is a diversified perfection that is shared in somehow by all real, actual beings. Not only men but also the other beings in the world have their own existence. The special structure of the human mode of being is no more endangered by this admission than by admitting that both man and the non-human world share in the empirical aspect of being. The fact that man exists as a reflective and free being is no ground for restricting existence to the reflective and free manner of existing. Current existentialism does not justify its exclusively humanistic and moralistic interpretation of the act of existing.

There are a number of distinctions in regard to our cognition of existence that Jaspers overlooks. The basic distinction is between existence as an actual perfection of a being and existence as signified in our understanding. In the former sense, existence is strictly ineffable and incommunicable from being to being. Jaspers recognizes this when he says that the communication of existence is impossible until there obtains a correlation between existence and reason, that is, until the existential act has been given intellectual expression. Now even with respect to our understanding of existence, realists hold that the finite mind cannot acquire a comprehensive grasp of any existent reality. The very act whereby a subject exercises existence cannot be known in its own intimate mode or objectified by any other being possessing finite intelligence. It is impossible for such an intelligence to exhaust the meaning of the existential acts of which it becomes aware. This fact drove Sartre back to an impersonal foundation upon which to develop his Cartesian theory of existential lucidity. We have noted some of the inhumane consequences of Sartre's refusal to accept the limitations surrounding our human grasp on existence.

But this is not equivalent to denying all knowledge of the existential perfection. Jaspers is correct in repeating with Kant that, if existence be regarded as a logical predicate, it has no distinctive meaning. There is no need, however, to follow Jaspers in shifting the entire meaning of existence to the act of moral freedom, which operates the other side of strict knowledge. Kant himself allowed for some categorial and objective significance of existence in the empirical order. The perfection of existing can be grasped through the act of intellectual judgment itself and expressed logically in the basic copula, *to be*. To know *that* a being exists is not the same as knowing *how* it exists in its own concrete act as an existent subject or the same as knowing all about its existential reality. Yet through the existential judgment, man does gain some minimal knowledge about the existential aspect of the beings of his experience and the beings implied by that experience. Since there is no need to transfer existential perfection entirely to the moral order, there is also no need to refuse to call our grasp of this perfection a piece of knowledge. It is not perfect knowledge, but neither is it the same as an act of faith or moral postulation.[24]

Finally, the existential judgment bears upon the very act of existing in the thing known and not merely upon the possibilities in time past or future for realizing existence. Here again, the moral mode of existing is not the only way in which existence exhibits itself. There is in ordinary experience a speculative affirmation of existence, an assertion that this being here and now before me does indeed exist. In this judgment, intellectual expression is given to the fact that this thing actually shares in existential perfection. It is not a case of physical assimilation or displacement of the existent thing, and hence there is no incompatibility between the concrete existential act and the cognitive affirmation of this act. The existential judgment expresses in an objective way the inalienable reality of that which constitutes the individual subject as an actual existent.

Jaspers' difficulty concerns a different situation, one where a man declares himself to exist. Now even here, Jaspers is compelled to admit some sort of speculative judgment of existence.

For he states that a man realizes his existence through a free act, that he can be only his actual existence, and hence that his existence eludes objective understanding. These are in fact assertions about the existential act, instances of knowledge. It is no objection to observe that a man does not exist merely as a given thing and that his minimal free existence does not assure his complete human perfection. These points must not only be granted; they are required in any theory of the analogical nature of knowledge about being and its ultimate actuation in existence. Jaspers has shown not that existence can be predicated of man alone but that the human way of existing involves a free nature, the full perfection of which is a task to be pursued during a lifetime. The moral aspects of human existence are further problems within the embracing context of an existing human reality.

Because he cannot admit, on his epistemological premises, that the human mind grasps actual existence in an act of genuine knowledge, Jaspers has been unable to develop a complete philosophy of existence. There would be no basis in his system for establishing the existential import of the natural world or of a speculative approach to man. Similarly, his interpretation of existence in terms of human freedom alone leads to a postulatory theory of transcendence, which Sartre deems just as hypothetical as his own postulatory atheism.

3. *Transcendence and the Transcendent.*

In working out his doctrine of transcendence, Jaspers returns to his fundamental analysis of situations. What is important now to observe is that, although a man can pass from this situation to that, he cannot pass entirely beyond all situations. Philosophizing begins with his recognition of himself as a being-in-situation. From his present horizon he can advance to another one, but he can never reach a unifying perspective or grouping of standpoints from which all being can be seen synoptically. He comes gradually to awareness that being is included within no particular horizon or situation. Rather, it must be characterized as the embracing, the enveloping, the comprehensive *(Das Umgreifende)*.[25] It is the "cosmic weather" or all-pervading atmosphere in which particular things are bathed and yet which transcends them all. All perspectives and situations derive from the enveloping reality and hence are partial and finite. They announce the presence of being, but being itself is never exhausted or completely revealed in its modes. Reason is the bond uniting the various modes of being. Correlative to reason is our own existence, as we face the various situations of life and attempt to integrate them under the unity of being.

Situations are not only many but of many sorts.[26] Some of them do not seriously involve or threaten our entire mode of being. Most of our everyday problems and decisions leave the foundations of our existence untouched. But there are other predicaments which do shake our sense of security and commensurability with the given world. Reason, for instance, tries in vain to achieve a stable synthesis between objectivity and subjectivity, the temporal and the eternal, the relative and the absolute. The antinomies of reason remain, despite its best efforts at overcoming them. And the existing self is the seat of other antinomies whenever it tries to seal itself off as a self-sufficient unit in the world. Certain situations serve to bring man's efforts at achieving autonomy to an abrupt and tragic halt. These are the fundamental limit-situations which bring a man to sudden awareness of his dependent, transient nature, the inadequacy of the empirical mode of being, and the ordination of existence to transcendence. Among these situations are man's condition as a mortal, suffering, and sinful being, together with his sense of historical decisiveness and fidelity, his absolute power of free action, and his need for communication with others. These limit-situations are, at the same time, the sure indices of our possible existence.

The effect of experiencing these situations is an abiding uneasiness, an inability to accept things as they are, or to feel at home in a torn and jagged world of empirical being. This sense of estrangement is connected not only with a Fall and a presenti-

ment of death but also with an intimation of man's need for transcendence. Human existence is harried by antinomies and limits
so that it will not forget its search after the Other, after being in
an inclusive, comprehensive sense.

Man organizes this search under the name of metaphysics.[27]
Its task is to discover the signs of the Other present in the various
modes of being. At first, metaphysical thinking seems likely to
reach its goal. In retrospect, the various modes of being and the
sciences of these modes can be arranged as so many stages in the
process of transcendence. This perspective gives at least negative
content to metaphysical judgments. It can be ascertained that the
transcendent reality is *not* the same as the empirical being of the
given world or the being of human reason and existence. It is
other than these forms of reality and, indeed, is the Wholly
Other. Jaspers claims priority over Barth and the crisis theologians in reviving a term that was once so pregnant with meaning.

In her study on our knowledge of God, the German phenomenologist and Thomist, Edith Stein, showed that the way of negation—the denial to God of finite structures and finite ways of
realizing unconditioned perfections—was supplemented by Dio-
nysius, the pseudo-Areopagite, and other philosophical theologians by the ways of eminence and affirmation.[28] But these latter
ways of approaching God are undermined by Jaspers, just as they
are undermined by Heidegger. Since the categories of ontology
are drawn from empirical, phenomenal being alone, they cannot
be used in the study of God. Not even our indirect awareness of
existence can be made to yield definite truth about the reality of
the transcendent. It requires an act of personal freedom in order
to direct our existence toward transcendence. This choice of a
transcendent orientation of one's existence is not made on the
basis of objective reasons but is a free decision to found our being
in the direction of *Das Umgreifende*. At least, there is no possibility of confounding transcendence and human existence. They
are contrasted as the one and the many, the unconditioned and
the conditioned, the actual-beyond-all-possibility and the region
of possibility.

Metaphysics, as Jaspers describes it, is not content with these negative determinations. It regards the empirical and existential modes of being as so many signs of the transcendent. Every effort is made to read the meaning of these signs, but they remain an unbroken code.[29] Whatever secret they are intended to convey remains locked up in the face of the metaphysical examination. The failure of the decoding project is apparent from the logical contradictions and circular reasoning in which the metaphysician becomes entangled. As crowning testimony of the metaphysical shipwreck, Jaspers adduces the impossibility of maintaining simultaneously the reality of a transcendent being apart from the world and the reality of a world confronted with such a transcendent being. Nothing is real to us except within the context of the *Dasein:* a totally other or nonempirical being would be an unreal one.[30] Conversely, if such a being did have reality, it would empty the empirical world of value and meaning. Since human existence occurs only within the empirical world, a transcendent being would also seem to rob man of status and significance. This is Jaspers' way of restating the objection he brought previously against Descartes for refusing to question religious beliefs purportedly derived by revelation from a transcendent God.

Metaphysics is bound to fail, but this failure is itself the redeeming sign of the power and reality of transcendence in human existence.[31] Jaspers welcomes the experience of failure as the master key that unlocks the entire code. It reveals that the impersonal transcendent has being and also that nothing more can be said about it. From our failure to assault the heights of the transcendent, the deepest lesson of existence is learned. We should develop the attitude of transcending by keeping our existence open in the upward direction. But man's existence can be worked out only within the sphere of empirical being. His duty is to embrace his failure and sorrow, resigning himself to them as the consequence of his presence as an existing self in the empirical world of manyness, time, and objectivity. From the human standpoint, reality is to be found only here, and man's greatness comes when he accepts his placement in situations with heroic patience. The reward is great. For it is precisely within this empirical world that the resigned man finds the absolute presence of being. His simple awareness of his own existence in a given empirical setting brings him the peace and rest that confute Sartre's view of existence as anguish without surcease.

How successful is this solution of the problem of transcendence? Mlle Jeanne Hersch, one of Jaspers' students, thinks that the theory of triumphant failure destroys every philosophical illusion by exposing Jaspers' own philosophy as the supreme instance of illusion and arbitrariness.[32] One way to avoid this judgment is by giving metaphysical weight to the theory of failure, but then it would have to bear the brunt of Jaspers' own devastating critique of metaphysics. On the other hand, Jaspers himself stresses the pragmatic consequences of the choice of an attitude of transcendence. He praises the personal intensity and resoluteness of the act in much the same way as does Heidegger. It engages the entire individual in his concrete existence and opens up for him an endless field of free endeavor.

What is difficult to see, however, is how this act of faith can supply a foundation for the two things Jaspers prizes most highly: a philosophy of existence and personal communication among men. Even when philosophizing is regarded as a personal action, it has its public aspect. Jaspers criticizes the philosophical attitudes of other thinkers and advocates a general return of philosophers to the sources of being, as apprehended by philosophical faith. Apparently, the grounds for making a common act of philosophical faith are found in the failure and its consequences, as described by Jaspers. He does not make clear how he has avoided proposing an objective truth, at least in the minimal sense of setting forth what others might expect to find, if they were to follow the same course. But to submit his notion of transcendence to such a test would imply that it shares something in common with propositions in the natural sciences and so-called ontology. This would, in turn, require a thorough reconsideration of the limitation of knowledge and objective criteria to merely phenomenal regions of being.

Jaspers' doctrine naturally invites comparison with the view of St. Thomas on transcendence, since this is a central theme in both outlooks.[33] Aquinas agrees that transcendence occurs in man and is performed by man in so far as he possesses intellect and will. Through his intellectual power, man can grasp the different modes of being, form a notion of being as such, and seek knowledge of the transcendent being. Furthermore, he can order his life freely towards God. But the common predication of being is neither a genus, having specific differences, nor the same as the being of God. The analogical character of the notion of being is quite foreign to Jaspers, so that he fluctuates between an equivocal view of diverse regions of being and a univocal theory of being as the embracing whole, of which the empirical world is merely an appearance.

The main difference between Jaspers and the Common Doctor turns about the pivotal distinction between ontology and metaphysics. The attempt to drive home a wedge at this point is common to all the existentialists of our time, although they differ on the significance of the distinction. The separation proposed by Jaspers can only be made in terms of the Kantian dichotomy between the phenomenal and noumenal worlds.[34] The only reason why a science of being that takes its point of departure in the empirical world would not be relevant for the study of God and the self would be the "noumenal emptiness" of this world. And the only reason for the failure of a metaphysics of transcendence is its postulated lack of an empirical basis. If the beings of the empirical world do not exhibit existence and other pure perfections of being, then—despite Jaspers' protestations to the contrary—the empirical modes of being can be nothing other than empty, deceptive husks. How these objects that signify nothing definite and convey no intelligible message can be called signs and ciphers is not readily apparent. Even to know that they do have further significance is to go considerably beyond the logic of Jaspers' position.[35]

Jaspers does not offer independent proofs of the impotence of metaphysics. He repeats Kant's charges about the circular and contradictory nature of metaphysical reasoning, without inquiring whether these defects would also occur in a metaphysics not systematically divorced from a descriptive basis in the existential world of sense experience. His major argument, showing the mutual incompatibility between a transcendent being and the empirical world, overlooks this realistic alternative. There is an essential identity between Kant's critique of the proofs for God's existence and Jaspers' contention that a transcendent being would seem unreal and meaningless apart from our phenomenal world.[36] The assumption common to both is that, in the speculative order, real, actual being can be ascribed to a thing only under the empirical conditions of space and time. Only on condition that all beings must conform to the given mode of *Dasein*, is there reason for declaring that a transcendent being seems to be unreal.

There is an ambiguity concealed in this last statement. "Conformity to the conditions of empirical being" may refer either to our knowledge of the transcendent being or to the internal constitution of this being. In the first sense, there is an empirical basis for knowledge of God in a metaphysics that rests upon an analysis of the traits of the empirical world and their implications. If the existence of God is required by the finite, contingent aspects of this world, then His existence will not seem unreal even from the empirical perspective. Affirmation of His existence will be in accord with empirical conditions of finite reality. But if the phrase quoted above refers to the mode of being belonging to God, then it is true that He does not conform to the conditions governing the realization of finite sensible beings. Jaspers thinks that such an admission entails the deistic conception of a God that is totally separate from the world, lacking in "possibility" or freedom, inactive, and permitting no relations between the world and Himself. There is no cogent reason for making this identification of deism and the doctrine of God's transcendence, however, unless it is already presupposed that being is not predicated as an analogical perfection. The doctrine of divine transcendence, as developed by Augustine and Aquinas, involves a correlative theory of God's immanence in His creation. This is evident from St. Augustine's famous declaration that God is at once more intimate to me than my innermost self and higher than my highest aspirations. A theory of transcendence that does not assure God's intimate presence in all created things has only a defective understanding of the divine transcendence itself. God's otherness from the world is the otherness of a creative, loving principle. Jaspers cannot explain how God is both pure act and first cause.

Another reason advanced for declaring the bankruptcy of metaphysics reveals the same set of principles at work. Jaspers states that metaphysics need not lead up a blind alley, if there be an intuition of God as the principle of this purported science.[37] Now except for certain phenomenologists working in the field of religion, there are few philosophers today who claim such an intuition. It is not unreasonable, indeed, to demand *some* sort of intuition as the starting point of metaphysical inference. This is a requirement common to both the Aristotelian and the Kantian conceptions of science. Realistic metaphysics is founded on a sensuous intuition, enabling the intellect to know the existence of material beings. This metaphysics is careful to respect the ordination of the human mind to the sensible world, even when it also permits inferential reasoning to explore something about immaterial existents and their nature. It makes being as such the subject of first philosophy, but being precisely as grasped by us in relation to the finite, sensible modes of being. God is not the point of departure of a realistic metaphysics, and within this context no claim is made that the human mind has an intuition of God. Knowledge of the existence and nature of God is not the principle of this metaphysics but the fruit of an inference from the being of the sensible world. God comes within the scope of a realistic metaphysics in so far as the implications of finite, sensible being permit and require inferences to be made about the first cause of all beings.

Jaspers has laid down, therefore, impossible conditions for the validation of metaphysics. Our finite, sense-dependent minds do not have an intuition of God in the present life, and neither is there an identity between being in general and the first being. But Jaspers' epistemological background forced him to specify these conditions and so to decree beforehand the futility of metphysical inquiry. Realism finds existence and other perfections of being exhibited in and by the things of the empirical world. Jaspers ties existence down to empirical conditions, but only in the sense that existence displays itself *in* empirical being but not *by* and *as* empirical being. The conflicting doctrines on transcendence stem from this capital difference. It could be predicted, before Jaspers began his critique of metaphysics, that the last word in metaphysics would be failure and would provoke him to make a desperate act of philosophical faith as a new foundation of inquiry.

Faith in the reality of the Other is supposed to have retroactive effect upon the entire metaphysical effort to decipher the signs furnished by the various modes of being. But even before this retroactive validation, Jaspers permits metaphysics to say a good deal about the Other. His entire negative theology provides a stumbling block to his contention that no knowledge of God comes within the scope of metaphysics. Jaspers reports the fact that metaphysics distinguishes God from man and the world through a series of contrasting comparisons, but he fails to probe the reason why these negative judgments are formed. It is not by any arbitrary rule that they are made, for instance, by an agreement to deny of God everything that comes within our finite experience. This explanation would not cover those cases in which the negative moment in natural theology refuses to make an unqualified denial about God. Thus it will deny to God the limitation of our finite way of realizing actuality or unity, but it will not simply state that God has no actuality or unity. Furthermore, many of the examples adduced by Jaspers do not belong properly to the negative moment. To say that God is eternal, unconditioned, and one is not to pronounce a mere negation of temporality, finitude, and multiplicity. It is rather a negative way of stating positive perfections about God, a way that yields some certain knowledge.

These difficulties show the impossibility of singling out the negative moment in natural theology as the prototype of metaphysical discussion about God. The *via negationis* is neither primary nor self-sufficient. It is a subsequent phase in the study of God and presupposes at least that His existence has been proven from an inspection of the given world. Now Jaspers fails to take account of the close connection between these two phases of natural theology. Like the American follower of Whitehead, Charles Hartshorne,[38] he thinks that the affirmation of God's existence is quite incidental to the problem of God's nature. Hence he leaves in complete obscurity the admitted fact that metaphysics shows that God has actual being. He does not see (any more than does Sartre) that therein lies the crucial issue. In a theistic realism, the negative and eminent approaches to God's nature are regulated by prior proofs of God's existence. It is only because God is proven to exist precisely as pure actuality that there is need of a negative moment of thought that will set off God from all other beings, which are not purely actual.

Failure to take account of this regulative influence of the proofs for God's existence upon the doctrine of His nature accounts for certain misunderstandings. Thus Jaspers speaks of God as undetermined being in opposition to the determinate beings in the world. Now this statement is at least verbally similar to the saying of Damascene and Aquinas that God is the infinite and limitless sea of being.[39] But Aquinas adds that God is in one sense the most undetermined (that is, unbounded) being and in another sense the most determined (that is, purely actual). A purely negative theology could not distinguish the different senses in which determination and indetermination apply to God. There is needed a general theory of the structure of being and the results of the proofs of God's existence in order to settle this delicate problem. Jaspers seems to identify the indetermination of God with the common character of being as the embracing or comprehensive whole. There is no way whereby he could correct himself, supposing that the formal object of metaphysics is transcendence and that negative theology is detached from prior proofs of God's existence.

As crowning proof of the contradictions of metaphysics, Jaspers cites two famous descriptions of God.[40] Plotinus says of the One: "It is what it is," whereas the Old Testament has God say of Himself: "I am Who am." Jaspers comments that this interchanging of *it* and *I* in reference to God is a confession on the part of both religion and philosophy that our minds make no penetration to the being of transcendence. It is an admission that the categories of reason are confounded with each other and yield absolutely no knowledge of that which is best defined as being the locus of non-knowledge. God cannot be said to be both a neuter entity and a person without discrediting the ability of our reason to discover anything meaningful about His nature.

In making this interpretation, Jaspers has recourse to the same terribly final historicism which motivated his dictum that Kant spelled the doom of ontology. When it is a case of disposing of other philosophies, Jaspers allows no recourse from the temporal displacement effected by history. But in actual practice, neither Jaspers nor any other metaphysician is condemned to accept without appeal "the verdict of history." There is no reason why the metaphysical tradition should stand helpless before this difference between the Old Testament and Plotinus. As a matter of fact, Christian philosophers from Augustine to Aquinas have noted this contrast and used it as a point of departure for fresh metaphysical developments.

From a purely analytical standpoint, a contradiction is not necessarily involved in referring to God as *it* and *He*. There are aspects of God's being which can be explored without making explicit reference to His personality. This is a procedure familiar to us in our treatment of man. We usually refer to human nature as *it*, even though a fuller explanation leads us to employ the personal pronoun in reference to the man, the concrete subject having this nature. Jaspers is prone to find contradiction everywhere among metaphysical positions, whereas the difference is often due to the various aspects of reality under consideration. Sometimes, it is merely a question of attending now to one aspect of the divine being and now to another. But there is also real progress in metaphysical thinking about God, so that further aspects of His being are gradually uncovered by different minds. Not every philosopher who fails to establish the personal character of God is thereby committing himself to a positive denial of His personality.

It must also be pointed out that the historical example chosen by Jaspers is singularly unfortunate for his case. It does not demonstrate that the religious mind and the philosophical mind become inexplicably and unalterably entangled in contradictions, where God is concerned. Gilson has recently shown that the Plotinian Intelligence, the second principle in the universe, is more comparable to the Christian God than is the Plotinian One.[41] Moreover, definite metaphysical reasons can be assigned for the contrast between Plotinus' One and the Christian philosophico-religious conception of God. The Plotinian One is at the peak because it is free from being and intelligibility; the Christian God is supreme and knowable because He is supremely existing being. Plotinus refers to his One in the only way in which it can be referred to: as an ineffable something lying totally beyond our ken. There is kinship between this conception and Jaspers' teaching on transcendence, because both Jaspers and Plotinus make the One nonexistential, unknowable, and impersonal. Now this position cannot be simply identified with "the" philosophical view of God: it is one philosophical conception and is based on a definite metaphysical option. On the other hand, the revelation to Moses has been a fertile source of philosophical speculation as well as religious meditation. It is the prime reason why Christian philosophers have felt compelled to revise their conception of being, and hence their entire metaphysical doctrine on God, in an existential direction. Hence Jaspers' historical example shows no more than that there are conflicts within philosophy as well as religion, and that he himself is not in a neutral position with regard to these conflicts. From this analysis, it may be concluded that conflicts concerning the transcendent arise from basic metaphysical options, which are neither unavoidable nor irremediable.

4. *Religious and Philosophical Faith.*

Jaspers does not show the same unbending hostility toward religion that antagonizes many readers of Sartre. Indeed, he never tires of pointing out the historical and social importance of a religious tradition. He believes that many of the basic philosophical convictions have been preserved for, and proposed to, mankind at large by religion, especially by the biblical religion of evangelical Christianity. But he also maintains that the sound core of religious insight has been perverted and overlaid by the authoritarian religious organizations. For this reason, there is often conflict between authentic philosophy and deformed expressions of religion.

Even with regard to the essential deliverances of religion, moreover, philosophy must retain a critical attitude. After it has purified religious tradition of its superstitious claim to exclusiveness, philosophy must then try to reappropriate the religious truth for itself. Although Jaspers is exceedingly vague on the relation between religious and philosophical faith, it does not seem to be doing him an injustice to liken his stand to that of Hegel and Goethe.[42] It inevitably calls to mind Goethe's famous quip that religion is the uncultured man's substitute for philosophy. As nearly as can be determined, Jaspers thinks that religious faith originally stemmed from the individual existent's philosophical adherence to transcendence and the comprehensive reality. Religious faith is an unreflective expression of this essentially philosophical insight. Where Jaspers differs from many Hegelians is in refusing to hope that religion can be transformed into philosophy within the prospect of human history. For the ordinary man, religion will continue to remain the primal source of truth about the modes of being and the only authority he will acknowledge in ultimate matters.

Nevertheless, Jaspers does look forward to a renewal of the wellsprings of a pure religious outlook. This is one of the effects of the existential inquiry into the sources and principles of being and knowing. Religion is not left unaffected by such an inquiry, since an effort to recover the intelligible meaning of religious faith leads behind religion itself to its philosophical substratum. "We are thus led automatically to interpret renewal of religious faith as a return to the primal source, as a renewal of the philosophical faith that is implicit in the religious, as a transformation of religion into philosophy (or philosophical religion)."[43] This is Jaspers' most explicit statement on this relationship. At least for the existential thinker, then, religious faith passes over into philosophical faith the moment the question of significance is raised.

Despite his insistence on the necessity and independence of religious tradition, Jaspers understands these attributes of religion in a relative way, as holding for the majority of men in their social and institutional relations. If all men were to embrace his existential philosophy (and Jaspers, unlike Nietzsche, does not reserve it in principle only for the few), they would transform religion into philosophy. They would know which fork in the road to follow in the search after transcendence: that which leads to flight from the world or that which leads to a more adequate penetration of this our world and its meaning.[44]

In view of the realistic doctrine on the divine immanence and the Christian doctrine on the Incarnation, it is difficult to see why the alternative is framed in this way. Jaspers cannot conceive the doctrinal relation between philosophy and religion as one of independent confirmation. Religion is tolerated by Jaspers only on condition of accepting a subordinate role, as far as intelligible content is concerned. Its distinctive contribution lies in the social and educational spheres. Whenever religion claims to be an original source of true doctrine, Jaspers regards it as the enemy of his philosophy and all philosophical tradition. Metaphysics is a failure if it tries to supply the theoretical basis of natural religion, and is a renegade to its own law of transcendence if it admits the possibility of an independent, supernatural revelation. Jaspers makes religious faith clash with philosophical faith rather than admit the older view of a harmony between a nonfideistic reason and supernatural faith. This is the ultimate measure of his criticism of Cartesian doubt and its Christian limitations.

The ideal of the existential thinker intervenes between Jaspers and any independent revelation from a supernatural source. The existential way of philosophizing is intensely personal, active, and autonomous. One philosophizes out of one's own possible existence and the result is *my* transcendence, *my* awareness, *my* God. There is no room in Jaspers' dispensation for a receptive attitude, wherein the thinker receives truth as a gift from another. He must not only appropriate truth to himself; he must regard as true only that which is an outflow from his own act of faith and original dynamism. In this unexpected way, Jaspers comes to agree with Sartre that any initiative taken by a personal, transcendent God would be an attack upon one's freedom, an intrusion from the outside. He defines philosophizing as the developed will to unity or as the defiant will to know. But he never explains why this "will" arbitrarily excludes effective communication of truth to us from the transcendent God. The attitude of defiant autonomy precludes sober philosophical discussion of other positions.

Instead of remaining prudently agnostic about the nature of the Other, Jaspers extends his negative theology into a positive denial of the tri-personal God of the Christians and of Christ as the unique God-man. For him, these doctrines are myths that at best convey some elements of true religious faith and at worst unleash man's shameful passions of intolerance and persecution. His manner of purifying religious faith leads eventually to a position wherein religious life becomes impossible. This is seen in the case of prayer. The philosophical recognition of the value of prayer becomes a deadly embrace, in which the reality of prayer disappears in the course of giving it philosophical meaning. As Jaspers admits, this process "marks a break with the concreteness of a personal relation to a personal God, which is one of the sources of religion, and a movement toward abstract philosophical contemplation."[45] Prayer thus conceived is not just compatible and fruitfully continuous with philosophy: it literally becomes an operation intrinsic to existential philosophy.

Philosophizing takes the place of praying in the existential economy recommended by Jaspers. It is the substance and sense of what ordinary religious men call praying. But without a personal bond with a personal God through prayer, the reality of religion vanishes. That is why Jaspers' closest French critics, Dufrenne and Ricoeur, conclude that Jaspers' philosophical faith remains ambiguously poised between atheism and religiousness.[46] It is neither of these, but it is doubtful whether it can respect the distinctive values of religiousness and still retain its own principles in their full rigor. Like Kant's rational faith, Jaspers' philosophical faith is, in principle at least, a counterprinciple to an autonomous religious conviction.

In many ways Jaspers has had a salutary effect upon contemporary philosophy. His criticism of scientism, idealism, and naturalism has reopened the question of monism and pluralism in being and method. One of his soundest contributions has been a defense of the plurality of the modes of being and the need for differentiation of method in dealing with different kinds of objects and attitudes. Within the existentialist camp he is distinguished by his respect for philosophical tradition and his defense of the rights of transcendence. His doctrine of transcendence is disappointing only because it rests content with the attitude of transcending and does not attain in some way to the transcendent. Transcendence is not for him a pathway to God but a fortification of the open and adventuresome spirit in man. Because of its Kantian lineage, this theory of transcendence does not succeed in reconciling the immanent world and the transcendent reality of God. Here, as well as in Sartre's case, the problem of such a reconciliation remains the problem of making fresh acquaintance with the world of sensible existents and interrogating them for their metaphysical implications.

Chapter IV

Marcel's Concrete Philosophy of Participation

Writing in 1944 in the liberation journal *La France Libre,* Claude-Edmonde Migny reported the shock she experienced in rereading the passage in Maritain's *Frontiers of Poetry* referring to Arthur Lourié's religious music as "existential." After a short passage of years, this term has come to receive a diametrically opposite meaning, signifying in France the standpoint of a godless humanism. Many critics of existentialism have been so short-memoried as to make no other use of the term than as a synonym for Sartre's philosophy. Perhaps this explains why Gabriel Marcel (1877——) presents a stumbling block in the way of some proposed general interpretations of existentialism. Helmut Kuhn, for instance, regards this movement as an analysis of a world from which God has been banished. If the fundamental existential experience is an encounter with utter nothingness, then there is little room for a philosopher who consistently studies such positive attitudes as fidelity and hope and worship. Consequently, Kuhn is forced to place Marcel at the periphery. For her part, Marjorie Grene thinks that Sartre is the tough-minded exponent of this trend of thought, whereas Marcel makes a sentimental flight from the stern prospects of existence without God. And because he disturbs the pattern of decadence which idealists like Guido de Ruggiero seek to superimpose upon existentialism, Marcel receives from them the label of mystic. Clearly, his approach is apt to upset the neatest definitions and generalizations about existentialism.[1]

Marcel himself regards this confusion among the critics as testimony to one of his major contentions: that the response to being is not determined for us but is a work of freedom. Since his first philosophical publication in 1912, he has been examining the nature of the alternative replies that can be given to the fundamental question about the nature of being. His starting point was the idealism so prevalent in France and Britain during the first decade of the twentieth century. He was profoundly influenced not only by Hegel and the classical German idealists but more especially by such contemporaries as Hamelin, Bradley, and Royce. Because he was satisfied with neither idealism nor its empiricist alternative as presented by Bertrand Russell, Marcel was forced to strike out on his own. He even developed a distinctive literary form, the metaphysical journal. Two complete sections have been published (the notes up to 1923, and those from 1928 until 1933), and Marcel continues to add steadily to this mine of personal observations.

Although his original researches seemed to take him far from settled country, Marcel found that he had some company along the way. Together with Nicolai Hartmann (who issued, in 1921, a stimulating treatise on the metaphysics of knowledge), he was moving in the direction of realism and a renewal of ontology. His *Metaphysical Journal* was published in the same year (1927) as Heidegger's *Being and Time*. Such themes as being-in-the-world, facticity, my body, the nature of the questioner, tools, and participation were common to both books. The similarity was due in part to a similar intellectual background, since they were both influenced by Hegel, Schopenhauer, the later Schelling, and Nietzsche. Reading of these sources also helps to account for the many resemblances between Marcel and Jaspers. Indeed, Marcel felt called upon both to acknowledge the deep impression left by a reading of Jaspers's *Philosophy* (1931) and to point out that as early as 1925 he himself had been exploring the meaning of fundamental situations, the enveloping character of reality, and the appeal to transcendence.[2] Marcel's relations with these three thinkers provide a striking instance of how certain ideas arise spontaneously and independently in minds that are sensitive to a common intellectual situation. Cases of "intellectual contagion" are common enough in the history of science, but they happen frequently in the history of philosophy as well, as the early years of the existentialist movement show.

There is an ironical aspect to the connection between Marcel and the French atheistic existentialists. Numerous entries in Marcel's published journals are concerned with what he calls the betrayal of being. These notes prefigure in considerable detail the doctrines more recently propounded by Albert Camus and Sartre. Camus' theory that suicide is the only logical attitude in an absurd world is given an anticipatory analysis from all angles in Marcel's notebooks.[3] Both the doctrine of radical unintelligibility and absurdity and the escape by way of self-murder are minutely outlined. Furthermore, the Sartrean hypotheses of an absolutely creative freedom and self-deification are acknowledged beforehand by Marcel as constituting the outlook most opposed to his own and yet possible within the context of man's interpretation of his situation. It is somewhat ridiculous, then, to have to refer to Sartre's acknowledgment of a theistic variety of existentialism as warrant for considering Marcel's philosophy. In his Gifford Lectures (1949–50), *The Mystery of Being*, Marcel's vigorous originality of thought is vindicated in his nearest approach to a "systematic" statement.

A comparison between Marcel and Kierkegaard is a somewhat delicate undertaking. Marcel did not come upon Kierkegaard's writings until his own views were firmly established in their characteristic outlines. Hence he has never been haunted by the doubtful ideal of achieving a latter-day revival of Kierkegaard's standpoint or of transposing it into a systematic, philosophical setting. Yet for this very reason there is a closer sympathy of mind and temperament between these two men than between Kierkegaard and any other existentialist. Marcel has reacted to neo-idealism in much the same way as did Kierkegaard to the original Hegelian position. Both thinkers offer a more realistic view of cognition and give prominence to the free individual and his fidelity to a transcendent God. The fact that both men profess the Christian faith and stress its relevance for the understanding of existence is, however, a ground for both agreement and disagreement. Kierkegaard regarded Christianity as a means of displacing philosophy, and hence his standpoint is that of Christian existence versus the prevailing philosophy. Marcel, on the contrary, admits not only the bare possibility of a legitimate rational discipline but the need for a renewal of philosophy itself in an existential direction. He is correspondingly reluctant to call his philosophy a "Christian existentialism," leaving that responsibility to his commentators and followers. He prefers to regard it as a concrete philosophy centered upon the mystery of being, although he grants that it is both compatible with Christianity and naturally disposes the individual toward receiving such a revelation from God.

One of the noteworthy points of similarity between Kierkegaard and Marcel is their common regard for esthetic insight and methods. Although Marcel does not operate within the triadic framework of esthetic-ethical-religious stages, he admits the importance of the esthetic factor in human experience. Kierkegaard once spoke about the need to inject new life into the old Christian and common-sense terminology, which he compared to a sleeping princess who requires a magic touch in order to awaken and reign again. Marcel feels a similar obligation to mint the language of philosophy afresh, not by producing neologisms but by recovering the immediate meanings of ordinary words.[4] Although his essays are free from the usual existentialist preoccupation with coining new terms, they do uncover an unsuspected freight of significance in words and ideas that have grown stale from superficial, heedless use. One of his criticisms of Scholasticism is its tendency to hide behind a formidable terminology that fails to make contact with our contemporary experience. His aim is to recast the perceptions of realism not in another ironclad technical terminology but in a precise and penetrating usage of the living tongue of present-day men.

Indeed, Marcel advocates a much closer co-operation between

literature and philosophy than is allowed either by Thomists or Kierkegaard. The former group tends to place poetic insight on the side of practical, connatural knowledge and to deny it any direct and comprehensive bearing upon a theoretical and abstractive discipline like metaphysics. For this reason, one of Marcel's most favorably disposed Thomistic critics, Jacques Maritain, holds that Marcel's analyses give only concrete analogues of metaphysical truths, without ever attaining to the formal and theoretical attitude required for speculative inquiry. But Marcel has remained faithful to his own conviction that there is a correspondence and ultimate convergence between metaphysical investigations and artistic representations, a closer relationship than even Kierkegaard would allow.

Marcel is a practicing playwright of long standing. He reports that the writing of plays was at first a means of extricating himself from the abstract whirligig of idealistic reasoning. In the drama, he was dealing with individuals and their free actions—realities that were slighted or misconstrued by the systematists. Gradually, Marcel discovered that a correlation existed between his dramatic and his theoretical advances. Many of the views which he later expressed in a philosophical way were first proposed in his plays. The plays expressed the import of human existence in a concrete, dynamic, and personal way: in them, metaphysical thought seized upon itself for the first time *in concreto*.[5]

The greatest danger is to reduce plays to mere occasions for illustrating a thesis, as Sartre has sometimes done. In Marcel's case, there has been an anteriority of dramatic representation over philosophical analysis, at least during his formative years. At present, he views his dramatic and philosophical works as complementary aspects of his exploration of human experience and its metaphysical implications. Art and analysis are regarded as the two poles of his reflective effort, and his aim is to achieve mutual solidarity between the two aspects. The many concrete descriptions that enliven the pages of his journals and essays testify to the influence of his artistic work upon his speculation; they also raise special problems in methodology and interpretation.

1. *Restoring the Ontological Weight.*

As a young man, Marcel dreamed of writing a great systematic work comparable to the idealistic classics of Hamelin and Bradley. But he found that he could not make the transition from his private notes to such a comprehensive exposition. The trouble lay not so much in his inability to make such a construction as in a theoretical reluctance to do so. For the assumption underlying every systematic project is that each man is privileged to write "his philosophy." This notion of "my philosophy" supposes that philosophy is a kind of private possession that can be disposed of at will.[6] Marcel's contribution to the tradition of perennial philosophy is a vigorous reaffirmation of the co-operative nature of philosophizing and its reference to a real world that cannot be reduced to a piece of property. We can share in the philosophical enterprise by means of our own researches, but no individual perspective on reality can be identified with philosophy itself or can be treated as an appurtenance for which its author is publicly unaccountable.

Furthermore, the idealistic custom of developing one system after another presumes that it is possible and desirable to encapsule the universe in a few first principles and deductive excursions. This can be done only by declaring arbitrarily that this or that fact which stubbornly resists inclusion in the system is "unimportant." Marcel would agree with the English metaphysician, Dorothy Emmet, that one of the least examined and most abused notions in philosophy is that of "the important and the unimportant." Systematists can rule out of court any embarrassing counterevidence by the simple (and circular) device of declaring it unimportant for the main issue. Like Pascal and Kierkegaard, Marcel employs the literary form of a journal as a protest against exaggerated systematism. Thoughts presented through the medium of a journal serve as a reminder that the individual thinker cannot embrace the totality of the real in his philosophy, that his reflections are constantly open to new incursions of experience, and that the "unimportant, transient" difficulties are frequently the generative source of new and balancing insights.

Despite his distrust of systems of thought, Marcel's own studies show a high degree of continuity. This is especially apparent in his attack on idealism, the point of departure of which is an article in the *Revue de métaphysique et de morale* in 1912 and the highpoint of which is reached in another article in the same journal thirteen years later.[7] In the former article, he offers a negative criticism and makes brief suggestions for replacing idealism by an intuitional realism. During the next decade, he worked on his *Metaphysical Journal.* The positive results of this period of intensive reflection are summed up in the second article, entitled "Existence and Objectivity." Marcel's anticipation of the other existentialists can be measured in terms of these publications.

Their purpose is to overthrow the hold of idealism on the contemporary mind and to open up a way of restoring the ontological weight to human experience. The effect of idealism and its empiricist counterpart has been to create a sort of "ontophobia," a horror of being, among men. Idealists have criticized being as signifying a dead and static thing which resists dialectical change and development. In its place, they propose to put the transcendental reality of the subject or the absolute idea. From the empiricist standpoint, this substitution is scarcely an improvement over the substantialist notion of being as an independent and rigid entity. Hence the empiricists seek to eliminate both being and any absolute from human experience. They interpret the real in terms of the elements of sensation or the control of practical life. As a consequence of this twofold assault, our lives have lost their metaphysical center. Contemporary man is no longer rooted in being and no longer recognizes the hunger for an intellectual and affective grasp on being. There has been a deliberate refusal to accept man's natural ordination to the ontological.

Marcel's entire philosophy, in its polemical phase, is a careful scrutiny of the grounds of this refusal. He agrees with Bergson that a beginning must be made from the empirical side by a closer examination of the data of experience. As against Kant, Bergson and Marcel maintain that we are capable of a non-sensuous intuition having relevance for the speculative order as well as for the practical.[8] This intuition is not some sibylline, mystic utterance but only our direct acquaintance with our situation in existence. It is not an exhaustive understanding of the mysteries of the universe but a cautious affirmation that something does exist. This intuition does not take the place of careful analysis but is its grounding in reality and its priming point.

Where Bergson and Marcel part company is over the more definite characterization of this immediate conviction. Bergson associates it with a grasp of human duration and regards it as a nonintellectual form of apprehension. To Marcel, the reality of internal duration is too narrow and precise a specification of this intuition. It is more global and indeterminate than Bergson's theory will allow. It is an affirmation of existing being which prescinds from the distinction between the inner and the outer, the specifically human and the non-human modes of being. Moreover, this primary act is an intellectual one. Marcel is not led astray by Bergson's attack on intellect, since it is clear that only a restricted and abused function of intelligence is vulnerable to this criticism. If intuition is valuable for our speculative investigations, then it partakes of the character of intellect in its more immediate and radical operations. Marcel rejects any suggestion that intuition leads to anti-intellectualism. Historically, this has often been the case, but this only proves the need to reconsider the nature of intellect and reason and their relation to being.

Instead of accepting Bergson's prejudicial contrast between intellect and intuition, Marcel develops another Bergsonian distinction: between *la pensée pensée* and *la pensée pensante*, a closed and an open manner of thinking.[9] Where reasoning respects its intuitional basis in an immediate apprehension of being, it keeps the circuit open between thought and reality. Thought is then pledged to return constantly to that which does not depend upon itself and which can never be captured definitively within our formulas. This open and dynamic attitude is the normal relation to mind and being. But when being is subordinated to the idea of being or absolute thought, the mind seals itself up within its own boundaries. The autonomy of thought-concentrated-upon-itself is expressed in systematic idealism.

Because he regards the intuition of being as an intellectual and speculative (as well as practical) affair, Marcel finds its natural prolongation in a dialectic of the open-circuit type. This dialectical employment of reason in the defense and penetration of being has two functions, a negative and a positive one. Its negative task is to expose the shortcomings of idealism; positively, it is called upon to analyze those aspects of experience which throw light upon the nature of being.

Marcel singles out the same postulate in Hegel that was the object of criticism for Kierkegaard and Marx: the ideal of pure thought, *das reine Denken*. Systematism is possible only on the assumption that there is no interval between being and the idea of being, and that any apparently independent instances of the former can be reduced to the latter. This position depends upon a sectarian interpretation of being, an identification of being and one of its modes, that of thinking. It is a kind of "realism of knowing," in which only that which has an ideal character is admitted as real. When the real is understood in this way, the claim can be sustained to include all real objects in an integrated system of thought. In this way, idealists from Hegel to Bradley declare themselves to be in possession of an absolute knowledge.

This equation of being and idea contains a contradiction, which prevents the actual completion of the systematic project.[10] Absolute idealism does not really escape from Kant's contention that a transcendental subjectivity is the condition of all knowing, even of an "absolute" sort. To avoid this conclusion, idealism would have to posit a kind of sur-being as the transcendental condition of the idea of being. But the status of a sur-being could never be determined with systematic satisfaction. For either it is knowable, in which case it comes under the conditions of idealistic cognition as a factor in the absolute idea (and then we are back at

Kant's original objection), or else it escapes our knowledge and *eo ipso* refutes the claim of the system to be comprehensive of all reality.

This does not mean that Kant's standpoint must be accepted, but only that absolute idealism does not provide a genuine alternative. It has made an incomplete analysis of thought, since there is an aspect of thought itself that is not reducible to the dialectical notion. This remainder is not an irrational surd but is the act of knowing itself, in so far as it is a real act of affirming. This reality cannot be reduced to the status of an object of thought or an idea, since it is that which posits or produces ideas. Thinking is first of all a mode of being, a participation in being rather than the idea of being. Using almost the same language as Nicolai Hartmann, Marcel calls for a counterrevolution that will call in question the legitimacy (at least in the philosophical sphere) of Kant's Copernican hypothesis of the conformity of being to thought. In the special sciences, such a view has some basis, since the sciences deal primarily with essential objects or mental constructs only remotely grounded in real things. But in philosophy, the mind is concerned with existent beings in their existential character. Hence the properly philosophical conformity is that of mind with the real thing. Thought is immersed and imbedded in being, and its ultimate significance is about being itself as the measure of truth.[11] Hence the only way to overcome Kant (and, a fortiori, Hegel) is by admitting the transcendence of thought in an intuition of being.

Marcel singles out three factors in our experience which are depreciated by idealism and yet which are sure indices of the apprehension of being: sense, "my body," and existence. Any adequate theory of being must take account of all three factors, for otherwise it will be on the road back to idealism. Marcel believes that it is this threefold test which distinguishes his efforts from the otherwise quite similar speculations of Louis Lavelle and the "Philosophy of the Spirit" group in France today. Marcel refuses to follow Lavelle in the project of a systematic ontology, since the note of systematism conveys a proprietary sense of dealing with objective things rather than with the act of being and personal existence. Furthermore, he suspects that Lavelle's analyses of the thinking self will promote an ontology in which sense, the body, and existence are in a subordinate position.[12]

A choice must be made between starting with the human condition as we find it in its integral connections or picking out one element in that situation for a privileged point of departure. The former method is arbitrary only in the sense that it refuses to make any such privileged selection, whereas the latter course is arbitrary in a way that can never find reasonable justification. Descartes begins with the epistemological subject, the self as a knower, rather than with the existent subject, which includes the cognitive operation along with other operations in the more comprehensive act of existing in the world.[13] Moreover, the being indubitably met with in the Cogito is precisely that aspect of being which is correlative to the human self construed as a thinking thing. Not being as such but the object of thought is the beginning of Cartesian speculation. Since an equation is established between pure intelligence and being, Descartes is forced to minimize the role of sensation in knowledge and the place of the body in the constitution of the self.

To the extent that empiricism presents a counterbalance to the Cartesian doctrine, Marcel shares the empiricist standpoint. The excessively dualistic view of the human self and the excessively intellectualistic view of knowing stand and fall together. To regard being merely as the object of pure intellect is to ignore the way in which objects become present to men. They are not the result of a sheer act of positing but depend upon a previous affirmation of being itself in us. Being is grasped in the first instance not through a purely rational determination but through its sensible presence, a presence upon which we must wait and to whose deliverances we must submit the mind. Sensation is metaphysically important not merely as a message but as a means of participating in the existent universe.[14] It insures our immediate presence in an *ambiance* of existent things and specifies this presence as one of sharing and receiving, as a condition for exercising our proper activity.

Sensation will always remain unintelligible and embarrassing until its twofold significance is appreciated. The fact that we understand the world only with the help of our senses is a sign both of our finite, creaturely nature and of the composite character of that nature. Being is not our own handiwork, and neither is it an inferior level to be conquered by, and subordinated to, our mind. Man knows only because he is first constituted as a being and receives within himself the self-affirmation of other existents. And he is open to others in his given reality as a fleshly being. The human self is not a thinking thing but an integral existent, having senses and flesh as well as mind and will.

What does it mean to "have my body?" Marcel is as concerned with this question as is Heidegger. His preliminary answer is intended to complete his critique of empiricism and the Cartesian Cogito.[15] Here he only stresses the fact that I must refer to it as *my* body. Within a strict empiricism, based as it is upon an analysis of the elements of experience, such a reference is meaningless. This particular body has no discoverable sensible quality about it that distinguishes it from other clusters called bodies. Marcel challenges the empiricist method of reducing experience merely to the "neutral" or "normal" elements which can indifferently constitute this self or that self. This procedure cannot deal with what is unique and freely affirmed in the individual's attitude toward his own body.

On the other hand, Descartes understands the relationship to one's body to mean simply the proprietorship which the thinking self exercises over a section of extended substance. But the instrumental relationship is not the primary sense in which this body is mine. It is mine as a part of myself, as *not* other than myself in the way in which the things around me *are* other. What transpires in my body is a constituent of my own experience. Man is an incarnate being, and his mode of cognition is that of an incarnate being. Marcel has referred to his philosophy as a metaphysics of incarnation, since it starts with man's fleshly presence in the world and the conditions which this manner of presence in being impose upon metaphysics.

In addition to being unduly intellectualistic and dualistic, the

Cartesian approach is nonexistential. This last mark follows on the two previous ones, since sensation is the true index of existence for men. The immediate participation of my body in the world of existent things is the way of access, for my mind, to a grasp of being in its existential fullness. It supplies the "existential indubitable," the assurance of my own existence amidst other real existents in the world. Whereas Kierkegaard and Heidegger stress the connection between existence and temporality, Marcel associates existence primarily with my body. Whatever bears a relation with my body can be called an existent.[16] Since it is clear that my own fleshly condition is not creative of the existents with which it is related, there can be no question of an idealistic production of existence as one moment in the dialectic of pure thought. Man enjoys an immediate sharing in the perfection of existence, without being its creative source. To know the existent is to acknowledge and adhere to that which can never be reduced to thought or a mode of the thinking self. It is to open oneself to being as it can be apprehended after the human manner.

Since existential knowledge is a participation and an adherence, it is not amenable to methodic doubt.[17] Existence is primary in being; it must be present at the beginning of philosophical inquiry or else it remains absent throughout the investigation. The first and most radical affirmation is that *this exists*. To call existence in doubt is to suspend this judgment and thus to break the indefectible synthesis between existence and the existent (this thing which does exist). This can only be done if existence is regarded as a predicate or as an adequate general idea, which one already has and is hesitant about applying in an indiscriminate way. Marcel admits the strength of Kant's contention that existence is not a predicate. But he goes beyond Kant and Jaspers by holding that the basic existential judgment expresses neither a particular existent in isolation nor the general idea of existence. It is rather an affirmation of the indissoluble unity between existence and the existent. Existence can never be completely abstracted from reference to particular existents: we know the perfection of existing in knowing the existential act of real beings of our experience.

What is given is a global experience of the world as existent.[18] Since the given existent is not yet particularized, doubt must either be complete or admit its inappropriateness as the privileged method in metaphysics. It is only in virtue of an arbitrary decree that Descartes divorces existence and the existent and then reserves from doubt one instance of an existent, the thinking self. But once this divorce is made, it is impossible to justify any particular case of existent being. The Cartesian Cogito is nonexistential, because it supposes that existence can be reduced to an idea or to some aspect of an essence. Similarly, the Hegelian derivation of existent actuality is illusory, since existence is no more derivable by a logical dialectic than it is reducible to reflection. Either the existential situation is accepted as the unity of existence and the individual existent presented to sense experiences or else metaphysical thinking must be resigned to a fate of moving among the phantoms which people a nether world deprived of existential act.

Thomistic critics, especially Marcel de Corte and Jacques Maritain, have warned against idealistic tendencies in Marcel's philosophy, but these are difficult to find.[19] Marcel regards himself as a realist but not a Thomist. He agrees with Maritain that thought is made for being as the eye is made for light and that the judgment of existence is the most properly metaphysical judgment. But characteristically, he asks whether intellect should not in turn be studied as a mode of being. He has found this approach an authentically modern way to overcome the primacy of epistemology. His own chief difficulty lies in another direction. Due to the close bond he establishes between existence and reference to the body, he is in danger of slipping into sensualistic materialism. Recognizing this possible outcome of his doctrine, Marcel strives to prevent it with the aid of a distinction between existence and being.[20] His example is that of a past event, which enjoys some reality without being existent. This is similar to Whitehead's speculation about the metaphysical status of the past. It becomes crucial in Marcel's case, once the question of God is considered. He is being in an eminent sense—Marcel states that the biblical *I am who am* is the only adequate designation of God. But it would be difficult to affirm the existence of God on this theory of a fleshly criterion. Marcel seems to be moving in Kierkegaard's direction: God *is* and Christ *exists*. His view of existence and corporeity is admirably suited for casting light upon the Incarnation, but it raises a special obstacle to the existential approach to God as transcendent of the world. For under this aspect, God escapes the existential orbit set up by the body. Perhaps what is lacking is a sufficiently emphatic distinction between our manner of knowing existence and the various modes in which existents can realize this perfection.

Although they leave unclarified the relation between existence and being, the notes on existence contained in Marcel's *Being and Having* (1935) are among the most penetrating remarks on this subject. On many points, they anticipate the later reconsideration of the matter by Thomists. Especially important is Marcel's refusal to allow an idea of existence. It is an act that can only be expressed intellectually through a kindred affirmation, the existential judgment. As Marcel puts it, "If I isolate existence from them [the actual existents], I think *it*, that is, I treat it as an essence or rather, to be more exact, as a pseudoessence. Does not this come to the same thing as saying that there is no *idea* of existence in the strict sense of the term? and this because existence is the limit, or, if you will, the axis of reference for thought itself?"[21] There is no priority of essence over existence, as idealists and rationalists are bound to maintain. Essence is not a realm lying beyond the existential, even though thought may, for certain limited purposes, prescind from existence. These purposes are proper to the special sciences, in so far as they are concerned with essential structures. But philosophical knowledge is a return to the plenary conditions of being. Hence the metaphysician must explicitly attend to the fact that all thoughtful exploration of essential structures transpires within the context of existence. He cannot be seduced by an imaginative picture of making a jump from the region of independent essences to existent things. There is only a transference of attention or what Marcel calls an intra-existential transformation. The mind may pass from one consideration to another but there should be no confusion of such a mental transit with an ontic one from essential to existential domains of being. The real order studied in metaphysics is the order of existent things. Essences are real and of interest to metaphysics in the measure that they bear a reference to this existential order.

Finally, Marcel refuses to regard the mind as completely passive in the face of being. Realism is compatible with a high regard for the proper activity of the human mind. Being is not a given factor, in the sense of something merely transferred from one inert container to another. It is given to the mind in such a way that it gives itself creatively and demands of the recipient an act in return. This new mode of being, proper to the human intellect, is perfected in the existential affirmation. "We must attach the 'being' of the copula to 'being' simply."[22] In this affirmation, the givenness of being and the responsiveness of our intelligence must be delicately balanced. Marcel proposes as a formula of the existential judgment in its reflective stage: *I affirm it because it is*. This unites directness of acquaintance with the existent and reflective concern to respect it precisely in its reality as an other. The mind and the existent become one in such a way that each retains its own reality. In the existential judgment, this oneness amidst distinction is directly experienced and reflectively guaranteed.

2. *Mystery and Problem.*

Marcel does not think that it is the task of metaphysics to make the primary affirmation of being. The recognition of being is rather the act of the individual man precisely as a human being.[23] It is a premetaphysical apprehension, in the sense that it comes within the ability of every man and is not contingent upon learning some special technique. Just as Kierkegaard satirizes the dons who arrogate all understanding to themselves, so Marcel punctures the academic pretentiousness of those who reserve the basic commitment about being for the philosopher in the specialized sense. Kierkegaard and Nietzsche like to expose the philosopher to ridicule when he reduces his outlook to that of a *Fachmensch*, a narrow specialist. Marcel is more constructive, since he points out that the initial attitude toward being is within the competence and responsibility of every man. He quotes with approval Peter Wust's remarks that each of us is required to make an act of trust or mistrust in being as the formative center of our character and outlook.

If today there is no clear recognition of this human birthright and duty, it is due to the antimetaphysical forces at work in our civilization, which Marcel usually refers to as "a broken world." Chief among these are the depersonalization of man and the reduction of all human tasks to the status of objective problems. The Cartesian Cogito and the Kantian transcendental subject are set over against the world. Their task is to institute order in a zone where it was not previously present, to establish practical relations with objects. The self is left fundamentally untouched and unnoticed. All interest is concentrated upon controlling objective forces and manipulating things. When attention is finally paid to the human person, it is regarded as but one object among the rest and hence as presenting another problem to be solved by technical methods alone.[24]

Marcel recognizes the value of the scientific and pragmatic intelligence, even in dealing with man. For there is a definite sense in which man is included with the other things that are subject to technical control and measurement. But the further claim that this is the only way in which man and other beings can be treated runs far beyond the evidence. One cannot legitimately appeal to the successes of scientific method, without assuming the point to be proved. There is an evident loss of human values when the problematic approach is made universal and exclusive. This can be seen in the prevalence of the impersonal way of determining theoretical and moral issues: "One says," "people think," "everyone is doing." Kierkegaard's critique of the crowd is continued in our day by Heidegger's critique of "the world of the impersonal 'one'," and Marcel's analysis of the influence of "what the man in the street says." Where the individual evades his personal responsibility by pointing to other people in the large, there is no room left for the sense of being. Anonymity and mass movements are inimical to the dignity of personal presence, upon which the ontological affirmation depends. The latter act is either personally performed or it is not performed at all. Man's responsibility toward being is not so much denied as smothered in our technical civilization.

Marcel suggests that a philosopher attempting to rewrite Hume's *Treatise of Human Nature* in terms of our own contemporary attitudes would have to entitle it a *Treatise of Man's Condition*.[25] Jaspers's concept of situation and Marcel's notion of the human condition are cognate. The pertinent character of this condition is its self-sealing function: it tends to make the problematic world of scientific techniques the only real world. Any data which cannot be assessed in measurable terms are declared to be irrelevant for man's condition and destiny. In a sense, this is correct. In so far as man is a problematic object, one controllable and useable thing among others, he can only be examined in accord with instrumentalist techniques and standards of evidence. From this standpoint, there is something "unreal, mystical, and unnatural" about any other view of man and the world. Yet this self-sealing autonomy of the naturalistic outlook is only a limited methodic device, justifiable on the nonphilosophical level. When it is erected into a philosophical standard, it results in unavoidable impoverishment of human personal existence.

That man can be looked at from another angle is shown by Marcel through the same sort of argument advanced by Heidegger.[26] Alone among all beings, man is not simply identical with his own life and factual reality. He is both a thing and more than a thing, for he can undertake an evaluation of his own life. This requires both an act of reflection and a moral judgment. This common experience raises the question: who is it that calls his life in question? Who is it that asks about the meaning of his being and of the being of the world? In inquiring about the nature of

the questioner, we are led to a perspective that embraces and surpasses the epistemological dualism of subject and object. The
dichotomy between the subject that posits its object and the being that is posited as an object obtains only within a restricted
field. Both the subject which asserts being and the being which is
objectively asserted are embraced within being and are seen to be
so contained, when one asks about the nature of the self-con-
cerned subject.

For the inquirer after being is more than what he asserts about
objects. He is himself an affirmation of being. He is made by the
affirmation of being within him and as himself. Being affirms itself
in him, so that he may be able to reaffirm it or give it intellectual
expression. His reality as an affirming subject is due in the first instance to that which is more than himself and which includes him
within its reality. The hold which man's intelligence can gain
upon being flows from the hold which being already has upon
him. This is not merely a reaffirmation of the realistic thesis concerning cognition: it is the foundation of metaphysics. For the
reflective mind recognizes that it participates in being as a prior
condition for constructing objective forms of being. More fundamental than the objective sphere, within which the technical
method functions, is the embracing domain of being as a global
whole, what Jaspers calls *Das Umgreifende*. The existential judgment refers to being as a totality, before the distinction into subject and object has been drawn. By gaining some grasp upon oneself and other entities precisely as existing beings, the mind is
given a foothold for exploring being itself in a new way.

This metaproblematic approach to being invites the inquirer to
study the mystery of being. Marcel's way of pointing up the contrast between the restricted sphere of objects and the whole realm
of being is to refer to the objective modes as the field of *problems*
and to being in its generality as the field of *mystery*.[27] The distinction between problem and mystery is also a distinction between scientific and philosophical knowledge. The order of problems is that of things that can be inventoried, characterized, and
manipulated. Problems are open to solution by the creation and

application of special techniques. Progress in a unilinear direction is possible here, since results can be measured in terms of output and increased control. The mind passes from one problem to the next, as Maritain also points out, without attempting philosophical penetration of an ever recurring mystery.

The problematic method is proper to the special sciences, since they study objective essences apart from the nature of the inquirer. But this method is not adequate for philosophical investigation, and this for several reasons. First, it is better fitted for establishing essential laws than for examining the existential act of beings. But a philosophy built upon essences is, in Marcel's graphic phrase, a house of cards and, like a house of cards, is easily swept away by a gust of sentiment or ill fortune.[28] Second, it is incapable of handling cases where the attitude of the subject toward a question is of crucial importance for understanding the problem. Evil, suffering, and death are instances where the entire situation is altered when the inquirer ceases to cut his own personal destiny off from the matter under discussion. The full force of the evidence is not realized until it is also envisaged as bearing upon his own life and conduct. Hence Marcel defines a mystery as a problem that is constantly encroaching upon its own data and hence going beyond the condition of a problem. In the face of a problem, the investigator retains his superiority and distance: when these are threatened and invaded by the direction of the study, then the threshold of mystery is crossed.

Marcel insists that no equation can be set up between mystery and the unknowable. His concrete ontology is neither agnostic nor mystical. In fact, he regards the unknowable as the limit toward which scientific or problematic methods are approaching. Mystery, on the other hand, designates the zone where the intellect acts in a new way in search of being. It is constituted by the mind's recognition that man as a personal subject participates in being as a creatively received gift from God. Hence mystery signifies the inexhaustible locus of being and meaning which is not limited to a duality of subject and object. Whereas the latter contrast marks the limits of epistemology, the proper field of metaphysics is mystery. There is no abdication of intelligence in metaphysics but an adaptation to further reaches of evidence. Transcendence is a deepening of the implications of experience rather than a break with experience.[29]

Marcel is the only one of the existentialists, including Kierkegaard, who has attempted to overcome Kant's theoretical agnosticism about the transcendent. His theory of problem and mystery is an illustration of the difference between his realism and the residual Kantianism of the other existentialists. Jaspers, for instance, places the transcendent One beyond all knowledge and beyond all knowable being. But Marcel's notebooks show that he is suspicious of any unknowable entity that is placed beyond intelligibility.[30] He sees a need to close the gap between truth and being, so that there will be no ground for a Kantian or Plotinian interpretation of his doctrine on being and God. This does not entail any impossible claim to exhaustive knowledge of being itself or of God. But it does forestall any limitation of knowledge to the phenomenal order or to finite things. Marcel holds that knowledge can be gained both in philosophy and in the special sciences, both in the order of mystery and in that of problem. Mystery is "metaproblematic" but that is not the same as being beyond the knowable. The distinction is intended to safeguard different ways of gaining knowledge rather than to circumscribe the field of knowledge in order to make room for philosophical faith. For Marcel, philosophical faith is not opposed to knowledge but to the technique of problematic solutions.

Marcel does not require a Kierkegaardian "crucifixion of the understanding" as the price of entering the region of being, mystery, and subjective truth. All that needs to be foregone, in this context, is one manner of research which is unfitted for examining questions about being as such, the divine being and the human person. Metaphysics, which addresses itself to such inquiries, has a method of its own, adapted to its distinctive range of interests. Its procedure is that of secondary, recuperative reflection or, in a word, *recollection*.[31] In reviving this Augustinian term, Marcel seeks to give contemporary significance to the African Doctor's advice to enter into oneself. Recollection is literally a recovering or repossessing of one's self. This regaining of the sense of one's existence is made by recognizing the divine source of the personal self. To enter into oneself is to find the gift of being as it comes fresh from God's hands: it is to discover that a man is not his own, that he does not belong to himself alone. The only satisfactory answer to solipsism is given in the metaphysics of participated being, not in the epistemology founded upon the subject/object relation.

As the tool of metaphysics, recollection is a kind of reflection, a reflective act raised to the second power (in Kierkegaard's language). It builds upon the original reflection or intuition of being which is available to every individual existent. There is no self-originating and self-sufficient act in philosophy: the indispensable materials are always furnished by man *qua* man, not *qua* professional philosopher. In this instance, the realistic source of metaphysical speculation is the original awareness of being. The acquiring of this primary apprehension is the responsibility of each individual man in his personal relation to existence. But it is a blindfold intuition, a non-self-conscious apprehension of existence in the existent thing. Although the totality of being is somehow involved in this affirmation, it is not clearly perceived and it is never open to direct inspection. But the primary adhesion and openness to being have a pervasive effect upon the individual's experience and his attitude toward the situations of human life. The task of metaphysics is to study the shadows cast upon our experience by the ontic intuition and, in this indirect way, to clarify the intuition itself.[32] Metaphysics works out the implications for human existence of the original trust or mistrust in being which is at the source of the individual's orientation in the world. Marcel's concrete philosophy develops through reflection upon the tension and dialogue transpiring "here and now" between the self and the depths of being.

Instead of accepting the Kantian contrast between knowledge

and faith, Marcel distinguished between profane or scientific knowledge and sacred or metaphysical knowledge. What is sacral about metaphysical knowledge is its concern with mystery rather than problem, with being as orientated to the existential act rather than to the self-enclosed essential construct. Inevitable misunderstanding will arise unless two points are made clear, in addition to the observation that metaphysics is an area of knowledge. "Sacred" does not mean "unworldly"; neither does it mean "supernatural." Marcel's conception of metaphysics is, if anything, more worldly than that of Jaspers. For he recognizes, in the very objects of problematic scientific study, a deeper aspect as instances of being. Mystery or the region of being includes all things in the world, viewing them in a more comprehensive way as participated modes of being and as individual existents. Moreover, the bond between the senses and metaphysics is a close one for Marcel. It is not by flight from the senses and man's incarnate condition but by a closer fidelity to these components of experience that the metaphysician gains some understanding of being.

Furthermore, the being studied by metaphysics is not a revealed mystery but a natural one. Hence metaphysics proceeds by way of a natural reflection upon the ordinary data of our experience. Metaphysical recollection is sometimes called by Marcel a hyperphenomenological reflection. By this he means that metaphysics must rely both upon an empirical diet, supplied by ordinary experience, and upon an exact description of the import of such experience as furnished by phenomenology. He has not clarified his own conception of phenomenology in relation to Husserl. He seems to regard phenomenology as a way of avoiding both psychologism and idealism. Thus he directs attention not upon subjective states of mind but upon the meaning or intentional signification of our attitudes. His philosophical interest in instances of dread or giddiness or fidelity is not a psychological or exclusively dramatic one but is integrated with the study of being in its general traits. Furthermore, Marcel states that phenomenology is not only free from total reduction of data to their essential structure but is founded on a recognition of something irreducible to thought. This is his justification for employing phenomenology against idealistic tendencies. But it does not take sufficient account of the historical difficulties raised by Husserl's attempt to make precisely such a total reduction in the direction of transcendental idealism. Perhaps the meaning of "hyperphenomenological" reflection is that the description of contents must be subordinated to study of their real foundation in existential acts and beings.[33]

Finally, Marcel refers to recollection as a form of detachment. Here, he is careful to distinguish between two sorts of detachment: that of the spectator and that of the saint.[34] The former is akin to the problematic attitude, in which the knower removes himself at a distance from the objects of investigation, maintaining a dominating control over them and never involving himself personally in the results. This objectivity is an indispensable requirement in scientific studies but in the fields of metaphysics and morals it may result in a self-forgetfulness that is fatal both to understanding and to rectitude. There is a way of overlooking personal issues which is equivalent to desertion from one's condition as a human being faced with issues which demand a personal choice and commitment. Here the attitude of the saint is helpful in understanding how detachment can mean closer participation. The saint withdraws from the world only in the sense of denying it his primary loyalty: he attaches himself to the creative source of the world and thus allies himself with the world from the divine perspective. Similarly, the metaphysician detaches himself from the closed attitude which regards the things in the world solely as objects of knowledge and control, and which views the self only as the noetic correlate to a set of objects. By recovering himself as a participator in being, the metaphysician also recovers the world of beings about him. This results in a more intimate attachment to the world than is possible from the purely problematic standpoint. Thus recollection is a form of detachment employed for the ends of a maximal metaphysical recognition of oneself and the world as common sharers in being and hence as likenesses of God.

3. Being and Having.

Not since the time of Hegel, Feuerbach, and Marx has there been such philosophical interest in the nature of having. Heidegger's analysis of "utensility" and the studies of Jaspers and Marcel on "having" mark a renascence of this line of investigation. Marcel fits his speculations on this point in with his general theory of mystery and problem. Mystery deals with being, while problem deals with having.[35] What I have, belongs to the objective order. It is something belonging to me rather than a part of myself. Over it I can exert a certain control; apart from it I can retain a certain aloofness and region of privacy. But in my own subjective reality as this particular person, having gives way to being. What I have serves the ends of what I am or come to be. Techniques can manage my possessions, but another selfhood must be approached by an invocation and a response. My relations with what I have are those between a *who* and a *what*: my relations with the personal being of another are those between an *I* and a *thou*.

Fortunately, Marcel does not press this set of distinctions too far. They do not become rigid in his hands, chiefly because he retains his dramatic interest in particular cases and focuses upon the concrete ways in which being and having are expressed. He has given special attention to two instances of having. Having a secret is a pure case of having, whereas having one's own body is the prototype of all other types of possession.

The secret one has is not the same as oneself, although it is contained in oneself. The self is not so much a container as a subject that "carries along" a container with it. This means that there is a receptive aspect of the self, such that it can appropriate objects to itself. The secret is under one's control, in that it is dominated by the mind into which it has been received. Moreover, this secret can be revealed, wrested from me, or even unwittingly betrayed. This shows a further trait of the order of having. It is the open flank which leaves one's being exposed either to the misuses of one's own freedom or to the assaults of others. One's being is vulnerable precisely at that point where it is prolonged in its possessions. To have things is not an unmixed blessing. The biblical young man who went away from the Lord in a sad mood, because he had many possessions, is a figure of those whose selfhood has been compromised by concern over the order of having. The danger of this sphere is its ability to transform the self into an object, to depersonalize a man so that his actions are governed by so-called impersonal laws and amoral considerations.

Marcel now returns to a study of "my body" from the standpoint of its belonging to me.[36] The body is the prototype of all cases of having, because the condition for all other possessions is that one first have dominion over his own body. The ownership of other things is an extension of ownership of one's body. Thus one's body is a focal point not only for significant acts of existing but also for objects and possessions. This convergence of being and object in "my body" obtains not only in respect to other things but also in respect to myself. There is an ultimate blending of being and having in the case of one's body. Corporeity or one's bodily life is simultaneously something that one has and something that one is. One's body is a possession and to that extent is at one's own disposal. But it is not merely a possession and hence is not absolutely at one's disposal, as the suicide pretends. A man cannot do entirely as he wishes with his life, since it is not merely a belonging. To be a man is not only to have a body but to *be* a bodily, incarnate being. Hence there is a limit to one's treatment of the body as a form of having. It must be respected as a component of one's personal being.

Recollection involves a recovery of oneself precisely as an incarnate being. The body is a reminder about the sort of being a man is. There is no way of deducing the presence of the body, any more than there is a way of deducing one's existence. For the body or one's life is the determinate mode in which a man does exist. He must accept his own being globally as a gift and a participation in that which does not depend upon himself for the initiative. The body is also a sign of man's proper condition. As a corporeal being, he exists through his placement in the world. Heidegger and Marcel wrote simultaneously that man is essentially a being-in-the-world.[37] But whereas Heidegger was usually construed as teaching that this mundane direction of human existing is a senseless fate, into which man is thrown, and a project to be accomplished, Marcel explicitly showed the other side of this relationship. (Thereby he anticipated the actual direction which Heidegger's thought has since taken.) To belong to the world is not to be abandoned to an alien milieu, for one's body is both a member of the world of objective things and a constituent of oneself. The world is not merely at hand as a potential tool of man's interests and projects. The having of something is an appropriation and assimilation, a process of making one's own that which originally was wholly other. By incorporation into the order of having, things become more than instruments: they partake of the dignity of the human person. Through the body, the imprint of personal value can be imparted to objects around us, so that they represent something more than an imperialist encroachment of man upon his surroundings.

Marcel's descriptive approach brings out the primacy of being over having by exploring the significance of sacrifice. There is a constant tension between being and having: the actual human condition often invites the subordination of being to having or requires the sacrifice of having to being. The New Testament speaks about this alternative as that of gaining the whole world at the loss of one's soul or of gaining the latter at the expense of one's possessions. The critical instance is martyrdom, in which one offers the world of having to God in the form of a sacrifice of one's life. The martyr and the suicide are the antitheses of existence in respect to the body and to the order of having.[38] Having can serve as a high wall against other people and as a barrier to personal communication. The man who subjects being to having is the man who entertains only "business relations" with other people. He is not at their disposal but regards them and the entire world as serving his ends. A life that is centered in having is one that is not available to others. Like Dostoyevsky's Kirillov, the suicide thinks that his final act is one of supreme freedom and self-management. This is his illusion, but it is a freedom that is turned barrenly against itself and a management that mistakes the field of what is at one's disposal.

The social function of martyrdom is to call attention to the perversion involved in subordinating being to having. The martyr shows by his sacrifice that the right order is one in which the individual's possessions minister to his personal development. Moreover, his action shows the direction in which this personal perfection lies. Not in self-centeredness but in centering one's life upon God; not in unavailability to others but in making oneself supremely available through love; not in dreams of autonomy but in a joyous recognition of one's participative status in being. The martyr does not dispose of his own body but offers it into God's hands for the sake of his fellow men. His action is a lesson in the right use and value of the body and material goods. By sacrificing the order of having, he calls to mind the frequent disorders in our attitude toward what we own. And by opening himself to God, he makes us aware of the only basis upon which men can communicate with each other as personal subjects rather than as indifferent objects and instruments of policy.

Unlike Kierkegaard, Marcel does not draw from his analysis of martyrdom the conclusion that all who are not martyrs are living unauthentic lives. The paradoxical purpose of martyrdom is to encourage restoration of a more humane order between being and having, persons and property, by proclaiming the divine foundation of human existence. In a world that tends to gloss over the role of a perverse will, the martyr stands out as embarrassing testimony to the supreme importance of our use of freedom. He prevents us from cutting off the sphere of having from its moral and personal roots. His example is a tremendous plea that we bear in mind our participation in being, the constant possibility of betraying this creaturely condition, and the loyalty we owe God in our visible and social acts as well as in our closet.

4. *Creative Fidelity*.

Marcel has been accused of pessimism, because he devotes so much attention to the dark underside of the soul as expressed in suicide, betrayal, and despair. His reply, like that of the other existentialists, is that these states are studied not for their own sake but for their illumination of human existence. He considers a certain vertigo—an understanding of, and even a tendency toward, the nihilistic aspects of reality—to be an indispensable condition of metaphysics. For only through such an unblinking appraisal of our precarious situation can we realize that freedom does place our lives at stake. Normality consists not in turning away from the knowledge of good and evil but in seeing the issues clearly. The basic fact is that being is constantly threatened. It is not a possession that can be managed handily and rendered secure by technical means. Even the technician is ultimately tributary to his own senses and fleshly condition: *percipio* rather than *cogito* is the first word uttered by man as man. An incarnate person is one who participates in being and yet can lose his hold upon it. To understand the hazardous character of being is to develop that salutary fear which is the beginning of wisdom.[39]

The actual state of affairs attendant upon our condition as corporeal beings not only allows for a refusal of being but positively encourages it. This is an issue upon which Marcel and Gilson agree.[40] They trace the differences among metaphysical positions not simply to a failure or perversion of mind but in some way to the very make-up of things. Gilson remains on the speculative plane in explaining the conflict of philosophies by the fact that existence cannot be conceptualized and hence invites either its reduction to a pseudo-idea or its removal from the realm of relevant questions. Marcel's approach is more concrete. He remarks that our placement in a space-time world recommends that we treat space and time as modes of absence, isolating individuals from each other, except for entertaining objective relations. It is easy to assume the role of spectator or social engineer in regard to others. Again, the fact of death may be taken as a reason for despair and for concentrating upon the pleasures of the moment. Suffering itself is an equivocal reality. The body is the foothold that suffering can gain in the self, since suffering attacks what we have in so far as it is also a part of ourselves. This can lead to depreciation of the body, to suspicion of all men and material forces, and to withdrawal into a fantasy world of complete immunity to suffering.

On the other hand, these same experiences may be viewed as tests wherein man is asked to make a right use of freedom. Marcel approves of the central role accorded by René Le Senne (a leader of the French "Philosophy of the Spirit" school) to obstacles as a means of developing human values. It would be all too easy for beings not subject to spatial separation or death to remain open to each other and to affirm the worthwhileness of existing. What a man is called upon to do is to maintain personal communion with others and a relation of prayer with God precisely under the conditions that specify our mode of being. It is in this sense that Keats called life on earth a vale of soul-making. Our souls are made or unmade by the quality of our response to being and the trials of bodily life. This response is not governed by the laws of technics but by the relations which hold between personal beings. Being cannot be objectively handled but it can be attested to by the attitude we assume toward it and its creative source.

A lifetime's attestation to being and free participation in its conditions are what Marcel means by *creative fidelity*.[41] He does not succumb to a common existentialist temptation to pay heed only to tragic situations and to the black heart of evil. Sartre is arguing in a circle, when he accords a privileged position to hatred and to its modalities and then declares that love and the virtues are vain ideals. Sartre's mistake is to frame the alternatives for man in such a way that he must choose between being a cold spectator of an objective drama and being completely absorbed in and defined by his choices. Man is first of all a witness to the being in which he participates and within which his cognition and freedom are exercised. A witness is neither a detached spectator nor an impossible self-creator of his situation. He acknowledges and invokes the being within which his own existence is comprised. His freedom is both an engaged one and a creaturely one. The existent individual is neither the idealistic spectator-god nor the Sartrean divine act of freedom unbounded.[42] He is a witness capable of both despair and creative fidelity.

Creative fidelity is opposed both to dead conformism and to a fantastic notion of freedom. Marcel adheres to Bergson's distinction between the way of things and the way of freedom, in the sense that man is not simply a product but a responsible agent who determines his own response to being. But Marcel does not appeal to a creative evolution, because of the possible implication that human freedom is under no moral requirement to acknowledge the ends of being. Freedom does not exist for its own sake but is a way of achieving our fuller participation in being. The soul is dedicated to the search after its integrity of being or, in religious language, its salvation. Because man shares in reality, he is a being who can either bear witness to the transcendent principle of being or repudiate it. His relation to God is not completely indifferent but follows, or repudiates, a natural exigency of his being to recognize the absolute presence of God.

Along with Louis Lavelle, once more, Marcel tries to cast some light on the mystery of human freedom as a participated form of liberty. Lavelle calls it a gift that is received and yet renders account of itself.[43] Marcel adds that human freedom transcends the Kantian antinomy between autonomy and heteronomy. It does not follow (as Sartre pretends) that because a free agent is nonheteronomous, he is therefore autonomous. Both these concepts are constructed with reference to administrable objects. They fit in with a view of the self as legislating for its objects and remaining itself above such determinations. But this antinomy of autonomy versus heteronomy is restricted to the field of problems, whereas freedom is metaproblematic. It is not a question of the owner and what he possesses but of the subject and what he is.

Being lies beyond the order of having and technical administration, and hence also beyond the alternatives of autonomy and heteronomy. The more I am, the less am I an autonomous legislator for objects. Metaphysical recollection studies man in so far as he is not his own belonging but a being who shares his reality from another (as Descartes' friend, Bérulle, put it). Freedom can only be approached in this theocentric perspective, because this is the only context in which freedom manifests itself as a mode of participated being.

For this reason, Marcel prefers to speak of his standpoint as a philosophy of being and freedom, not a philosophy of freedom alone. His reflections on freedom rest on an act of ontological humility or recognition that man is a created being, not an autonomous god. There is a receptive aspect of human being, but this is not the same as asserting that man is passively determined by another. On this score, Marcel declares his preference for the Aristotelian notion of potentiality. The powers of man are potential; they need to be actuated. But his acts are truly exercised by man and, in the case of his free actions, are performed on his own responsibility. His freedom is both received and self-originated, as befits the action of a being which *shares* in reality and *is* according to its proper mode of self-determination.

Fidelity expresses itself in the vow, the declaration that a certain relation will be regarded as indefectible for oneself. Is such a pledge presumptuous? André Gide answers in the affirmative, declaring that no man has the right or duty to bind himself with regard to the unknown future. There is no way of assuring the continuance of the same feeling, and hence Gide counsels us to remain true only to the present moment, which alone is surely within one's grasp. This advice is reminiscent of the esthetic attitude of pursuit of momentary enjoyment, as portrayed by Kierkegaard's character, Johannes the Seducer. Marcel admits that no one can give surety for the future states of his feelings. But the vow refers not to the flux of sentiments, taken by themselves, but to one's adherence to the ruling principle of existence. A commitment can be made, because a man can transcend the moments of his life-flux sufficiently to give his loyalty to God and, in God, to his fellow men. It is in God's presence that a pledge bearing on the future is made. Fidelity is an appeal to God for strength and constancy amidst temporal changes and uncertainties. It bears testimony to the ontological permanence proper to a temporal person: not a pretended immutability in a world of essences but constancy of purpose and loyalty throughout a novel course of events.

Fidelity is not merely Christian faith in disguise. It expresses the natural ground bass of human character, as founded upon an invocation of the transcendent being. Along with Josiah Royce (the great American idealist, whose philosophy he explained in a long series of articles, in 1918–19), Marcel considers loyalty to the absolute self to be the highest act of existence. But he does not regard Jaspers' theory of the attitude of transcending as a sufficient analysis of man's ontological relation. This relation cannot be established without having regard for whether or not there is a real, creative source of being. Unless the source of participation does have being and is knowable as the transcendent principle, the attitude of transcendence will be betrayed. Transcendence requires some experience of the transcendent being, in order to fulfill its nature. For this attitude is an intentional one. It does not feign the existence of its object or remain indifferent to whether or not God really does exist. Transcending occurs only as a renunciation of human self-sufficiency and as an unequivocal affirmation of God's existence. On the other hand, Marcel does not accept the Thomistic proofs of God's existence at their face value, as being strict demonstrations.[44] He maintains that they are based upon a previous acceptance of God and are only formally stated clarifications of this original adhesion. He asks how they can be irrefutable proofs and yet fail to convince so many people. This would be a scandal, could one not point out that the question of conviction or skepticism hinges upon the prior act of the primal response to, or refusal of, being.

Marcel's difficulty with the classical proofs arises from his peculiar, rationalistic notion of what it means to prove something.

For him, proof is only a process of pointing out the logical implications of certain admitted definitions and propositions. The demonstrative process is a logical deduction, moving exclusively in the realm of essences and conceptual constructs. On this account, there could never be an existential demonstration, and demonstrations that claim to be existential would be laboring under either confusion or pretense. According to St. Thomas, however, proof may sometimes bear upon the implications of a given existent and thus may move from an existential datum to an existential conclusion. If the starting point of inference lies in some apprehension of an existent, then reasoning may proceed in an a posteriori way to certainty about some other existent, whose actuality is required in order to account for the original point of departure. Hence Aquinas regards his proofs of God's existence as giving demonstrative certainty about the actually existing first cause of the sensible world. In order to join issue with Aquinas, Marcel would first have to subject the rationalistic notion of proof to critical scrutiny and then compare this view with other theories of demonstration. Apparently, the existential foundation of the Thomistic theory of a posteriori demonstration was not sufficiently stressed in the textbooks consulted by Marcel. But to omit this aspect is to pass over the distinctive procedure in Thomistic metaphysics.

Nevertheless, a philosophy which claims to rest on existential demonstrations should also explain why many honest minds are unmoved by these proofs. This explanation should be given, even when it is held that there is a distinction between the intrinsic force of an argument and its ability to convince this or that person, under particular circumstances. Here, Marcel's descriptive approach is valuable, just as Pascal's or Newman's psychological observations on the causes of skepticism are indispensable. Marcel discloses a prephilosophical drama, in which the individual either acknowledges the participated and contingent nature of his hold upon existence or closes out all thought of an absolute source of his being. The whole of Marcel's philosophical reflection is centered upon this unavoidable alternative and upon the consequences of this primary choice. A denial of our creaturely openness and sharing in being results in a radical infidelity to the human condition. What Thomas Hardy called man's unhope is the outcome of refusing to extend credit to the universe in the direction of its transcendent source. And the fruit of unhope is despair.

Marcel does not identify his concrete philosophy of being with a Christian existentialism.[45] One can accept this philosophy without being a Christian and without being under a logical necessity to become one. It is based on an analysis of concrete human experiences that are not confined within confessional boundaries. On the other hand, the purpose of philosophy is to elevate experience rather than to castrate it. In our historical situation, the influence of Christian ideas cannot be discounted. Their irradiation makes it easier to discern the need for fidelity and the presence of an ontological mystery at the heart of a world arranged according to problematic requirements. The human experiences upon which this philosophy relies are deeply affected by the Christian orientation of life. Without formally relying upon Christian revelation, Marcel's interpretation of existence accords with revealed religion and admits its existential influence. In this factual recognition, he agrees with Jaspers. But unlike Jaspers, Marcel refuses to close off his thought from reception of the gift of revealed truth as such.[46] If philosophy is not a closed system but an open participation in the mystery of being, there is no sound philosophical reason for placing an obstacle in the way of such a gift.

Chapter V

Heidegger's Recall of
Man to Being

1. Heidegger and His Critics.

Martin Heidegger (1889——) did his early studies with the intention of entering the Catholic priesthood. Acquaintance with the problems of modern philosophy soon led him along other paths, although he never lost his early interest in the terminology and method of the Scholastics. He attended the lectures of Windelband, Rickert, and other representatives of the Neo-Kantian, Baden school of values. The most decisive personal influence came from his association with Edmund Husserl, under whose direction he wrote his dissertation on the theory of meaning and categories in Duns Scotus (1916). Heidegger taught for some years at Marburg, where he issued his fundamental treatise on *Being and Time* (1927). The following year, he was called to Freiburg to succeed Husserl in the chair of philosophy. Heidegger's professorship there continued until 1945. He is now professor emeritus, lives in the outskirts of Freiburg, and continues to give annual lectures and seminars at the University.

Heidegger became a controversial political figure, due to his acceptance of the rectorship of Freiburg University in 1933. In his rectoral address, he called for wholehearted support of the newly elected National Socialists. He felt that their stated aims provided the inevitable way for the self-assertion of German scholarship. As Karl Löwith remarked, people who listened to Heidegger's official speeches were never quite sure whether to resume their study of the Pre-Socratics or to don the uniform of the Storm Troopers, so close a connection did he make between learning and political life.[1] Disillusionment came rapidly in the wake of this initial enthusiasm, however, leading him to resign the rectorship the following year. He found it difficult to generate the right quality of resoluteness and dedication in an atmosphere pervaded by suspicion, conformism, and force. Furthermore, his appeal for a reaffirmation of German selfhood and self-determination carried some specific implications which he regarded as excessive, even though he could not avoid conveying them in view of his officially sanctioned position.

After his resignation of the rectorship, Heidegger continued to teach at Freiburg until the end of the war. Unlike Jaspers, he was naturally held in disfavor by the Occupying Powers. For a time, he went into retirement in his ski hut in the Black Forest, confining his discussions to small, private groups. In English-speaking countries, his political associations with Nazism continue to stand in the way of a careful examination of his thought. During the war, it became customary, even in respectable philosophical journals, to refer to his "demonic personality" and to substitute political denunciation for direct consideration of his reasoning.[2] But since his views give every evidence of surviving the collapse of Nazism, it is no longer possible to evade the philosophical task by remaining solely at the pragmatic level. He has raised a number of significant issues which must be faced for their own sake.

Among the matters discussed in *Being and Time* were many typically existential themes. It contained long accounts of dread and fear, death and repetition, time and historicity. Unfortunately, only the first part of the total project was published, leaving wide room for interpretation and even misrepresentation. Heidegger was both acclaimed and attacked for the most variant reasons. Kantian scholars like Cassirer and Levy repudiated the attempt he made in *Kant and the Problem of Metaphysics* (1929) to interpret Kant in conformity with his own standpoint,[3] whereas other critics concentrated upon exposing the Kantian and idealistic roots of his speculation. On the strength of the

topics mentioned in *Being and Time*, as well as his analysis of
the naught and boredom in *What is Metaphysics?* (1929), he
was classified with the growing company of existentialists. Heidegger and Jaspers were customarily linked together as the leading German existentialists, the difference between them turning
mainly upon the religious issue. It was supposed that Heidegger
represented the atheistic, completely this-worldly wing of existential thinking. His own cryptic utterances in *On the Nature
of the Sufficient Reason* and the other short treatises issued during 1929 did not clear up the confusion of critics about where he
stood in relation to contemporary currents and perennial problems.

What seemed to be a new direction in Heidegger's speculation
began with the publication of a lecture on *Hölderlin and the
Essence of Poetry* (1936), which was followed by brief studies
on several of Hölderlin's poems. Instead of taking his text from
the rationalist philosophers, he now turned to the Romantic
poets. Instead of restricting himself to an analysis of human existence as projected into a world of technical relations, he considered man in a wider natural setting and in close intercourse
with apparently supernal powers. Chthonic wisdom and inspira-
tional utterances seemed to replace the sober phenomenological
inquiries of a former time. It became apparent that either Heidegger's original position had been misunderstood or he was undergoing a profound intellectual revolution within his own mind.
For the continuity between the earlier writings and the exegesis
of Hölderlin was evident neither methodically nor doctrinally.

The exact nature of this development may never be known in
its details. But we are fortunate to this extent, that Heidegger has
spoken out clearly, during recent years, concerning his present
views and their significance for understanding his past achievements.[4] Some of these later writings are positive expositions of
doctrinal and historical matters: *Plato's Theory of Truth* (1942),
On the Essence of Truth (1943), and *Forest Trails* (1950).
Three important essays are devoted, however, to polemical purposes: the Introduction and Postscript to the later editions (1943

and 1949) of *What is Metaphysics?*, together with the *Letter concerning 'Humanism'* (1947). These latter pronouncements are, in effect, Heidegger's answer to two decades of critical studies of *Being and Time*. He considers both general interpretations of his philosophy and the criticisms made of particular theories and terms. Although the sequel to *Being and Time* may never appear, the author has now provided an authentic guide to this difficult and perhaps incorrigibly ambiguous work.

On Heidegger's own reckoning, very few students of his master work have grasped its true meaning.[5] His own explanation for this almost universal misunderstanding is that the meaning of being has fallen into oblivion, obscuring the minds of even his most sympathetic readers. The best evidence he adduces for the need of making a fresh start in ontology is precisely the diversity of critical opinion concerning his essay in fundamental ontology. There are, however, a number of intrinsic obstacles against reaching agreement upon its import. For foreign readers and even for many trained Germans, it requires a long tussle with the text in order to master Heidegger's very free use of German words and constructions. Like Whitehead, he has been forced to use familiar terms in entirely new significations and to coin new words in order to convey original insights or nuances. Many of his arguments have a linguistic rather than a material foundation, making appeal to peculiarities of the German tongue which cannot easily be rethought or verified in some other language.

Rudolf Carnap, the logical positivist, has made huge fun of Heidegger's treatment of the naught.[6] From the positivist standpoint, his abstract way of stating metaphysical themes is proof enough that metaphysics consists in nothing more than a clever manipulation of terms having only pseudo-meaning. Certainly Heidegger's earlier publications remain consistently on an abstract, general plane, where it is difficult to recognize familiar intellectual landmarks. When the common touch is applied, as in his appeal to certain moods and attitudes, the descriptions seem bizarre and unconvincing to those who are unacquainted with Kierkegaard. The extreme situations of dread, anticipation of death, and encounter of other selves seem to be either overstated or out of place in a philosophical analysis. Whereas Heidegger's intention in employing these existential themes is to overcome an exclusively intellectual or rationalistic approach, their effect is often to alienate empirical-minded people as well.

Heidegger refused to be classified with the other existentialists under some general heading. In a communication sent in 1937 to a *séance* of the French Society of Philosophy, he stated that although he treated human existence at length and was indebted to Kierkegaard, he should not be ranked as a philosopher of existence.[7] Even in *Being and Time*, he qualified his admiration for Kierkegaard with the remark that Kierkegaard's entire philosophical outlook moved too exclusively in the shadow of Hegel. For this reason, Heidegger found Kierkegaard's *Edifying Discourses* and other religious writings more profitable than his more formal treatises. (That this preference is in the authentic Kierkegaardian spirit, he did not seem to note.) As for his interest in human existence, this is not the focal point of Heidegger's philosophy but a means of attaining a view of being as such. The movement of his thought is from existence to being rather than a constant preoccupation with man's condition.

In this same communication, Heidegger distinguishes his stand from that of Karl Jaspers. He terms the latter viewpoint "existential" and his own philosophy "existentialistic" (Werner Brock has proposed these renditions of *existentielle* and *existentiale*). The difference concerns whether or not a general theory of being is possible. Since this is denied by Jaspers, he is limited to making systematic descriptions of the various traits of human existence and its frustrated efforts at making a universal synthesis. Heidegger himself not only accepts the possibility of a fundamental ontology but offers his own efforts as proof that it can be worked out in some detail. Whereas Jaspers contends that thought is brought to a standstill in attempting to search out the origins of things, Heidegger defines "essential" thinking as that inquiry into the foundations of being which must successfully precede every other use of thought.

Heidegger's *Letter concerning 'Humanism'* is an answer to a set of queries sent him by the French student of existentialism, Jean Beaufret. He takes this occasion to repudiate the usual coupling of his doctrine with that of Jean-Paul Sartre. In numerous ways, he shows that Sartre's theories have "not the slightest thing in common" with his own. The basic contrast arises from Sartre's anthropocentric view of human consciousness and freedom. For Sartre, man is all in all, with respect to both meaning and practical projects. For Heidegger, being is what counts most and provides a measure for human comprehension and freedom. Lapsing deliberately into French, Heidegger explains that thinking is "l'engagement par l'Etre pour l'Etre" and not merely "l'engagement dans l'action."[8] Sartre fails to see that human conditions and situations are determined primarily by being rather than by creative human consciousness. Hence if Sartre be taken as the representative existentialist, Heidegger wishes to separate himself definitively from this movement.

At the same time, Heidegger takes cognizance of the fact that most of his Scholastic critics have attributed to him doctrines which would make him the forerunner and pattern for Sartre. This is the case not only with minor contributions but also with the two best studies on Heidegger made by Scholastics: Alfred Delp's *Tragic Existence* (1935) and Alphonse De Waelhens' *The Philosophy of Martin Heidegger* (1942).[9] Both of these works are conscientious attempts to grasp the sense of Heidegger's enigmatic text. They avoid the more egregious errors made by those Scholastic critics who fail to take account of the new meanings given to "essence," "existence," "possibility," and other terms that also find a place in the Scholastic vocabulary. But they both conclude to Heidegger's fundamental atheism, nihilism, tragic finitism, and creative production of the world and its meaning. They agree with Maximilian Beck in describing his philosophy as a sort of Schellingian idealism of the will, from which all reference to a divine principle has been deleted. Heidegger explicitly denies all these charges and recalls indications in his early works which could be taken as pointing in a contrary direction.

It may be, as J. B. Lotz warned in a review (1944) of De Waelhens' book, that Heidegger's critics did not appreciate the degree to which his position, as outlined in *Being and Time*, was still indecisive and open to further clarification.[10] Several factors may have concurred in removing the original ambiguity. Since 1927, Heidegger has been using the mystics and poets in order to break the hold of Kant and Schelling upon his mind. This process of liberation from idealism has doubtless been hastened by the Scholastic and Sartrean interpretations, which performed the valuable service of working out one consistent line along which his thought *could* move. A clear statement of this alternative has aided in clarifying his position, even though it means a rejection of the Sartrean possibility. Heidegger's warning at the end of *Being and Time* should be taken seriously: he does not propose these views as definitive conclusions. They are meant to rekindle questions and to prepare for their solution in the perspective of being.[11]

Most of his critics agree that the promised ontological sections of this book cannot in principle be forthcoming. They feel that Heidegger has reached an impasse in attempting a completely immanent interpretation of human existence and that no bridge can be thrown from his existential analytic to the anticipated fundamental ontology. For his part, Heidegger maintains that this verdict is only partially correct. He speaks of withholding the second part of the book not because of an intrinsic hindrance but because of the failure of language to convey his meaning.[12] The accepted philosophical terminology is laden with certain prejudices about the nature of being which it is his purpose to challenge. The reception accorded to the first part of the new theory of being has made Heidegger extremely wary about making systematic statements in the conventional language of philosophers, even with the aid of his own linguistic innovations. This accounts in part for his preoccupation with the poetic use of language and with finding "original" words that can name things afresh.

At the end of the Introduction to the published portion of *Being and Time*, Heidegger set forth the plan for the entire work.[13] It was to consist of two parts, the first of which was further subdivided into three main sections: an analysis of human existence, an account of the temporality of human existence, and an approach to being as such from the horizon of time. In the second part, he proposed to undertake a phenomenological destruction of the history of ontology, working back from Kant to Descartes, the medievals, and Aristotle. Only the first two sections of the first part of this project were published as *Being and Time*. The crucial third part, in which the fundamental ontology proper was to be contained, was later referred to as *Time and Being*. This is indicative of the reversal of perspective from which things were to be viewed in the light of their openness to being. Whereas his critics uniformly held that Heidegger had failed to prepare an adequate basis in the first two sections for making this transition, Heidegger himself reported that a contrary relationship obtains. It was only because he had *already* come to view things from the standpoint of their relation to being that he saw the need to reopen the questions of man's being and the nature of time and history. Hence the only sure way of appreciating the analysis of these latter points is to approach them from their prior basis in an account of being as such.

Despite his withholding of the remaining portions of his systematic work, Heidegger has given precious indications of his views on the history of ontology, the nature of being, and its relation to man. With the aid of these hints, it may be possible to reconstruct the background of *Being and Time* and hence to clear the way for a reliable interpretation of its major doctrines.

2. *The Destruction of the History of Ontology.*

Heidegger no more than Jaspers is motivated by an antimetaphysical animus in his desire to "destroy" the previous accomplishments in ontology. The overcoming of ontology is attempted not in a parochial and obscurantist spirit but on the basis of a respectable historical knowledge and a guiding principle of evaluation. In Heidegger's case, this principle leads at once to the heart of his thought. He expresses it pithily in the observation that metaphysicians are constantly talking about "being as such" and forgetting the nature of being. Ever since the lines of speculation hardened with Aristotle, there has been a fundamental confusion between *Das Sein* and *Das Seiende*, between being itself and this or that concrete instance of that-which-is. Metaphysicians declare themselves to be investigating the nature of being, whereas their statements really bear upon *this* being, *a* being, beings, or the totality of that-which-is. That in virtue of which each being or mode of being is what it is—an instance of being, a manifestation of being-ness—has been obscured in the effort to explore and universalize some particular region of being. Hence the constituent standpoint for an ontology or theory of being as such is lacking. The history of so-called ontology is not false or worthless, but it suffers from this fundamental deficiency. What Heidegger wishes to "destroy" is the claim that an ontology can be founded without bringing the discussion back to considerations more primary than those so far considered in the history of philosophy. His aim is not to lead to agnosticism about being, as is the case with Jaspers, but to clear the ground for a radical comprehension of being.

Appeal is made to Descartes' famous comparison of philosophy to a great tree, the roots of which comprise metaphysics, the trunk physics, and the branches the practical sciences of mechanics, medicine, and ethics. Heidegger asks: What is the soil into which the roots of metaphysics are plunged?[14] Unless this question is deliberately raised, philosophers will continue to regard the tree of philosophy as a self-sufficient organism, instead of one that is nourished by a supporting earth and atmosphere. The fruitful soil of thought, the presupposition of metaphysics, and the entire philosophical inquiry, is being. This is a simple consideration, regarded in itself, but it cannot be taken seriously unless the philosopher is willing to take a step backwards, going behind what is usually taken to be metaphysics or first philosophy.

Because they have been unwilling to take this step, the great philosophers from Aristotle to the present have been led astray about the nature of being. The various general explanations of reality in terms of mind, matter, subjectivity, and the will to power provide striking testimony to the confusion between being itself and some aspect of that-which-is. In each of these conflicting descriptions of the real, some particular kind of being has been proposed as characterizing being as such. The Greeks, for instance, made an unwarranted extension of the categories. In their original sense, the categories were taken as the widest discoverable traits of the objective world about us. But the ideal of a metaphysics or generalized doctrine on being led to the application of the categories to man himself, to God, and to being as such. This interpretation of all entities according to the standard of one domain of being placed a greater burden upon the categories than they were capable of supporting. Its distorting effect was felt especially in the Greek conception of time.[15] Despite their insight that time provides a point of departure for studying being, the Greek thinkers understood time and being in terms of a static present (*ousia* in terms of *parousia*). Time became for them a series of present moments dominated somehow by an immanent principle of permanence or eternity. No room was provided for a peculiarly human kind of temporality or for history in the full sense. Both human duration and being itself were modelled upon the flow of *nows* or motions in the physical world. The "numbering" of this process by the human mind was not seen to involve a new set of factors irreducible to the categories.

Heidegger exposes the equivocation hidden in the Greek conception of metaphysics. This science is supposed to be now the theory of the widest traits common to all beings and now a discourse about the highest being, God. But it is at least questionable whether a transition can be made from the first to the second meaning of metaphysics, with the sole aid of the categories. That there is at least a problem here is suggested by St. Paul's well-known contrast between the foolishness of God and the wisdom of the world or Greek philosophy.[16] Heidegger suggests, indirectly, that Christianity contains a principle that should challenge the twofold view of metaphysics and perhaps prevent any direct application of the categories to the religious reality. He is openly critical of the entire tradition of Scholastic philosophy and theology for taking over unchanged the Greek approach to metaphysics. No matter how much they extended and refined this tradition, the Scholastics never submitted it to the kind of radical revision and refounding declared by Heidegger to be a philosophical necessity.

This accounts for Heidegger's deep-seated reluctance to employ the word "God" or to deal with those problems which are usually included in natural theology.[17] He is not ruling out God from his philosophy but is literally rendered speechless before the task of treating of Him in a way consistent with his criticism of Scholastic ontology. For he regards the "God" of the Scholastic treatises as merely the highest *Seiendes*, the supreme instance of that-which-is. To call God the first cause, the highest good, the last end, and the other designations of metaphysics is, in Heidegger's estimation, to understand Him merely as the superlative among those things that are. To apply the categories of the objective world to God is to implicate Him as but one among the other beings in the world and hence to overlook the distinctive character of the divine. From this criticism, it is evident that Heidegger is using the term "category" in the broadest sense, so as to include cause, the transcendentals, essence, and existence, as well as the usual technical list of the categories. All the conceptual tools of Greek and Scholastic metaphysics are fashioned after the objective world and *hence* are relevant only here. Heidegger regards the latter inference as self-evident, since he never discusses the Scholastic theory of analogical predication of transcategorial concepts like cause and the good.

Descartes did not make as complete a break with the past, and modern philosophy is not as sharply opposed to the ancient and medieval traditions, as is customarily supposed.[18] He contributed a good deal towards the modern conviction about the sharp distinction between man and the beings around him, and for this end he demanded new methods and new ideas. Nevertheless, he continued to measure man by comparison with one particular mode of being rather than in relation to being as such. Just as the Scholastics patterned their notions of God and man after the Greek image of the physical world, so Descartes and his successors followed the lead of mathematical physics or the modern scientific world view. On such a basis, man is seen to be other than the rest of nature, but his distinctive reality is studied only by way of contrast with the prevailing notion of the physical universe. Man the thinker is still correlated mainly with the order of extended things; the human spirit is still taken as a peculiar type of substance, although counterpointed with the substantial things of material nature. And whatever Descartes says about God and being as such is also framed within this set of references to the zone of that-which-is.

Heidegger's criticisms of Descartes and Kant are significant. He offers two main objections, the first of which tells most heavily against Descartes and the second against Kant. First, they are too rationalistic in elaborating a theory of human nature primarily in terms of knowledge and reason. Despite their liberal interpretations of the nature of thought and reason, they overlook other ways in which man is related to the world. In *Being and Time*, Heidegger shows the immense significance of the practical and productive relationships, the emotional responses, and the whole complexus of tools. This is the empirical and even pragmatic side of his mind. But he does not award the primacy either to man the knower or to man the maker, since both conceptions specify man only in his connections with other beings. Prior to either, and more distinctively human, is the existential relation of man to being as such. This perspective escapes the notice of both rationalism and empiricism.

The second shortcoming is the epistemological convention of designating man as a subject-in-opposition-to-the-object. Defining man in this way is no more adequate than defining God by contrast with creatures. It fails to grasp that aspect of human nature which sets it off unmistakably from every other sort of being-which-is, and for this reason it fails to determine the horizon wherein the problem of being can be broached. Kierkegaard provided the decisive clue in referring to a kind of subjectivity that is anterior to the distinction between subject and object. Heidegger's own existential analytic is an attempt to capture some of the existential (rather than categorial) traits of human being. This approach seeks to overcome the antinomy between objectivism and subjectivism and hence to lay bare the point of departure for a treatment of being as such. Heidegger's own interpretation of Kant's *Critique of Pure Reason* regards it as an ontological answer to the question: What is man?[19] What Kant referred to mysteriously as the transcendental unity of apperception or transcendental imagination is a halting approximation to that aspect of man wherein he is regarded precisely as an existent being, orientated to being as such.

Surprisingly enough, Heidegger accepts Hegel's evaluation of his own system as the culmination of all metaphysics.[20] Heidegger's interpretation of this claim entails, however, a reappraisal of Hegel's achievement and a more precise definition of *metaphysics*. As he now understands this science, it is the general theory of that-which-is as such and in its totality. This gives to metaphysics a valid but limited field of inquiry. It can no longer be accepted at its face value as the study of being as being; rather, it investigates the nature and field of that-which-is, *die Seiendheit des Seienden*. In the course of such a study, being itself is connoted but never formally considered under its own conditions. Hegel's glory is to have given the completest conceptual formulation to the proper object of metaphysics in this restricted sense. His claim to have brought being "to the concept" is justified in respect to that-which-is but not in respect to being itself. Hegel offers the most comprehensive formulation of the Western view of being in the mode of that-which-is.

In order to complete his "destruction" or undermining of the history of ontology, Heidegger is sometimes compelled to minimize the significance of conflicts among different metaphysical systems. He remarks that it is futile to attempt to refute any particular system, since the pros and cons belong equally to that strife of things and thoughts which the early Greek philosophers perceived to be at the heart of the things that are. Hence Heidegger is unduly indulgent in accepting Hegel's synthesis of all previous doctrines as a successful accomplishment rather than as a one-sided claim. He is anxious to recapitulate all Western speculation in a culminating philosophy and then to point out that this philosophy, along with all its subaltern systems, remains within the restricted sphere of that-which-is. No fair hearing is given to those who interpret the development of metaphysics in terms of a number of fundamental challenges, shifts of viewpoint, and genuinely total disagreements about being as well as about the things that are. Particularly unfortunate is Heidegger's failure to consult the effort of St. Thomas to resolve the dualistic Greek view of metaphysics. In the Thomistic outlook, there is a fruitful and humanly unavoidable tension between the subject and object of metaphysics. Our mind finds being as exhibited under the categorial modes of finite, sensible being (the subject of metaphysics). The object of the metaphysical enterprise is to obtain as full an understanding of being as such, the diverse realizations of the act of existing, and the supreme causes of being, as is humanly possible from the starting point in sense experience. A metaphysics of this sort is not a mere interlude between the Greeks and Hegel. Hence it is not properly dealt with in Heidegger's historical criticism of metaphysics as a study of that-which-is.

Having limited metaphysics in this way, Heidegger is compelled to adopt some version of the commonplace existentialist distinction between ontology and metaphysics. Instead of accepting the Wolffian equation between general metaphysics and ontology, he usually refers to his own standpoint as a *fundamental ontology*.[21] This is one of the conventional terms which can be misleading, if given the usual connotation. For Heidegger does not mean that his doctrine is one among many varieties of ontology but that it is occupied with exploring the fundaments of ontology. More precisely, ontology is the study of the foundations upon which metaphysics and all philosophy rest: it is the study of the soil in which all speculation of a right sort is rooted. Metaphysics is truly the theory of what is first in philosophy, but what is first in philosophy is not first in every respect. What is unconditionally primary for all thought is being; consequently, fundamental ontology is the unconditionally first investigation.

Despite several efforts to clarify his meaning, Heidegger has not yet settled the consequences of his distinction between metaphysics and ontology. His "destruction of the history of ontology" amounts to a demonstration that what was taken to be fundamental ontology was a succession of metaphysical solutions, valid in their own field but incompetent to determine the nature of being. The proposed fundamental ontology is to effect an overcoming of metaphysics, not in the sense of a refutation and obliteration but as establishing limits and providing foundations that cannot be supplied by metaphysics itself. Yet there are indications that Heidegger also conceives this process as one of *self*-reform and *self*-foundation of metaphysics. Although pointing out the discrepancy between the verbal definition of metaphysics as the study of being as being and the actual practice, he does not deny that further historical developments are possible, in which metaphysics may close the gap. The limitation of metaphysics to the field of that-which-is is based upon a historical survey rather than upon a theory of the sciences and the intrinsic nature of metaphysics.

Furthermore, Heidegger calls man a metaphysical animal in virtue of his existent reality. Although human existence is *de facto* faced in the direction of that-which-is, it retains an intrinsic freedom to inspect its relation to being and being's relationship to human selfhood. A change in human existence, a turnabout of our interests and speculations, is the condition for becoming aware of our placement in being. But to be a man is precisely to be such a possibility of revaluing and redirecting our existence. Since metaphysics *is* the fundamental occurrence of human existence, it shares this power of returning to its own foundation in being.[22] The transformation of human existence, as it passes from primary concern for the things of the world and man in correlation with his environment to primary concern for being, should find speculative expression in a transformation of metaphysics. If Heidegger is reluctant to refer to reflective thought on being as metaphysics or first philosophy, it is because of his historical interpretation of metaphysics and his initial deprecation of metaphysical "categories."

3. God's Absence and Man's Homecoming.

Heidegger does not make a sudden bound from Hegel to his own project of a fundamental ontology. Recognizing Kierkegaard's religious protests as an informal anticipation of his own critique of metaphysical systems, he also comments on a twofold philosophical reaction to Hegel. Both Marx and Nietzsche corroborate the thesis that Hegel reached an extreme limit in metaphysical thinking. It is their joint witness that no hope lies for man in concentrating upon that-which-is, to the exclusion of being. Heidegger terms the Marxian theory of human alienation the most profoundly realistic appreciation of man's fate elaborated in recent times.[23] He contrasts it explicitly with the humanistic views of Sartre and Husserl which lack a historical foundation and an anchorage in material circumstances. Yet Marx does not grasp the significance of his own indictment of Hegel and capitalism. He frankly accepts the view that every being or *Seiendes* is valuable only as providing material for work and for the further conquest of nature. The wholly technical outlook of Marxism is more critical than a Platonizing metaphysics but is no more effective in removing the root-cause of human self-estrangement. As long as man is dedicated wholly to the ends of that-which-is, he cannot gain full possession of himself. For the principle of self-possession is to arouse in man a sense of his responsibility to being and his power of making room for being in the world of that-which-is.

A long essay in *Forest Trails* is devoted to an analysis of Nie-

tzsche's philosophy.[24] Heidegger combs through the entire Nietzschean corpus for evidence that will throw light upon Zarathustra's famous announcement that God is dead. Into this saying,
Nietzsche concentrates his disillusionment with the whole tradition of Western metaphysics, which he identifies with a Platonic
appeal to a supersensuous realm of ideal powers. The supersensuous God and the ideal motives that formerly sustained our efforts
have lost their hold upon our minds. The world beyond has no
more power to vivify us, and so metaphysics has come to an end.
Nietzsche regards his own philosophy as a countermovement to
the metaphysical dualism of two worlds, but like every other
"anti-" movement, his thought is specified by the views it attempts to combat. His appeal to the superman and to the eternal
return of the same is still within the metaphysical tradition of
that-which-is. Heidegger concurs with Jaspers' judgment that
Nietzsche failed to make the radical break with the past which
was supposed to culminate in his tidings of God's death.

The lasting value of Nietzsche is to have underlined the homelessness of contemporary man and to have suggested that there
is more involved in nihilism than a simple negation of all values.
Homelessness is another way of expressing the self-alienation observed by Hegel and Marx. For all the energy and genius ex-
pended upon the control of nature, man today feels less at home
in his natural setting than he did in the time of the Greeks.
Naturalists would contend that this is due to his still incomplete
attachment to nature or the realm of that-which-is. Heidegger
suggests, on the contrary, that man may have failed to fulfill an
indispensable condition for acquiring the sense of being at home,
namely, a recognition of the presence and power of being as the
foundation of all that is. Man cannot be at home in the world
until he learns to be at home with being and to domicile it in the
center of that-which-is.

Heidegger lists the opinion that his philosophy is a doctrine of
nihilism as one of the major misconceptions of his position.[25] Its
plausibility is due to the importance he attaches to the naught,
which forms the central theme of *What is Metaphysics?* and

which is treated at length in most of his other writings. Those who charge him with propounding nihilism fail to consider the way in which the naught is opposed to all that is. Here the example of Nietzsche is instructive for an appreciation of Heidegger's own treatment of the naught. When the "philosopher with the hammer" demolishes the dualism of an ideal ground and a phenomenal world, all is not thereby negated. In sweeping aside the Platonic metaphysics, Nietzsche is making a tremendous effort to think that-which-is as a whole, to include all beings within a single order and unity. He is obliged to clear out any God who is merely a support for dualism. For either God is degraded to the level of one among the other beings in the world (in which case, Nietzsche correctly concludes, there is no longer a God) or else He transcends the entire order of that-which-is. Nietzsche does not give serious consideration to the latter alternative, any more than he gives thought to whether being itself can be identified with the totality of that-which-is. To raise such questions, however, is the function of a constructive and thoroughgoing nihilism. Heidegger has suggested that being is *not* the same as the totality of that-which-is and that therefore being takes on the aspect of a naught from the perspective of this totality. He hints also that Christianity is similarly nihilistic in denying of God that He is like this or that being of our experience or like the world as a whole.

There is a special historical sense in which Nietzsche's declaration of the death of God is true. In order to elucidate this authentic meaning, Heidegger comments upon some lines written by the German poet and friend of Hegel, Friedrich Hölderlin:

> Near and
> Hard to grasp is the god.
> But where danger is,
> The deliverer too grows strong.
> In the darkness dwell the eagles. . . .
> But fearless man remains, as he must,

Alone before God, simplicity protects him,
And no weapon needs he, and no
Cunning, till the time when God's failure helps.[26]

To Heidegger, Hölderlin appears as the herald of the contemporary era, the most prescient mind of the nineteenth century. Like Matthew Arnold, Hölderlin grasps the importance of the general loss of religious faith and the anguish of men caught between a dead world and one yet unborn. Hölderlin's attitude, however, is not one of agnosticism but of expectancy and basic piety. In Heidegger's eyes, Hölderlin has set a pattern on the artistic level for human existence in a transitional period, when the old gods have departed and the God of the future has not yet come. This situation of man, living between what is no longer and what is yet to be, characterizes our time culturally, religiously, and philosophically. In Hölderlin's writings are contained hints as to how man should deport himself under these circumstances and what his reasonable hopes may be.

The original thinker and the sensitive poet occupy neighboring peaks and can speak to each other across the space.[27] They have in common a solicitude for words, a care for the "right" words that will name what they intend. The poet's care is for the holy, whereas the philosopher's is for being. One can learn from the other and in turn help his neighbor. Our age is a time of need in a dual way, since there is a lack of both the holy and being itself. The manner in which the poet relates himself to a world from which the holy is absent, provides a clue for the philosopher who lives in a world that does not recognize being as such. In turn, the philosopher's search after being opens up the horizon wherein alone the questions of the holy, divinity, and the word "God" can be considered. The foundation of being in the world is at the same time the initial step in making intelligible to men at large the poet's private quest of the holy. Heidegger conceives his own relation to Hölderlin (as well as to the poets, Rilke and George) somewhat after this fashion.

Hölderlin's poem, *Homecoming*, provides by anticipation a

response to Nietzsche's analysis of the homelessness of modern man. Instead of speaking loosely about the death of God, Hölderlin refers to God's *Fehl*, His "absence" or "failure."[28] This means that the holy has withdrawn itself in proportion as men have failed to live reverently and in a consecrated way. When the total energies of a civilization are directed to immanent ends, there is no longer a presentiment of the holy or a response to its demands. God fails us by ceasing to cast pearls to swine. Yet in this absence, the holy does not cease to be present in its independent way and attractive power. Men are not swine, no matter how resolutely they shut out the transcendent from the range of their effective interests. They remain *capax Dei*, capable of receiving God, and it is to permit the *free* realization of this capacity that God fails to appear in our age.

Hence there is a special function to be fulfilled by those who are aware of our plight and of God's assuring absence. Both Hölderlin and Rainer Maria Rilke view their poetic office as that of an "angel" or messenger, who recognizes and calls the attention of others to the traces of God even in an age of His absence.[29] Hölderlin hails the broad earth and the course of light as tokens or angels of the holy, somewhat in the manner of Beethoven's *Pastoral Symphony*. He draws close in his poems to the treasure at the heart of being, yet approaches it always as a reserved treasure. This is the paradoxical meaning of the words: "Near and hard to grasp is the god." For it is only our own abandonment of the holy that estranges us from it. In our homecoming, however, we return to the holy as it is in its own nature, that is, precisely as a mystery. A mystery is approximated by being respected as a mystery. In an age of God's withdrawal, the poet draws close by waiting confidently for the gift of the word that will name the holy for his own generation, even though this word has not yet been given.

Heidegger regards the thinker's attitude toward being as similarly determined by the historical situation. Being remains a hidden treasure in a world centered upon that-which-is. The thinker who has been called to the task of essential thought is aware of the authentic basis of human dignity. Man is not primarily the over-lord of that-which-is, as pragmatism and the technical mentality maintain. He is first of all the shepherd of being.[30] Only on con-dition that he fulfills this office, is he able to establish control over that-which-is without degrading himself. Homecoming for the thinker means dwelling in the proximity of the mystery of being. The essential or primary thinker obtains and retains his existence in the neighborhood of being. He must be loyal to the guardian-ship of being, protecting it from hasty identification with that-which-is and at the same time assuring it a dominant place in the world of that-which-is.

Being as such can never be reduced to the state of obviousness, where no mystery and challenge remain. It cannot, in Marcel's language, be levelled to the status of a problem. On the contrary, the thinker is related to being as to a hidden presence, a reserved treasure, a vivifying absence. Just as holy names are lacking to-day, so is there a dearth of names for being. The poet, Hölderlin, refers somewhat hesitantly to the Joyous One, the High One, the Serene; but these names do not pretend to do more than hail the holy from afar off. Similarly, the thinker must be just as spar-ing in language as he is rigorous in thought. He does not have the adequate ontological names at his command, and neither are they present in common currency. Yet the word is not merely an ex-trinsic index attached to something that is already known and mastered. Being only *is* for us when we express it in the essential word, the naming act that enshrines it in our existence. Heideg-ger's difficulty about finding an adequate language in which to cast the discussion on *Time and Being* is traceable to this rever-ence for the word as well as to the misinterpretations made by his critics. In a world that places a premium upon catchwords, facile phrasing, and articulateness, he defends the value of silence, speechlessness, and halting testimony. We must learn to live with the nameless and to endure this condition.

Homecoming is closeness to the truth of being. Such proxim-ity belongs only to *essential thought*, which Heidegger defines as thought that at once listens and belongs to being, making a free return to its source.[31] This mode of thinking is "of being" in two ways: it is owned by being and it attends to being. To be a man in the most essential way is nothing other than to acknowledge the claim of being upon oneself. Being takes the initiative and retains the primacy. For the relationship of man to being can only develop within the fundamental and constitutive relationship of being to man. In explicit opposition to Sartre, Heidegger holds that man is not alone in a chaos of that-which-is. Being is his element, as it is the element for every other instance of that-which-is. Hence essential thought is an engagement by being and for the ends of being. Not man but being is the essential: Heidegger declares this to be the simple truth animating *Being and Time*, which is a phase in his own attempt at essential thinking.

A simple truth need not be an easily grasped truth. This is seen in the case of essential thought, which involves a radical reversal of the usual trend of speculative and technical interests. As a homecoming or return to origins, essential thought does not overcome metaphysics and technical attitudes by transcending them but by getting behind them to "the poverty of existence," to the situation of the "shepherd" or responsible thinker, whose sole office is to care for being. Essential thought precedes not only the distinction between subject and object but also the division of thought itself into theoretical and practical.[32] Heidegger has been accused of at once elaborating a theoretical framework from which no practical, ethical results can issue and exalting man's practical, instrumental relationships. Neither of these contradictory charges takes account of the plane on which he develops his view of essential thought. He regards it as the initial act which supplies the basis for all particular actions, since it founds our actions firmly upon the basis of being. At the same time, this act formally consists in nothing else than the free saying of the truth of being. Its total and proper effect is to domicile being in a human way by bringing the unspoken word of being to language in fitting words. It studies the light of being, which precedes every theoretical investigation, and the power of being, which precedes every active project.

This account of essential thought enables Heidegger to clarify two propositions, advanced in *Being and Time*, which most Aristotelians unavoidably misunderstood. There, he stated that the possible is better than the actual, and that there is being only as long as there is human existence.[33] These statements were immediately taken to imply a subversion of the classical relation between act and potency and a creative idealism. In his essay on Humanism, Heidegger replies to both these objections. His answer shows the difficulties he experiences in expressing his position and also the pitfalls that attend even the most conscientious study of his philosophy.

By "the possible" he means neither sheer conceptual possibility nor potency (as opposed to act in the Aristotelian sense) nor essence (as that which is actuated by existence or actuality). These notions are infected with the "categorial" standpoint of that-which-is. Rather, it designates that in virtue of which a thing authentically is and takes a hold on its essence. In this sense, being itself is the supremely possible, the enabling power whereby whatever is *is*.[34] As the enabling power with respect to man's essential thought and essence, it permits thought to realize itself as an affirmation of being and hence constitutes man in his essence as what he *is*: a participation in being. This explanation comes close to the Thomistic doctrine that existence is the proper effect of God, regarded as an active power or efficient cause. Heidegger beats a hasty retreat from the resources of Thomistic metaphysics, without considering whether this metaphysics also attempts to overcome the limitations of categorial thinking.

The second proposition does not signify that the Cogito-subject of modern epistemology produces being. For being is the altogether transcending reality, which conditions the things that are and is not created by them. A clearing must be made for being, however, so that its presence in the midst of that-which-is may be recognized and reverenced. Only when this clearing is made, is being rendered accessible to man. Human existence is the place that is cleared for the advent of being, and yet being itself is the clearing. Being is essentially broader than any instance of that-which-is, including human existence, and clears a place for itself in man. The act whereby man domiciles being in the essential word is itself destined by being. To say that, as a consequence, "there is being" (*es gibt das Sein*), means that being gives itself to the world of beings through giving itself to human existence and human essential thought.[35]

In answer to Jean Beaufret's question as to how the adventuresomeness of philosophy can be maintained without making philosophy an arbitrary adventure, Heidegger emphasized the fact that thought is responsible for the enunciation of being.[36] Thought is bound to being by essential ordination and reaches its perfection only with the advent of being. This ordination is not set by thought itself but is the work of being, so that the recognition of being is man's way of meeting the prior claim of being. There is a remarkable consistency in Heidegger's speculation concerning the primacy of being over human existence and the entire range of that-which-is. In a letter to Karl Löwith written in 1924, he confesses that his destruction of the philosophical and theological tradition is not made in the interests of any definite system. In this respect, he consciously differs from Kierkegaard, the defender of Christian existence, and from the proponents of this or that cultural ideal. His pure resoluteness and intensity of thought are dedicated to the acknowledgment of being, no matter what the results be for man and the world. This same ruthless pursuit of the meaning of being is reaffirmed in the Postscript to *What Is Metaphysics?*, where Heidegger speaks of the sacrifice of all human interests for the sake of preserving the truth of being.

The dangerous and adventuresome element in fundamental ontology arises from man's freedom to make this sacrifice and hidden act of thanksgiving for being. Although the guardianship of being is man's destiny, he may refuse to accept it and may bury himself in the cares of that-which-is. His homecoming to being can never be forced: homelessness may be deliberately preferred. The claim of being upon human existence is what moralists call a moral necessity, a demand that is unconditionally made—upon our freedom. The danger and challenge of being are greatest precisely for those who become aware of the vocation of man to being and of his power to refuse or accept this grace.

4. *Man, the Horizon of Being.*

Heidegger refers to the philosopher as one who is constantly en route as a wanderer in the neighborhood of being. He is unwilling to enter into full possession of the treasure, if such possession means the abandonment of our historical predicament. With all the other existentialists, Heidegger gives an ontological ring to the religious notion of a call to repentance or change of mind.[37] To be lost in the cares of the world means, in this context, to center oneself exclusively upon that-which-is. The philosopher's function as a "wanderer," a *homo viator* (in Marcel's terms), is both to respect the incomprehensibility of being and to offer guidance to his fellow men. This guidance is best given by convincing them that they are indeed wanderers or pilgrims, who are in search of a homecoming to the truth of being. There are certain aspects of human experience that illuminate this hidden tendency of man to the proximity of being. All of Heidegger's phenomenological analyses are directed to the recall of man to being, through an interpretation of these indicative signs. His hermeneutic of existence is an effort to orientate existence in the neighborhood of being.

Heidegger is very sparing in his criticism of Husserl. Much of it is presented indirectly, especially his reply to Husserl's charge that fundamental ontology is a revival of psychologism and the anthropocentric viewpoint in philosophy. Heidegger's repudiation of Sartre is simultaneously his answer to this indictment. The center of gravity is being rather than man: what counts in human existence is not the subjective states but the bond with being. On certain fundamental points, however, Heidegger proposes an explicit counter-reform of phenomenology itself. He is not satisfied with the usual explanation of his relation to Husserl, as though he merely removed the brackets formerly placed around existence and thus hoped to draw out ontological conclusions from the phenomenological method. If this were the case, Husserl's starting point in a purified transcendental subjectivity would still provide the measure for what can be derived with the aid of his method. Sartre's mistake is to accept this account of the relationship between ontology and phenomenology.

The manner in which metaphysics is overcome is a clue to Heidegger's treatment of phenomenology, since in both instances there is an attempt to get behind the given sciences. This entails a challenge of Husserl's claim to have made the most radical start of thought in a presuppositionless way.[38] From Heidegger's standpoint, phenomenology makes a presuppositionless beginning only within the context of logic; but logic itself has presuppositions in the comprehension of being. There can be no pure logic, if by "pure" is meant complete autonomy with respect to being. Heidegger agrees with Kierkegaard and Marcel in calling in question the major assumption of systematic idealism. He observes that consciousness is not sufficient to establish the original overtness of that-which-is, the intelligibility which renders it accessible to us. Furthermore, consciousness stands in need of a prior act of freedom whereby man opens himself to the significance of that-which-is, allowing it to stand over against the mind as an object. In sum, Husserl fails to explain the intentionality of consciousness: it is not an irreducible, given fact but a consequence of man's establishment of an open relationship with the things that are. Only a fundamental ontology can illuminate the ground of intentionality, and in doing so, this discipline discredits the phenomenological claim to absolute presuppositionlessness.

Heidegger's intricate and somewhat tenuous discussion of *the naught* becomes more pertinent when viewed as a critical response to Husserl's theory of a pure logic.[39] The naught is the veil of being or the veiled way in which being appears to us by contrast with particular instances of being. What is said about the naught applies to being and, indeed, is an indirect way of inspecting being itself. The naught is not a logical negation or denial, but is the condition rendering such logical acts possible. It is more original or primary than our negations. We encounter rather than constitute it, and we are able to encounter it because it is first given to us for acceptance. Hence the naught cannot be demonstrated from a prior premise. It is not an a posteriori explanation but the anterior principle for both our logical acts of negation and our understanding of particular instances of being. A logical method that attempts to be utterly self-founding is soon converted into a doctrinaire logicism by glossing over the radical rectification of thought by being and its surrogate, the naught.

Unlike a nihilistic philosophy, Heidegger's analysis of the naught is intended to pave the way for an experience of being precisely in the naught. There are two positive effects of this study of the naught. When being is understood as completely other than this or that being-which-is and other than the totality of beings-which-are, then for the first time the entire realm of that-which-is is revealed in its proper nature. Confusion is no longer possible between being and the totality of that-which-is, once being is adjudged as *not* identical with that-which-is. At the basis of the various calculative sciences (what Marcel calls the problematic approach), dealing with the world of that-which-is, lies this clarifying proposition that the entire field of investigation is distinct from, and dependent upon, being itself. Thus the essential thought which is responsible for this proposition underlies phenomenology and the other sciences. It deals with a subject matter that is too simple and originary to become the object of a calculative investigation, after the manner of phenomenology.[40]

The second consequence of a discussion of the naught is to prepare a place in our experience for the truth of being. This result serves to correct the usual interpretation of *Being and Time.* It was a widespread opinion that, for Heidegger, human existence, or *Dasein*, is a brief moment of light shining between two abysses of utter nothingness. Man is thrown from whence he knows not and advances whither he knows not. Nothingness has cast him up on the beach of that-which-is and has made his essence to be a care of death, leading to total extinction and return to the void. The things that surround man in their brute presence have no intrinsic significance. They are simply present to him, and acquire meaning and value as tools in his milieu. Human projects succeed in organizing a network of tools, a global relationship of instruments of human purpose. But for each individual existent, the world is experienced in time from the standpoint of the *Dasein*, which is already fallen into that-which-is and hurtles by anticipation of the future into the final "whole" of death. On this reading, Heidegger makes of human life an idiot's tale, which in the end literally signifies an empty nothing.

That there is a positive significance hidden in the experience of the naught, and revealed by means of dread, is the central contention of Heidegger's fundamental ontology. The defect in the notion of dread, as expounded in *Being and Time*, is that it remains wholly within the confines of human existence. But from the standpoint of the relation of being to man, dread takes on a new meaning. It is the basic mood overtaking a man when he first comes to realize the contingency of that-which-is as such and in its totality, as well as its complete otherness from being. The total response of man to the contingency of the world, including himself, is not terror of annihilation but a sense of our otherness and distance from being. It is dreadful anguish before the withdrawal of being. This is not unmingled dread but dread blended with awe.[41] For a sense of the deliberate absence of being is founded on a certain manifestation of the presence of being. Only because man is capable of responding to the call of being, is he also capable of feeling dread at the situation in which being reserves itself from that-which-is. Because it is both the foundation of that-which-is and other than the totality of particular beings, being opens itself to man as a kind of nothingness. The power of the naught over human existence is nothing other than the powerful presence of being to that which is other than itself.

It is being which throws man into the zone of that-which-is and destines him for a return to his native attachment to being. Man is free either to accept this destiny or to attempt to ignore his calling to being. The latter state is that of inauthentic existence, what Heidegger (along with the other existentialists) calls the world of anonymity and "what one says."[42] The rule of the anonymous herd seeks to destroy the belongingness of man to being by sinking him in the affairs of that-which-is. Genuine selfhood and freedom are constituted only when man stands open to being and thus makes the overtness of being the effective principle within himself. In the Introduction to *What Is Metaphysics?*, Heidegger inserts a warning concerning the relation between selfhood, consciousness, and existence.[43] He accepts the existential commonplace that whereas other beings *are*, only man *exists*. Only a being capable of existence can be a self. But from this it does not follow that selfhood and existence are the same or that existence is only an affair of consciousness. Husserl's accusation of psychologism is probably founded on this unwarranted inference.

In *Being and Time*, Heidegger places emphasis upon one's self-being, acquired through acts of freedom, in order to show what is peculiar to man. Man is not merely a substance, like other things in the realm of that-which-is, and not merely a cognitive subject correlated with noetic objects. These assumptions of the modern philosophies of man are inadequate. He is above all a center of responsibility for his own nature: he becomes truly human when he accepts this responsibility for developing a mature self. But this analysis, while fitted to its designated purpose, does not exhaust the description of human existence. Critics of Heidegger's main work noted that he did not give an answer to the question of why man exists as a being that is constantly projecting meanings. They concluded that the doctrine of a projective mode of existence is only a voluntarist restatement of the main thesis of absolute idealism. This inference is perhaps inevitable, on the assumption that the analytic of human existence is complete in itself.

Actually, Heidegger's later ·theories of truth and *Dasein* require a revision of this judgment. He does not regard the world of non-human things-that-are as being devoid of meaning, except through human projects. There is intrinsic significance in the world of that-which-is: ontological truth consists in letting that-which-is *be* and hence reveal itself in its own import.[44] Freedom is the foundation of all explanation and truth, in the peculiar sense that man must freely assume the attitude of letting things become present to him in their overtness. In this sense, Nietzsche was right in pointing to an act of will at the basis of all science. Man's freedom to stand open to that-which-is and to conform to its demands is the ground of truth and the binding force at work in every instance of a search for truth. What Marcel calls man's humility before being is a free act, without being an arbitrary one creative of anthropocentric meanings.

This casts a new light upon the *whither* and the *why* of human projects or transcendence.[45] The fundamental directions of transcendence is not the horizontal one to the world of practical materials and tools but the vertical one to being. To this extent, Heidegger approaches closer to Jaspers than either is willing to admit. Concern for the world is conditioned by, and contained within, the anterior attitude of openness and orientation to being itself. Moreover, it is not merely a brute fact that man is of such a nature as to be a projection. His existence is of this sort because of the special relationship of being to man. Being determines man to be nothing else than the place where being manifests itself in the world, and for this end man must be an orientation to being and the world together. Transcendence is expressed primarily in the relation of being to that-which-is and then in the reciprocal, free relation of man to being.

It is only in this perspective that the full meaning of the term *Dasein* can be appreciated. Heidegger repudiates Sartre's exegesis on this key word. *Da-sein* does not signify the absurd and irrevocable fact that man *is there*, hurled up on the beach of that-which-is . . . and let no more be said about it. In its primary sense, it means that man is the *there* for being, the point of insertion for being as such amidst the things that are.[46] Man is the focus of the relationship of being to the totality of that-which-is, the temple where being can make a clearing shelter for itself. The truth of being can be realized in man, because his mind can establish a relation with the overtness of being. Hence for man to exist is to be the place of the truth of being. *Dasein* is not identical with the truth of being and does not exhaust it. Being can be without that-which-is, including man, even though that-which-is cannot be without being. But man cannot enjoy his proper mode of being, his existence, unless his fundamental project be to open himself in true, essential thought to the manifestation of being.

When Heidegger writes that man's essence is his *Dasein*, he is not secularizing the Scholastic proposition that God is His own existence. He does not have in mind any Scholastic pairing of essence and existence as potential and actual co-principles of created being. Like Kierkegaard, his treatment is not so much in terms of created being generally as in terms of the basic, free orientation of human life. It would be more correct to say that he presents an ontologized ethics than that he favors ontology at the expense of ethics. This is evidenced by his practical restriction of existence to man. *Dasein* is man's self-presence or essence, in the sense that he is most truly and distinctively a man when he relates his essential thought to the openness of being, recognizing his own contingency and that of the world in respect to participation in being. Man's essence is the realization of the truth about the proximity of being. His care is not a self-centered worry or a nihilistic obsession but a solicitude to realize this essence and so to become truly human.

This is the only sense in which Heidegger acknowledges his philosophy to be a humanism, and it is also the only kind of pre-suppositionless beginning that he admits.[47] He interprets humanism as the doctrine that man's essence is essential for truth in such a way that truth is not due to man as such but to his call to the guardianship of being. This explanation is in direct conflict with Sartre's theory of truth as a purely human invention. But Heidegger is not far removed from the Thomistic teaching that man enjoys the privilege and responsibility of giving a unique, created expression of truth, both in his intellectual judgment and in the rectitude of his conduct. In Heidegger, the notion of a call to the guardianship of being serves to remove any lingering equivocation in his doctrine on human existence as a project. The human project does not create being because it is a project that is thrown. Rather, the thrownness of *Dasein* is the human side of the call to make a clearing for being. Being itself is the thrower and the caller: human existence is a project or throw only because it has been destined and thrown by being.[48] Thus the thrownness of man's being is not a dereliction and abandonment to the world, but a mission or sending forth to live in the neighborhood of being. Only he who wills to exist in a final mode of inauthenticity refuses to heed this invitation by despairing over the environing naught. Man lives in the world not under a ban but with an importunate summons to enter into free relationship with being and thus to give recognition to the presence of being in that-which-is. As the older theologians would express it, man is called to render formal glory to God both on his own behalf and on behalf of all creation.

During the past decade, Heidegger has used the term *existence* *(Existenz)* in a more comprehensive way than in his earlier writings. Previously, he limited the term to mean the tendency of human *Dasein* in a forward direction as constituting the basic temporal mode, the future.[49] He referred to the various modes of time (past, present, and future) as ec-stacies of *Dasein*, its historical projections in the world. In the perspective of fundamental ontology, however, history is primarily the history of being, within which is incorporated the temporal activities of man. This is the sense in which time and history constitute the horizon of being itself. The basic ec-stacy or outward striving of man is toward being itself. In its authentic mode, existence is ec-static first of all in the direction of being. Heidegger now speaks of "ex-sistence," as a reminder that man becomes a genuine existent in so far as he accepts the call to attend to being. He does not deny that, apart from man, *Dasein* could be found in some other form of that-which-is, provided that it had the capacity to recognize being as such. Its essential structure could have a non-human realization: this is Heidegger's safeguard against anthropomorphism. But within our experience, *Dasein* is realized only in human ex-sist-

ence. To ex-sist is to open a sheltering clearing for being and
to express this vocation in carefully chosen words and deeds. To
make a presuppositionless beginning is not the work of logic but
the first act of ex-sistence. Kierkegaard's leap expresses this act
better than does Husserl's transcendental reduction, since it is in
the nature of an encounter, a free response of man to the call of
being. Ex-sistence "leaps" into being by engaging in a pure finding
of being, a finding of that which is already present as a gift to us
and a demand upon us.

5. *Being and God.*

The problem of God still remains the crucial one in Heidegger's
philosophy, despite the recent elucidations. In an interview
granted to R. Scherer (in 1947), as well as in his *Letter concerning 'Humanism'*, this situation is recognized by Heidegger himself.[50] In these remarks, he explicitly rejects what the philosophers
usually call God. The attributes of prime mover, first cause, and
highest value are all taken from the region of immanent, objective traits of that-which-is. In Heidegger's eyes, their attribution
to God is sacrilegious, since He is not contained in the order of
that-which-is, even as its highest instance. Like the religious phenomenologist, Max Scheler, Heidegger discerns a wide gulf between the Christian concept of God and the metaphysical view.
He also agrees with Scheler and Pascal that God is given to religious experience rather than to philosophical analysis. His own
philosophy refrains from pronouncing anything about God, not
out of indifference but because of a respect for the limits of philosophical inquiry. Philosophy is a study of being and of that-
which-is. God is not identified with being, and neither is being
the same as a world-ground. Heidegger admits that the absolute
reality is somehow connoted in the idea of being as such, but philosophy is incapable of establishing this absolute as God. From
the philosophical standpoint, God does not emerge from His
hiddenness, as He does in revelation.

Heidegger, *qua* philosopher, makes no decision about theism. The resolve of the philosophical thinker is one of openness to being and restriction within its limits. If there is a divine actuality, it transcends both that-which-is and being itself, and hence falls completely outside the thinker's purview. But Heidegger maintains that his fundamental ontology opens up the dimension within which the problem of theism can be raised. It is perhaps for this reason that he made the surprising remark to Scherer that he could go along with a liberalized Thomism. The four tasks facing our historical era—the age of the absence of God—are: the recovery of the meaning of being, the arousal of the sense of the holy, the search after the Godhead or divinity, and a settlement of the question of the meaning of the word "God." The first objective is assigned to the philosopher and the second to the poet. Heidegger has not specified the way of approaching the two latter questions, although it is probable that a study of the mystics would provide a valuable lead, as Bergson suggested.

It is difficult to evaluate Heidegger's position on God, since his remarks have been few and guarded. The main problem is why a study of the truth of being should keep the philosophical thinker from approaching God. There are some indications that the reasons for this restriction are to be found in still uncriticized portions of Heidegger's philosophical heritage. He accepts the phenomenological principle of a rigorous correspondence between modes of experiencing and modes of being. On this basis, Scheler had once argued that no bridge can be thrown across from the God of Aristotle and Thomas to the God of Abraham, Isaac, and Jacob, so different is the intentional object in each case. Although Heidegger has not explained his position in this regard at sufficient length, he may be reasoning in a similar way. If this be the case, then he is allowing the phenomenological method to govern his thought much more effectively and decisively in the question of God than in the question of being as such. He has not asked whether different intentional and experiential approaches may not be used to arrive at the same reality and whether there is not a positive set of relations between the religious and metaphysical views of God. He has not made clear how and why being as such may bear an indirect reference to God, or why philosophy cannot grasp what is thereby connoted about God.

There is perhaps a more urgent reason for Heidegger's hesitation. In *What Is Metaphysics?* occurs the following statement: "Being itself is finite in essence."[51] This is merely a passing remark, which is unsupported by argument but which may be the regulative principle in his speculations about God. If by "God" is meant an unbounded reality, then this reality is placed not only beyond everything that participates in being (the order of that-which-is) but also beyond being itself or what is knowable through philosophical means. The likely source for the view that being is essentially finite is Kant. Heidegger has not yet specified the extent to which he continues to accept and adapt to the language of ontology Kant's key notion of transcendental apperception or imagination. Heidegger's persuasion about the essentially finite character of being itself may have its source here. In *Kant and the Problem of Metaphysics*, he places the humanness or finiteness of reason at the source of metaphysics. This shows that our knowledge of being is finite but not that being itself is essentially finite. It is more difficult to determine the Kantian influence here than in the case of Jaspers, who also places the transcendent beyond being and philosophical knowability. But Jaspers would not allow an independent and perhaps superior religious apprehension, which remains at least an open possibility for Heidegger.

The doctrine on the categories remains just as central and as embarrassing for Heidegger as for Kant and Jaspers. His denial of their applicability to man is made more in a dogmatic spirit than in a critical one. For it rests on the assumption that all traits discovered *in* a certain region of being can be relevant only *for* that region. But not all the traits present in one order of being are limited to it. Heidegger himself inadvertently admits as much when he defines man as that instance of that-which-is which is in the mode of ex-sistence. Although man is a special sort of *Seiendes,* he does have at least something in common with other beings.

Hence it is difficult to maintain a rigid distinction between categorial and existential traits.

It is even more difficult to speak about being as such, without using concepts drawn from some instance of that-which-is, either categorial or existential. Although he avoids the use of the term "cause," Heidegger conveys its meaning through several synonyms. Otherwise, it is difficult to understand how being gathers, holds, clears a place, throws, calls, relates, and destines. These dramatic substitutes remind us that some adjustment must be made in the meaning of causality as it applies to different "enabling powers," that causality has a special reference to being, and that no comprehensive and univocal notion of causality can be gained. But they also show that the causal relationships discovered in the objective world are only special instances of the causal process, not its exhaustive exemplification.

Heidegger's thought is still developing and changing under the impact of new insights. This is evident not only in terminological shifts but also in the careful revisions and additions given to his writings in later editions and in the new problems to which he continually addresses himself. One of the problems still in a fluid state is that of the predication of being. It is not always clear in Heidegger, any more than in Kant, when the discussion concerns the concept of being and the judgment of existence and when it concerns real being and the existent. Heidegger's "being" (like that of Husserl) bears an undeclared affinity to Kant's "condition for the possibility of experience in general." In commenting on the proposition, "There *is* Being," Heidegger notes that the "is" which attaches to being is not the same as the "is" of that-which-*is*.[52] This remark can be taken in two senses. It can mean either that no particular instance of being fully realizes the perfection signified in the *concept* of being or that that *reality* of which being *can* be unconditionally predicated is different from those things of which it can only be predicated in certain respects. The exact import of the qualifications "as such" or "in itself" or "essentially" is never specified in the case of being. But Heidegger does remark that perhaps the term "is" can be most properly applied to being, even though common usage reserves it for that-which-is. This is an indication that there is some indetermination in the meaning of "to be," such that an analogical predication is required in order to apply it both to that-which-is and to being.

It remains an open question whether the predication of "to be" may not be extended also to the reality of God. The concept of being, as resident in our minds, is certainly finite. But its signification need not be exclusively finite. Some intrinsic adjustment is required, so that Heidegger can say of both being itself and that-which-is that they *are*. Moreover, he recognizes that it may be applied more properly in the former case than in the latter. The way is open for extending the meaning of being beyond the act whereby finite things receive finite being. Although Kantian metaphysics is essentially limited to the finite modes of being, the truth of being, to which the thinker is called, is not restricted to the truth of the participation of being in its finite modes or even to the notion of participated, finite being itself. Heidegger's own attempt to "get behind" this viewpoint indicates the prospect of an ontology of both infinite and finite beings. Being must somehow bear upon the absolute reality, if the latter is connoted even indirectly by this concept and if it can be meaningfully referred to as a reality of an absolute sort.

Finally, the relation of Heidegger to the theology of crisis needs to be determined, especially with regard to the problem of knowledge of God. Heidegger's reference to the Pauline repudiation of the wisdom of this world is in the spirit of Kierkegaard, Barth, and the earlier Brunner.[53] His limitation of philosophical reason to the finite order, denying its competence in the cognition of God, finds its parallel, if not its source, in the strictures passed by the crisis theologians. Heidegger shares with them a deprecation of the philosophically elaborated concept of God. Although he does not lend positive support to their claims about the revelation of the Word of God, he does frame the possibility of approaching God in such a way that it could be achieved only through such a "vertical revelation from God downwards."

Until Heidegger reveals more about his links with Kant, religious phenomenology, and dialectical theology, only tentative criticism is possible. He has removed a good many ambiguities in his own thought and repudiated certain interpretations of his basic work. But he has not yet made accessible to critical inspection the grounds upon which he makes a reaffirmation of being. He has shown the direction which such a reaffirmation takes in his philosophy, as well as its systematic consequences for the analytic of human existence. The actual development of the assertions about the presence of being and man's guardianship of being remains locked up within the promised treatise on *Time and Being*. This indispensable bridge between program and conclusions is still in the condition of much of Hölderlin's insight: "lyre music, a song without words."

Chapter VI
Five Existential Themes

Perhaps the greatest danger facing students of existentialism is that of giving a premature, one-sided definition of the entire movement. If, for instance, Sartre is designated as the typical exponent of this philosophy, then his position becomes the touchstone for testing the orthodoxy of other theories. A doctrine will achieve existential standing only in the measure that it approaches the Sartrean standard. This a priori method has disconcerting consequences. Marcel and Jaspers are banished posthaste to the outlands, whereas Heidegger and even Kierkegaard are remade to the image of postulatory atheism. Similar absurdities follow whenever one particular explanation is regarded at the outset as the basic expression of existential thinking.

A less arbitrary procedure is to begin with a mere nominal definition, accepting the conventional grouping together of a number of thinkers under the banner of existentialism. There are some advantages to the policy of postponing an attempt at summary statement until the philosophies of these men commonly called existentialists have been examined in their own right. It is a precaution against ruling out of court major sources of evidence and against prejudging the testimony to be heard. Only after each of the representatives has been heard at some length do the common elements in their viewpoint begin to emerge. Hasty and unbalanced generalizations are most deftly exposed by comparing them with the actual relationships seen to obtain among the existentialists. The fact that there is a good deal of internecine strife within the existentialist household should make us wary of all attempts to impose a uniform, simplistic description. Thus Julien Benda's thesis that existentialism represents merely the revolt of life against reason calls to mind the conflicting existentialist interpretations of reason, as well as the various efforts to vitalize reason and rationalize life.

The inductive approach also shows the wisdom of defining existentialism more in terms of its problems and methods than its doctrines. There is no Kant or Hegel to provide a central, generally accepted body of doctrine. In this respect, existentialism has broken away from the school-philosophies of the nineteenth century and has advocated pluralistic freedom in the ranks. Common ground is provided by methodic and problematic commitments more than by a definite set of solutions or by a sacred text. By recalling the broad themes of existentialist speculation, justice can be done both to the divergent opinions and to the points of real similarity. The five topics chosen for synoptic study here are: the nature of philosophizing, descriptive metaphysics, man in the world, man in society, man and God. Existentialism is a concrete manner of reflection upon these themes, paying special attention to their foundation in individual existence and freedom.

1. *The Venture of Philosophizing.*

The existentialists have given currency to a line of Fichte's, contained in a youthful letter to Jacobi: "We philosophize out of need for our redemption." Although not going to any length of calling philosophy a salvation-knowledge, they agree with Dilthey and Scheler that the gap between intelligence and life must be closed. Moreover, it must be closed in some other way than that proposed by absolute idealists from Fichte to Cassirer. The latter school would identify life abruptly with the vital activities of the mind and the workings of an ideal dialectic in history. The danger of such a reduction of life to its ideal structures is its deprecation of those individual traits and stray qualities which are recalcitrant and defy a priori classification. It is better to expose the discrepancies between our intellectual cadres and actual existents than to perpetuate a false sense of philosophical adequacy.

Whatever their success in trying to liberate themselves from idealistic categories, the existentialists have subjected the notion of an ironclad philosophical system to concentrated fire. They have taken to heart Kierkegaard's warning that a logical system of existence is impossible of human achievement. Everything depends, however, upon the reasons advanced for this alleged impossibility. When these reasons are scrutinized, the existentialists are seen to be partners to Kierkegaard's equivocation in the use of the term "system." From definite historical reference to the meaning of this term in the context of Hegelian idealism, it is easy to slip into universal skepticism about the mind's ability to give a coherent, generalized explanation of reality. Because they tend to oscillate between these two senses of the attack upon systematic reasoning, the existentialists do provide grounds for the charge that they foster irrationalism in the course of criticizing the idealistic exaggerations about philosophical reason.

Although Sartre espouses an ontology of the absurd, it is perhaps in the philosophy of Jaspers that the dialectic of irrational situations is most subtly cultivated. The very finesse with which the project is carried out contains a paradoxical note. Jaspers subjects the contradictions of systematic thinking to coherent, systematic analysis; his philosophy is a successful study of the failures to which all philosophical efforts at understanding being must lead. He plots a cunning course, so that logical reason cannot but run aground on the shores of personal existence and transcendence. Philosophy is thus conceived as a salvage activity, which can only begin to function properly after there has been a shipwreck of the traditional categories. Behind this figurative language lies the typical existentialist conviction that we can philosophize only in the spirit of taking a dare and a risk in the face of constant philosophical failures to understand existence. System is opposed here in the sense of an assumption that the main outlines of reality have already been ascertained and that the work of our generation is only to fill in the details on the map and make application to contingent circumstances. Courage to face the as yet uncharted areas, rather than devotion to achieved certitudes, is the fundamental virtue demanded of a philosopher in an age of crisis. The philosopher, in Gabriel Marcel's phrase, is not a man of congresses: he must be prepared to go his solitary way and assume sole responsibility for his doctrines. Thus he provides an example for everyone who wants to become an authentic individual existent.

In this same vein is the prominence accorded to personal activity as a condition for philosophizing. The existentialists speak sparingly about philosophy but quite freely about philosophizing. They think it more important to follow Plato's advice of philosophizing with one's whole soul than to become fluent about this or that historical theory. They share the Greek view that philosophy connotes first of all a habit of mind or intellectual virtue and only thereafter a body of doctrine. Only he who has made a personal effort to uncover and appropriate truths is on the road to wisdom. The philosophical tradition does not subsist independently on an empyrean plane but only in the minds of individual thinkers, who must rethink their premises in their own generation. This accounts for the apparently antithetical attitudes of existentialism toward the philosophical past. Like the rest of history, it can be regarded either as a dead weight, from which we must be rid, or as a possible heritage of insight, which must be made our own. Often, however, the *possible* nature of this tradition and the correlative obligation to make personal appropriation and test of its claims are overlooked. Existentialism is in rebellion against the notion that transmission of the philosophical heritage is an automatic, impersonal and uncritical process, involving no risk or radical revision. Philosophizing is kept vital precisely by the resolve to re-vise or see reality with fresh vision.

The drawback of this emphasis upon the subjective side of philosophy is the encouragement it may give to idiosyncrasy and fantasy. Heidegger's praise of sheer resoluteness in thinking may generate a healthy radicalism, fearless of the practical conse-

quences of a new discovery. But it may lead with equal readiness
to one-track fanaticism. The danger is lessened but not entirely
removed by developing historical studies. For the "destruction of
the history of philosophy" may issue not in a quickened appreciation of long overlaid original meanings but in an arbitrary reading of the texts. This subjective simplification is seen in Heidegger's own restriction of all previous metaphysical systems to the
realm of particular modes of being. It is even more apparent in
Sartre's statement that all philosophies anterior to his own have
held the primacy of essence over existence and have merely postulated, without proving, God's existence. Neither of these assertions can be verified outside the narrow cycle running from
Hegel to Husserl. Deliberate narrowness and sustained intensity
of feeling are counterbalances to the formalism and vapid universality of many traditional standpoints. But these attitudes cannot be cultivated apart from a plain love of truth, without im-
poverishing philosophy in another way.

   The golden mean between these extremes is found in the ideal
of a perennial philosophy. All the existentialists pay homage to
this ideal, admitting thereby that the positive features of their
conception of philosophizing need to be integrated with other
views that stress historical continuity and doctrinal content. By
nature, a perennial philosophical tradition is not a partisan affair.
It had adherents among the medieval Scholastics, who were careful to maintain the lines of communication with Plato and Aristotle, Augustine and Proclus, Avicebron and Averroes. It found
an enthusiastic proponent in Leibniz, who sought to do for the
classical modern period what Thomas Aquinas did for the high
Scholastic age. Despite Hegel's employment of the notion of a
perennial philosophy as proof of the culminating character of his
own system, it has been revived by the existentialists. The discipline of history provides one way of correcting the excesses that
sometimes result from the existentialist concentration upon the
responsibility of the lonely individual thinker. He may be alone
in respect to the final shape of his own outlook, yet he cannot cut
himself off entirely from fruitful dialogue with fellow philoso-

phers without inviting the philosophical madness of talking only to and about himself. Co-operation among many minds across many ages is a necessary complement to the responsible work of the individual thinker.

Gabriel Marcel has wrestled with the problem of detaching perennial philosophy from the idealist view of the history of philosophy. He notes the paradox entailed by the practice followed by each successive philosopher of writing "his system," wherein he claims to present the definitive theoretical encapsuling of the universe. It were better for the philosopher to regard his doctrine as a limited participation in the meaning of being. Marcel's use of the journal-form of communication is intended to forestall any claim to have exhausted the intelligibility of the real in a single set of formulas. The constant increment of fresh insights and problems removes the illusion that the philosophical logos can be captured apart from the co-operative inquiries of many thinkers or that it can ever be given definitive incarnation in a particular system. The objection may be raised that, in attaching speculation so closely to individual experiences, the thinker is logically forced to withdraw into silent contemplation of the ineffable instant and its purely private significance. Marcel's reply is contained in his view that individual experience is itself constituted by participation in an order of being which is commonly available to all experients. A philosophically relevant reflection would thus be one which captures the ontological import of our experience and throws open a door for communication among the joint participants in existence.

The personalist approach to philosophizing also serves to counteract the influence of scientism. Against the latter standpoint, existentialism maintains the distinctive character of philosophical understanding. It is not merely a summation of scientific findings or a reflection upon scientific procedures. Existentialist opposition to the idealistic assumption of a monism of method is extended to the similar claim lying behind naturalism. Naturalism and revised, dynamic materialism have not yet specified the kind of adjustments required in applying scientific method to various regions of being, especially man, but this is not the main issue. Existentialists readily admit that some application of scientific techniques of investigation can and should be made to human nature. But they challenge the naturalistic inference that only those aspects of human existence which can be ascertained by a fundamentally univocal method have an assured standing in philosophy. Although it is historically true, for instance, that naturalistic analysis of religious and esthetic states is still in a pioneer stage and can be expected to yield a rich harvest in the future, this does not justify a methodological exclusion of other approaches. Well-founded expectation of scientific conquests should not be converted into an argument for the sole competence of a biologically patterned method of inquiry, such as Dewey proposes.

The existentialists accept Kierkegaard's distinction between objective and subjective truth. Heidegger sets off categorial from existential traits, calculative from ontological disciplines. Marcel has a similar contrast between problem and mystery, and Jaspers a contrast between the logic of the world and the clarification of existence. The pivotal distinction is between man regarded impersonally as a given natural thing and regarded in a reflective way as a free existent, responsible for setting his own attitudes. From this angle, philosophizing is not only the work of the individual but also takes its point of departure in awareness of individual selfhood. This is the proper basis of an existentialist philosophy which locates the act of existing primarily in the individual's free moral orientation. The existing self may be specified with Sartre as the prereflective Cogito, or with Heidegger as the point of confluence between being and the world, or with Marcel as the incarnate consciousness. In any case, its nature is accessible to the philosopher only on condition that he respect what is distinctive about man and about a perspective that arises from and implicates one's own nature. Man is the one being in whom there is reflective coincidence between inquirer and subject of inquiry. Man alone asks questions with reflective deliberation and with himself as a primary subject under inquisition. It is almost a proper existentialist definition of man that he is capable of posing questions about his own being and being in general. Appreciation of this unique capacity is the constitutive mark of the existential manner of philosophizing.

Finally, the existentialists make common cause in defense of the practical orientation of philosophy. There is a jejune sense in which most thinkers admit the need for both speculative and practical philosophy. But because of the close connection established between awareness of human freedom and philosophizing, the existentialists are obliged to break down this classical distinction. Their polemic against naturalism has led them into a similar exaggeration of the practical factor, although considered this time in a moral context. They are forced to deny that speculation is genuinely philosophical (in the sense of having existential import) unless it takes formal cognizance of man's free actions. They have introduced a practical, moral differentia into the very conception of philosophy as such, because of their inability to discover a distinctively speculative aspect of existence. Along with Kierkegaard, the truth they seek is the edifying truth. To be rated as philosophical, an inquiry must make a difference in one's practical attitude. Hence it is not surprising that, with few exceptions, existential investigations have subordinated the traditional ethical field to metaphysical and anthropological problems. The latter problems are handled in such a way that any distinct development of a moral philosophy would be a work of supererogation. This comes close to saying that the good existential philosopher and the good man are identical.

Fichte's remark about philosophizing out of a need for salvation is given a special metaphysico-moral twist by the existentialists. A great burden is placed upon the operation of philosophizing, since it is almost asked to take the place of conscience and individual acts of prudential judgment. The only way to pass from everyday, deceitful living to authentic human existence is to become aware of man's proper situation. This awareness is not a mere theoretical ascertainment and generalization but arises from a moral transformation of the individual's dynamic direction of will. Existential philosophizing is akin to Nietzsche's transvaluation of all values. It is a reconstruction of our existence from its roots. It not only has a practical end in view: it *is* the basic operational reordering of human attitudes and practices. This is the pragmatic import of existentialism.

2. *Descriptive Metaphysics.*

By whatever name they call it, the existentialists are striving after a renewal of metaphysics. To seek the renewal of a discipline implies that it has fallen on evil days and stands in need of reformation. The existentialists combine respect for the analogical unity of a perennial philosophy of being with strenuous criticism of the actual historical representatives of the metaphysical tradition. Somewhat uncritically, however, they consider the nineteenth-century idealistic systems to be the apogee of all past metaphysical speculations and hence the breakdown of these systems to be the confessed inadequacy of all previous approaches to being. This is the main support for the existentialist contention that a new context must be provided for the insights of the past, if they are to retain their germinal power of stimulating metaphysical research.

The existentialists share the convention of beginning the metaphysical inquiry with an analysis of the questioning self and its situation. Existence is reached most immediately and certainly in the existing self, although not even the existentialists can settle among themselves upon the exact nature of this self as revealed in a primary inspection. But they agree in according to the human mode of being a privileged position which it does not hold, for instance, in the initial moment of the metaphysics of St. Thomas or recent naturalism. For both existentialism and Thomism, metaphysics is ordained to a study of existence as the ultimate act of being. But since in the Thomistic view the act of existing is not restricted to a free human act of transcendence, but is the perfective act of every actual being, this perfection can be examined as analogically realized in all natural things. Moreover, the dependence of human intelligence upon sense perception seems to indicate that the primary affirmation of existence is made with respect to a natural thing, falling within the scope of the senses as well as of the intellect. John Dewey has often pointed out that many of the most widely distributed traits of existence are first observed, and sometimes best observed, in their non-human embodiment. This difference of opinion concerning the starting point of metaphysics suggests that the human self cannot be the sole foundation of an existential analysis.

What prevents the existentialists from accepting the theory of the complementarity of man and the rest of nature in regard to being is a fear lest it compromise the uniqueness of human existence. Can this uniqueness be preserved without limiting existence to man? The affirmative reply of Thomism is linked with its doctrine on the mutual proportion between the existence and the essential nature in *every* type of being. The more perfect the nature, the more perfect its proportionate existential act. Because man embodies the traits of natural being in the most comprehensive way, the act whereby his nature is placed in real existence is the most adequate one in the order of finite, material existents.

Another route is explored by Whitehead, who thinks it possible to universalize the libertarian notion of existence and yet maintain the special place of man in nature. All the marks of human existence, including a certain freedom, sensitivity, and striving, are attributed in varying measures to the other participants in concrete being. In this instance, the main concern is to assure not so much the distinctiveness of human existence as the natural foundation of its outstanding features. The Whiteheadian method rests on the premise that only those aspects of human being which are universally distributed in nature can be given philosophical standing.[1] This contention bears a curiously inverse relation to Sartre's notion that only those attributes can be asserted of the world which are traceable to some project or founding intention of the self. Whereas Whitehead is anxious to find analogies of human traits in the rest of nature as a condition for making warranted application of them to man, Sartre and Husserl admit in the make-up of the world only those factors which can certify a foundation in the constitutive act of human freedom.

The subject/object dichotomy is another favorite existentialist way of defending metaphysics. Kant pointed out how an affirmative answer might be given to his question about the possibility of metaphysics. Although it is not admissible as a science on the same footing with physical and mathematical sciences, it does fulfill a role in the analysis of practical life and its postulates. Here is one reason for the moralistic interpretation of philosophizing and existence so much in favor with the existentialists. Kant's distinction between the phenomenal world of objective necessity and the noumenal world of human freedom is the fountainhead for Heidegger's contrast between mundane categories and humane existential traits, as well as for Jasper's contrast between an ontology of the world and a metaphysics of human freedom and transcendence. The Kantian bifurcation enables Jaspers to assign a definite territory and method to metaphysics. Existential subjectivity, communication among persons, free search after the absolute, and the interpretation of the ciphers of transcendence fall within the scope of metaphysics and of metaphysics alone. But this distinctive standing is gained at the cost of a considerable narrowing of the field of metaphysics and a dualistic depreciation of the ontic significance of the objective world. Events in the natural world are at most ambiguous pointers, which refuse to yield up their message about the transcendent and which therefore frustrate the metaphysical project.

A further complication is introduced with the phenomenological reduction. It is possible for Sartre to distinguish between two ways of investigating existence: a pre- and a post-reductive method. Ordinary metaphysics attempts the hopeless task of understanding existents without having first reduced them to their essential structures, as intended by the self. This approach is fruitless, because it starts with a particular order of contingent existents, instead of arriving at the particular and contingent as moments in a universal, necessary explanation. If Sartre is the philosopher of freedom and contingency, it is only because he is first of all the phenomenologist of how a world in general *must* be constituted. The dualism between consciousness and material stuff, existence and given being, reappears in this phenomenological ontology. No ultimate unity of the science can be achieved, because there is no purely descriptive way to overcome the antinomy between the conscious subject and its environing setting of being. Rather than follow Husserl in his radical reduction of everything about the object to the transcendental self, Sartre bases his ontology on an acceptance of the absurd. There is no accounting for the morass of being, and the self-accounting of the projects of consciousness does not extend to a self-foundation in being. The only hope for this sort of ontology is a lucid appraisal of the futility of seeking after truly sufficient reasons.

It is the challenge of this Gidean paradox which gives point to the efforts of Marcel and Heidegger to discover a somewhat less attenuated basis of metaphysics. Marcel's restoration of the thinking self to the incarnate person and his recognition of an intellectual intuition of being, beyond the cleavage between subject and object, lay the groundwork for liberating existentialism from Descartes and Kant. The problem of metaphysics is given a new direction when the role of the senses is admitted in the judgment of existence. The co-operation of sense and intellect was methodically underplayed by Descartes in favor of a first truth grasped by an act of pure intelligence. Kant, on the other hand, limited the immediate grasp of being to sensuous intuition. Consequently, he refused to allow any strict knowledge of the supersensuous order of reality. Thus metaphysics was divorced from sensuous existence and ordered to the study of human subjectivity. Marcel regards the dilemma of sensuous versus intellectual intuition as an artificial predicament, caused by overlooking the properly human way of knowing. Human cognition is a synthesis of intellectual and sense factors, both of which are involved intuitively in the immediate affirmation of existence with which metaphysics begins.

Because our original acquaintance with existing being is intellectual, metaphysics need not be limited to the sensible, objective modes of being. Yet because the senses are also operative in the existential judgment, metaphysical knowledge is grounded in actual, sensible beings and does include an analysis of their way of existing. The initial apprehension of being is never attained in separation from particular, sensible instances of being. Hence Marcel regards the sensible world as a gateway to the transcendent, although it might be expected to serve some more permanent function in a philosophy which recognizes an infrangible union between being and incarnately grasped beings. At least, the minimal thesis is established that metaphysics treats of the transcendent only because of a discoverable orientation of sensuous existents in that direction. Metaphysics need no longer be described in Wolffian fashion as a quest after "the soul, the world and God," a trinity of ideal entities ungrounded in sensuous experience.

In specifying the method of existential metaphysics as a concrete one, Marcel believes himself to be in opposition to the Thomistic theory of abstraction. It is not entirely clear, however, whether he has an exact understanding of either the doctrine of "abstraction" or the provision made for the concrete in Thomistic philosophy. Aquinas regards metaphysical thinking not as a withdrawal from the reality of the concrete existent but as a means of grasping that reality in an intelligible way. The intellect does not empty out the concrete sensible existent from thought but at once affirms its immediately given reality and denies that the existential act must be confined to the material mode of being.[2] Thus the constitutive act that calls forth the metaphysical approach to things has its broad basis in sensible entities and our interior experience of an immaterial mode of existing. The various principles of being entering into the structure of material and immaterial modes of being are nothing other than the principles of concreteness, since finite being is realized only in individual, concrete acts of existing. Marcel himself illustrates the need to grasp the concrete otherwise than according to its own ineffable mode. In defense of the attitude of fidelity, for instance, he invokes man's power to disengage himself from immediate involvement in the vital stream, in order to make a comprehensive evaluation of his life in the light of supratemporal principles of permanent and universal import. Far from being inimical to the concrete qualities of human existence, such an abstractive act is the condition for understanding and promoting these traits.

Neither Marcel nor Heidegger is content with making a metaphysical analysis of human existence within its own limits. They regard this investigation as a means of access to being as such and to other modes of being. In order to escape from Husserl's transcendental solipsism, however, a descriptive method is not enough. For it tends to make existence a subclass within the wider sphere of intentional being or essential meaning and to accept as real only that which can eventually be given a direct appearance in consciousness. Description finds its proper realistic supplement in the method of causal implication and the discovery of principles of real being. Phenomenological description is a first phase in the metaphysical enterprise, but it cannot be followed exclusively without converting the study of being as being into a study of consciousness and its acts. Metaphysics is transformed into philosophical anthropology, unless description of human experience is supplemented by an attempt to draw out the existential implications of that experiential situation.

Marcel advises the metaphysician to dig or excavate rather than expend himself upon imposing but foundationless superstructures. In like manner, Heidegger seeks to get behind the particular modes of being of man and the world. These are precepts which outstrip the process of phenomenological description. For they call attention to the real causal conditions which determine the structure of human existence, the material world, and even the intentional world of purified consciousness. Without any formal recognition of the fact, there has been a renascence of the conception of metaphysics as a study of being in its causes and principles as well as in its existential act. Far from being incompatible (as Heidegger supposes, in accordance with

his narrowly categorial interpretation of cause), these aims are
coessential for giving contemporary meaning to the ancient formula of metaphysics: "the science of being as being."

3. *Man in the World.*

The most generally accepted existentialist proposition is that existence means having one's being as a human individual in the
world. From the conjunction of man and the world, the existentialist dialectic invariably takes its rise. Albert Camus sees in this
bond between the world and man an absurd juxtaposition of a
blind, relentless environment and a being incorrigibly given to
planning, hoping and seeking response from nature.[3] Camus
makes capital out of the evolutionist warning against reading
human purposes into nature and viewing the environment as
benevolently disposed toward man. He also translates Franz
Kafka's tales about the individual's bewilderment before natural
events and social conventions into a semiphilosophical theory of
universal nonsense and frustration. The only virtue is a dignified
acceptance of our Sisyphean tasks, with no illusions about ever
attaining permanently significant ends. This doctrine of absurdity is in open revolt against loose and sentimental interpretations
of the Christian belief that God has ordained material things to
minister to man's needs.

   Although there is a similar undercurrent of theological *res-
sentiment* in Sartre, he places his own theory of man-in-the-
world on a surer footing by employing the notion of intentionality. Franz Brentano, the great Viennese teacher and bridge
between Scholasticism and phenomenology, conveyed to Husserl something of the Scholastic teaching on the objectivity of
knowledge.[4] The intentional character of thought means that our
ideas are primarily about something other than ideas themselves.
This provided Husserl with a tool for overcoming psychological
subjectivism. Objects, not merely empirical states of consciousness, constitute the field of scientific knowledge. Furthermore,

particular objects fall within the general region of objectivity and submit to the general conditions determining the world. This is the phenomenological basis for explaining the common sense conviction that men work out their lives in the world. It also provides the background for existentialist descriptions of the mundane context of human existence.

Because consciousness intends a world in general, our mode of being is necessarily implicated in a world. Husserl's analysis concentrates upon the originary act whereby transcendental consciousness (which is taken as individual but not empirical) constitutes the world of meanings and relations within its own immanence. Sartre follows along the same path, with a significant reservation. He holds that consciousness itself, no matter how purified and autonomous, arises in an unintelligible way within the womb of unconscious being. Hence the founding act of consciousness produces a world order on the surface of amorphous being, without producing this inactive reality itself. Man's consciousness is the projective source whence proceed the meanings which are related as a world order. The world as an organized whole of rational purposes and relations is a human product, but this world is precariously carved out of the given *en-soi* and soon collapses into it again. Absurdity is here extended to the very meaning of a stable world, not merely to its relation to man, as in Camus' outlook. Camus' world is senseless because it pays no heed to human pleas and cajolings; Sartre's world is intrinsically senseless because it is overladen with human designs, seems to be independently ordered, and is nevertheless destined to relapse into an irrational quicksand.

In addition, Sartre finds it difficult to refer to *the* world. Men are individual existents and hence individual centers of consciousness. Each individual makes his own project of endowing a world with meaning, organization, and teleology. But the public world of science and intersubjective experience poses a problem for phenomenological reconstructions. Sartre prefers to attack it primarily in terms of personal relations, but Jaspers has the merit of facing it on the scientific level. He re-examines the Kantian distinction between empirical and transcendental consciousness. Although neither Kant nor Husserl implied that these represent two different spheres of being, they did leave the relation between empirical and transcendental consciousness sufficiently unspecified to allow for a public world based upon consciousness "in general." Jaspers does not ask whether this lack of specification is a convenient vagueness permitted precisely for achieving this end. Kant and Husserl wanted to preserve the reality of both individual conscious existence and scientific generality, but they wanted to do so within the framework of a theory of a priori constitutive forms of experience. Hence the dualism of aspects of consciousness was tailored to fit this purpose.

Jaspers is satisfied to account for the objective being of the world within the Kantian framework, so that existence may have a place of reference. Like Heidegger, he notes that the special sciences operate within the assumption of the world as a given whole. The aim of his philosophical logic is to gather all the objects of experience under their widest aspect. Kant's transcendental doctrines on space, time, and the categories are appropriated and enlivened by the influx of recent scientific findings. Jaspers renews Kant's correlation between consciousness in general and the world as the total set of conditions for the possibility of experience and empirical knowledge. The most general a priori traits constitutive of the world are rooted in the common structure of consciousness found among all human individuals. Hence we can all intend and agree upon the public world and the public standards of verification for our widest scientific propositions.

This explanation of the constitution of the world would be acceptable to modern Kantian philosophers of science and to those logical positivists (headed by C. I. Lewis) who assign an a priori origin to analytic truths.[5] Nevertheless, it labors under certain handicaps, some of importance to empirical realists and others of importance to existentialists. The former maintain that there is no more need to suppose the constitutive function of consciousness and its pure forms in the case of basic analytic propositions than in the formulation of empirical scientific laws. Both areas of truth rest on the fundamental submission of the mind to a given minimal, intelligible structure rather than to a given chaos, and on the willingness to test all propositions by their conformity to experience, whether it be actual or predictive. To reply that the "mind" in question is only the empirical aspect of consciousness is to assume that the source of intelligibility in nature can only be mind, in a nondivine sense. Scientific explanation prescinds from the question of a divine creator of the universe. In a theistic realism, the world derives its broadest unity and intelligibility from God, whereas our knowledge of this order is radically dependent upon the world itself. The mind must, indeed, render this organizational whole actually intelligible through its experiential discoveries of order and its practical production of order. But the predictive and practical attitude towards nature does not exclude the wide area in which a realistic openness to the actual ways of things is the only road to understanding.

From the existentialist standpoint, the chief difficulty concerns the relation of individual existents to universal, a priori categories. There is danger that what is "really real" about the individual will turn out to be a common mind, somewhat after the fashion of Averroes' separated intelligence or Hegel's Absolute. Even though Jaspers would deny a separation of transcendental consciousness from the world, he is obliged to define the sphere of immanence by the extent of a common form of consciousness. This is a circular procedure which leaves unclarified the kind of reality accorded to consciousness in general and the kind of necessity placed upon individual existents of sharing in this form. Jaspers recognizes this problem to the extent of declaring that the scientific explanation of the world is just as beset by antinomies as is the older metaphysical theory of Wolff and the rationalists. A philosophy based on the Newtonian conception of the world is liable to two errors. It tends to identify being as such with the phenomenal, objective being of the sensible universe and it prizes the human self mainly as a bearer of general categories. Jaspers objects that, though freedom and transcendence have their reality only in a being which is placed *in* the world, they cannot be reduced to modes *of* the objective world. Here again, the distinction between the subjective world of freedom and the phenomenal world of scientific objectivity becomes operative.

The challenging purpose of Marcel's philosophy is to accept the correlation between man and the world and yet to dissociate existential metaphysics from Kantian dualism. He has seen that if Jaspers' theory of consciousness in general is rejected, significant modifications must be introduced into the existentialist doctrine of the world. A first step in a new direction is made by holding that the sensible world is not only the habitat of existents but also possesses some existential traits in its own right. It is not sheer phenomenal objectivity but in the first instance is a participated mode of being. In and through our own bodies, the sensible world notifies us about its existential significance. Existent actuality is present not only *in* but *as* sensible modes of being, although the plenary form of existence is found in man's interior life of recollection and fidelity to the transcendent. The distinction between problem and mystery is not identical with Kant's distinction between scientific understanding and practical reason. Mystery bears upon the sensible world itself and gives theoretical knowledge about being even in its non-sensuous actuations.

There are several indications, however, that Marcel has made only a preliminary survey of this new perspective. He admits that the relation between being and existence is not fully clear. This relation is of utmost importance not only in the problem of God's existence but also in that of the world of things. The difficulty is more metaphysical than epistemological, since it is admitted that the non-human world has being. But it would seem that existence in the pregnant sense can be attributed to the world only in so far as it affects human freedom through the human body, as associated with the self. Marcel's primary interest in the material world is as a field for personal attitudes.

Space and time, for instance, are implicated in the sphere of existential mystery as having a bearing upon human destiny and the use of freedom. Like Louis Lavelle, Marcel gives existential recognition to the spatio-temporal world mainly on the ground of the moral problems raised by distance, separation, and endurance as a personal test.[6] The opportunities for betrayal, fidelity, and spiritual growth supply the space-time system with its chief claim for inclusion in the existential analytic. Whether this reference to man's spiritual trials is the *exclusive* ground of existential significance is not fully settled. At least, some indirect reference is apparently required. The human body becomes, in William James' figure, the storm center for all existential currents, theoretical and moral. Things in the world carry existential import as being sensibly related to my body. The natural region for bodily activity is a realm of existence because of its contribution to the individual's dialogue with fellow men and God. But is this all that is meant in affirming the global being of the world? Marcel does not fully integrate the theoretical affirmation of global being and the ethico-religious existential approach to the sensible world.

At this point, the distinctive character of Heidegger's problematic becomes apparent. His study of being-in-the-world is undertaken in order to effect the transition from a Kantian outlook to that of a new metaphysical realism. Against classical scientific mechanism, he stresses the practical character of the objective world. The scientific ordering of materials under organizational categories is not for the sake of arranging an epistemic spectacle but primarily for facilitating human control over the environment. This instrumentalist view is corroborated by noting that things take on meaning in the degree that they enter into human plans. Heidegger analyzes at length the distinction between brute entities as merely there before us in an indeterminate way and as definitely available or "at hand" in their status as tools. The truly human milieu is constituted by natural things in so far as they become incorporated into a network of human utensils. The scientific world is the world of useful things; it stands in the

service of the existential world formed by the individual self
with other existents.

It is into the world of tools or useful categories as well as into
the social world that the existent individual is plunged. This
world may well appear to him as something already completely
and impersonally formed: he need only fit himself into it in the
least conspicuous and least strenuous fashion. This is the attitude
of mediocrity or banal living, and it is literally death-dealing to
the dynamic aspirations of existence. The everyday interpretation of our predicament makes no special problem out of the
world. But the world retains its infraproblematic status only as
long as the self is content to remain a thing determined mainly
by outside forces and its proportionate responses. Fortunately,
life contains earthquakes, shocks of existence that rock the solid
basis of the impersonal outlook. The purpose of dread, care, anticipation of death, and like sentiments is to convince the individual that his soul or selfhood is under threat. Heidegger refers
to the voice of conscience as a device of the individual self for
assuming responsibility for its own being. A man assumes responsibility existentially by becoming aware of his situation as
a being already launched out in the world and headed toward his
own determination of the world. To become a self is to appreciate the power of human projects in organizing a world of significant temporal and historical relations, yet a world ordained
to one's own death.

Instead of arresting his analysis at this stage, however, Heidegger has gone on to inquire into a further dimension of man's
relation to his milieu. Two hints from nonphilosophical sources
have been particularly helpful. There is a line of religious testimony extending from St. Teresa of Avila and Pascal to Kierkegaard, the main burden of which is that "we are already
embarked," already placed in the world by God to work out our
salvation. This suggests that the placement of man in the world
is an ineluctable condition of his existence, indeed, but not a
senseless one. Man still retains his freedom of interpreting his
presence in the world and toward death. His plunge into the

mundane order may be regarded as something more than a brute hurtling into chaos, even though it remains true that the significance of human history requires the co-operation of our conscious projects. Man's being-there in the world may be seen as his being-sent-forth on a mission from being and toward being. The world would then bear still other traits than those imposed upon it by our practical, scientific interests.

This suggestion is confirmed by the second independent source consulted by Heidegger: the poets. From Hölderlin to Rilke, these lovers of beauty have been calling attention to other aspects of the natural world than those which are of technical and scientific importance. Man's presence in the world is that of a witness as well as of a master planner. He must tend to the demands of being as well as to his own needs, and he must see in nature something more than a storehouse for satisfying his desires and supporting his projects. The world is of esthetic, religious, and ontological significance, as well as being serviceable to man. Even its usefulness to man is thus extended, since it helps to recall him to his nobler vocation as the spokesman of being in the midst of beings.

Heidegger's present task is that of reconciling the viewpoint of saints and artists with that of scientists and metaphysicians. He is groping toward a philosophy of being which will do justice to both sets of deliverances, which will uncover the common ground between the "Hymn to Brother Son" and the "Treatise on the Cosmos." His own hesitancy reflects the general existentialist division of opinion about the significance of man's orientation to the world. The existentialists have not yet developed a metaphysics of existence based squarely upon the theoretical affirmation of existential act and the implications of this affirmation. Until such a basis is secured, the existentialists will have no central tableland from which to evaluate the scientific and ethico-religious notions of the world. The differences between the objective and the reflective approaches to man's mundane condition cannot be emphasized indefinitely in the face of the similarities and convergences. A synoptic treatment of the question is required, so as to take account of both methodological differences and areas of mutual reinforcement and communication between science and existential reflection.

4. *Man and Fellow Man.*

There is no sharp distinction between the problem of the world and that of the human community. For one's fellow men also belong to the zone of the other and must first be approached through the medium of things. Just as the individual self must pass from the condition of a given thing to that of a responsible existent, so a similar transition is required in the individual's relations with his fellow humans. At first, social relations belong to the undifferentiated problem of the self and the world. Only as the individual comes to have awareness of his own distinctive nature, does he also realize the special quality of his dealings with other centers of subjectivity and freedom. The social relationship is not established in its distinctive nature until the possibility of transcending the network of things and tools is recognized by the self.

There is, however, a remarkable correspondence in existentialist philosophies between the general doctrine on man-in-the-world and the theory of society. This is plainly seen in Sartre's case, since he decides social issues on the basis of his general commitments on the nature of the world.[7] He rejects the hope of his fellow existentialists that communal forms of being can be placed on a satisfactory basis. This denial is not the fruit of direct inspection of the whole gamut of societal existence but is, a rigorous deduction from his phenomenological premises. Sartre's concern is not so much with intersubjective knowledge in the scientific sense as with the personal efforts at mutual understanding and the emotional acts that bear a social reference. The existence of other egos presents no trouble to him, even though their reality is by no means evident from his starting point in the transcendental consciousness of the individual self. His example of the stare of one person outstaring another or embarrassing another is a psychological argument which is perfectly compatible with transcendental solipsism. Within the purified consciousness of the individual there is room for conflicts and disintegrations among the empirical attitudes.

In addition to allowing the existence of other selves, Sartre also admits a deep-seated desire for social harmony among men. It would be as futile to try to account for this social tendency as for any other given fact of our existence. Man is just as irrationally devoted to seeking an understanding with other men as to attempting to become divine or to constitute a world. Indeed, it is in function of the direction of consciousness to the world and God that Sartre settles the social question in an a priori way. Every entity other than myself figures in my consciousness as an object in my world. My native inclination is to order all the objects I encounter according to the pattern of my private project. Some of these objects are recognized as being other selves, but they must also submit to the general law of the subject and its subordinate objects. However, the resistance of selves to my imperialistic designs is different than that of things, since other people are also centers of consciousness and freedom. Each man has his own subjective perspective, within which he tries to fit other men as facets reflecting a central brilliance. Thus there is an inevitable clash of private worlds and personal projects.

Since social life is a mutual robbing of the other man's subjective integrity, the basic social form is hate. All other attitudes are variations on the dominant theme of hatred, either in an overt or in a concealed, hypocritical way. Sartre is especially insistent on the impossibility of overcoming hatred through motives of love, personal respect, or belief in God. It is just as natural to desire a loving, interpersonal, human community as to desire to become God—and just as impossible of fulfillment. For love tries to unite the self as consciousness with the beloved *as* an ordered element in one's cosmos, *as* a thing which regards the self as an absolute. Love therefore conceals an explosive contradiction that is bound to revert to hatred. It hides a desire to trick the beloved into becoming an object in the lover's world, a worshipper before his own divinity. Since the beloved is motivated by a similar purpose, all social efforts are doomed to failure. Sartre pours his empirical analyses into this rigid mould, choosing only those instances where some sort of hatred and lust are implicit.

Sartre's extreme doctrine has not met with acceptance from the other existentialists. But, like every pure position, it has had the salutary effect of clearing the atmosphere of equivocations and challenging a radical reconsideration of the problem. It has confirmed Marcel's view that phenomenological description is not adequate for all philosophical tasks. This method must be founded on a prior apprehension of being and subordinated to a further reflection. Unless its claim to autonomy is removed at both the initial and the terminal points of the phenomenological reduction, there is no way to emerge from the inclosure surrounding the lonely, purified consciousness. Other selves can figure only as factors within one's self-consciousness in a view which does not begin with an affirmation of the absolute givenness of being. Being is shared in by many participants and yet surpasses them all. Like the world, the human community is a relationship founded upon a perfection distributed among all the members, without owing its origin to the projective consciousness of a purified individual ego.

Apart from a basic reformation of method, Marcel also suggests that a fresh descriptive approach should be made to social situations claiming to be founded on love. Love is present only on condition that the beloved is respected as another self, an inviolable source of personal freedom. What is asked of the other is a free response of love, a response that can be given by the other only *qua* a personal subject, irreducible to the status of a captive thing. Social union motivated by love finds its typical expression not in an act of appropriation and submission, modeled after Hegel's dialectic of master and slave, but in a mutual giving of selves and sharing in a common activity, after the manner of friend and friend. Friendship is destroyed when the victor-vanquished attitude intrudes, but there is no metaphysical necessity for such an intrusion. A free, moral decision to universalize the phenomenological method lies at the bottom of the Sartrean self's refusal to treat other men in any other way than as potential materials for the construction of his own world. This refusal deliberately closes the way to the creation of a shared social reality rather than proves its impossibility.

Marcel has helped revive the insights of Feuerbach and Kierkegaard into the I-Thou relation.[8] A humane community rests upon the moral resolve to treat another man as a person rather than as a thing, as a *thou* rather than as an *it*. One's social conduct is thus regulated by a cognitive appreciation of the reality of other personal existents. Yet recognition of the thou-character of another means more than classification of him in a privileged group of objects. It stems from an awareness of that in the other entity which is not objective and which does not coincide with mere thinghood. Just as the existential judgment affirms the actuality of that which can never be reduced to my mental states, so the personal nature of another is irreducible to an objective component in my field of intentional projects. Far from frustrating the social design, this realistic self-restraint before the inalienable personality of another is the condition for community life. When this recognition animates practical behaviour, it serves to differentiate the attitude of the friend and lover from that of the technician and conqueror.

Incisive reasons for the personalist foundation of human society are advanced by Jaspers.[9] He notes that the individual, in treating the other as a fellow existent or self, not only contributes to social reality but also perfects himself as an individual. The other is a mirror of one's self, and to love the other is to treat him as oneself. Learning how to act properly toward another person is a lesson in self-knowledge as well. The individual self does not attain his mature growth of self-possession until he has developed his capacities for social intercourse. When the other being passes from the status of an *it* to a *thou*, there is a corresponding transformation in the self, who discovers the meaning of being related now to an objective thing and now to the subjective integrity of a person. There are some aspects of his own freedom which refuse to reveal themselves as long as a man restricts himself to the subject-object relationship. Not until the differences between impersonal control and interpersonal communion are practically experienced, can a man realize his full potentialities as a person.

Personal existence is coexistence not with things but with fellow men. All beings make some sort of response to the individual existent concerned about them. But, as Heidegger observes, the quality of our concern becomes differentiated when it is engaged first by things and then by other selves. Genuine solicitude is only forthcoming when another free form of being is involved, for in this case there is room for response at the same level. Jaspers' psychological studies substantiate this philosophical conviction that human society rests on mutuality among fellow selves. The *we*-form of being develops only between individuals who respect each other as free subjects. The various kinds of societies bring out different phases of the communal mode of existing. Jaspers employs two criteria for determining the authenticity of social modes of existing and the value of their free projects: their aptitude to promote the attitude of seeking beyond the finite world and their contribution to human communication. Achievement of mutual understanding through personal communication is among the major goals of the existential dialectic of transcendence. The main lines of tension in existence run from man to man and from man to God. For both Marcel and Jaspers, the availability and openness of one human self to another correspond to the openness of existence as a whole to the transcendent.

Marcel, who holds that God is personal as well as transcendent, adds that the trust which is needed for stable communal life among men is generated along with our mutual fidelity to the divine Thou. One way to learn how to remain loyal toward a fellow human person is to be mindful of one's religious intercourse with a personal God. Furthermore, the pledge of one's self for the future, so essential for constituting reliable human social bonds, rests in the final analysis upon our hope in the eternal and its powerful presence in time. Marcel sees an analogy between approaching God as a person and approaching other men as persons, since in both cases the basic social virtues of fidelity and hope are the animating principles of the social mode of existing. Without the strength of these virtues, the individual will be fearful of opening himself by way of just dealings and love for others. His social situation will remain one of dire necessity and mistrust, approximating his attitude toward things. It is this degeneration of community life which Sartre regards as its highest flowering.

Sartre's scepticism about the social views of the other existentialists derives partly from his denial of God and religion and partly from his methodology. He argues that if the religious quest is vain, it is also vain to look for a sanction and support of secular social enterprises in a religious prototype. In reply, it will be noted that descriptions of existence, even within a secular and finite frame of reference, show the presence of genuine social orders which do not manifest themselves as disguised forms of hate. Co-operation in games, scientific research, family life (which, as such, is overlooked by Sartre), and civil society can be instanced. In the philosophical order, Heidegger's account of "being-there-with" or human coexistence is the best example of a nonreligious but existential analysis of adequate societal modes of being.[10] Far from widening the chasm between selves, Heidegger's investigations show that the possibilities of existence are only incompletely actuated until they give birth to a manner of being along with other selves in a common work of freedom.

Heidegger's theory of *being-with* as a fundamental mode of human existence forces Sartre to retreat to his last bastion: the exigencies of phenomenological method. He contends that Heidegger's postulation of a social reality is similar to his postulation of the world, time, and history. Heidegger establishes a most intimate connection between the self and the space-time world in which it exists. He has given an anthropological interpretation of Kant's doctrine on space and time as forms of sensibility and transcendental conditions of all experience. The individual existent is by nature a transcending project in a forward direction. Hence its very existential dynamism temporalizes and exteriorizes itself as a temporal and spatial world having history. Similarly, the existent self projects itself in the direction of other selves, attempting to organize other free selves within its own world. Sartre presses the analogy between Heidegger's theory of the transformation of brute natural things into handy tools and the transformation of other individual existents into components in my milieu. Each of these other selves, in turn, constitutes its milieu in terms of a subordination of the remaining selves who are jointly there in the world. Hence Sartre claims that his own conclusion follows logically from these premises, despite Heidegger's intention to the contrary.

Unfortunately, Heidegger has not yet completed (or, at least, published) his revision of the analytic of existence in the light of his general ontology. But he has indicated the effect of his later position upon his former theory of the world, thus undermining Sartre's principal line of exegesis. The technical world produced by man does not exhaust the ontological significance of the natural beings gathered on "the earth." Respect must be had for the intrinsic intelligibility and organization of beings independently of human technical projects. Man can share in these traits and discover their import for existence without destroying them or converting them into a humanly derived pattern, but this is possible only because the phenomenological reduction is itself overcome. Whether a similar revision will be made in the doctrine on time, history, and coexistence remains to be seen. There is a hint that this is being done in the case of time and history. Heidegger refers briefly to the significance of history not only for understanding the temporal and historical structure of the existent self but also for grasping the relation of being to the world of beings.[11] It is reasonable to expect that similar modifications will be introduced into the doctrine on coexistence, since Heidegger has consistently bound it up with his general view of the world and time.

To exist means to be there in the world along with other selves.

Heidegger agrees with Marcel and Jaspers that mutual relation among selves is required for the perfection of human existence. Other existents cannot be approached as utensils but only as free selves, jointly present in and to the world. Sartre's objections center around the way in which the existent self constitutes itself as existing along with others in a mutual world. Heidegger's revision of the radical phenomenological constitution of being can be extended to include the Sartrean theory of mutually conflicting personal worlds, if the latter be proposed as the necessary and sole form assumed by human society. Just as there can be some effective union with the beings of nature apart from the projection of a world, so there can be a way of access to other selves otherwise than as a subject relates itself to its objects or to its possible conquerors. The stewardship of being is not the exclusive concern of any one existent individual but can be shared by him along with others. This sense of a joint vocation may have a retroactive effect upon one's attitudes concerning other forms of social union. An individual's solicitude for others and with others for the common ends of society stems naturally from a common solicitude for assuring the recognition of being in the world. Once more, it is not metaphysical necessity but a free decision that leads to Sartre's despair about man's social use of freedom.

5. Man and God.

The existentialists take seriously the widespread withdrawal of intelligent men from God and religion during the past century and a half. They are dissatisfied with the more facile and complacent explanations of this alienation made in the name of economic materialism, social democracy, and evolutionary rationalism. Since these current shibboleths fail to touch upon the predicament of man as an individual existent, they explain away without touching the real problem. The existentialists attempt to harmonize their account of this defection with their broader positions on man and transcendence. They also regard the investigations on God and religiousness as having the highest practical import in an age of religious crisis. This is in conformity with their common concern for the practical fruits of philosophizing.

The existentialist approaches to God run the gamut from atheism to Christianity, with philosophical faith and discreet refusal to make a philosophical commitment serving as intermediate steps. Yet the various representatives agree upon two propositions. A fresh appraisal of the nature of God is imperative, and a movement of transcendence towards the infinite belongs to man's connatural drive. The first or historical thesis is compatible even with Marcel's Christianity, the second or descriptive thesis even with Sartre's atheism.

The existentialists resemble Kierkegaard in being correctives of their age in matters religious, critics whose judgments are admittedly conditioned by particular historical circumstances. They inquire how such a swift passage could be made from Hegel's philosophy of religion, apparently the apogee in the philosophical defense of God and Christianity, to Nietzsche's pitiless shattering of the religious idols. Sartre, in this instance, makes full acceptance of historical determinism. In the person of Nietzsche, Western consciousness has passed irretrievably beyond the capacity for honest belief in God. Hereafter, such belief may be treated as a sign of weak evasion or deliberate bad faith. Sartre regards himself as the headsman of the Hegelian dialectic, depriving it of the Absolute as the origin and end of temporal process. Unhappy consciousness, or the sense of futility surrounding all our projects of transcendence, is no longer to be regarded as a transitional state, spurring men on to a real transcendence of their limitations in the self-consciousness of the Absolute. On the contrary, this mood expresses the permanent human condition, from which there is no deliverance, except in its deliberate acceptance as our fate. Nietzsche's *amor fati* is given a somewhat activistic and strident interpretation by Sartre, who fears lest it lend semblance to the charge of moral quietism. He points out that not even Husserl's notion of the self can bring tranquillity, since consciousness is a thoroughly immanent and ungrounded event. One cannot attempt an absolute constitution of being, without providing a secular counterpart to the pitiful religious conatus towards self-divinization.

Another solution of the Hegel-Nietzsche problem is advanced by the other existentialists. They look upon Hegel's philosophy as the most comprehensive expression of previous metaphysics but not as the supreme expression of Christianity. Their caution on the religious issue reflects Kierkegaard's critique of the Hegelian philosophy of religion. They agree with their Danish predecessor that religion is not merely a moment in the absolute dialectic which must be sublated in order to attain the complete philosophical synthesis. Decapitation of the Hegelian dialectic can be made in the interests of religious autonomy as well as in an antireligious spirit. The Judaeo-Christian religious outlook springs from the living God of Abraham rather than from the logical nudity of the Absolute Idea, and hence it resists incorporation into the final concretion of the Absolute as a total philosophical system. Marcel and Heidegger agree that the Hegelian philosophy of religion is no more an adequate theoretical statement of Christian truth than is industrial capitalism its characteristic social embodiment. Hence they regard the attacks of Marx and Nietzsche as inadvertent means of purifying Christianity from philosophical and social distortions rather than as mortal wounds dealt the substance of religious life. Jaspers is more reserved, since he is in partial sympathy with Nietzsche's strictures against ecclesiastical institutions.

Unlike Kierkegaard, however, the existentialists who admit a distinctive religious standpoint are not opposed to a philosophical treatment of existence. It has taken over a century for absolute idealism to complete its disintegration. But its dissolution coincides with the beginning of a new period of philosophical speculation on existence freed from the spectre of Hegelianism. Jaspers, who is most akin to Hegel in this respect, regards the content of truth in the religious tradition as at least theoretically reducible to a basic philosophical faith. To philosophize about existence "from the origins" is to become aware of the common springs of both religious and philosophical faith. But it is an error of rationalism to suppose that a historical and cultural reduction of the one tradition to the other is feasible, universally desirable, and inevitable in the dialectic of history. Jaspers regards it as a practical necessity that most people receive their nourishment of existential truths from religious sources, which are present in factual independence of philosophy. He is willing to strike a balance at the practical level between philosophical rationalism and the historical biblical expression of religion. Only when the Christian Church makes claim to unconditional autonomy and exclusiveness of revelation does the spirit of compromise fade. For in this instance, Jaspers sees a threat to the integrity of philo- sophical faith and to the social bonds among men of good will everywhere.

Heidegger is not convinced by Jaspers' argument that direct and adequate revelation from God is incompatible with the ex- istential values of communication and transcendence. Hence he is ready to grant at least the possibility of revelation of the word of God as well as the existence of God. But he is no more moved than Marcel by the classical proofs for God's existence or by conventional Christian apologetics. It is as necessary to rethink the problems of God and Christianity as to recast metaphysics and philosophical anthropology. Marcel goes beyond Heidegger in affirming that the forces of renewal are actually present within the Christian communion itself. Hence his concrete philosophy does not stop at the threshold of the possibility of God's exist- ence. It is a new positive defense of theism and of those natural virtues which provide the normal subsoil for the Christian life.

The inconclusiveness of the descriptive method is illustrated by the existentialist theories of transcendence and its attendant states of soul. The inherent dynamism of existence prompts the individual to seek outside himself, to become ec-static in the non- mystical sense of being mindful of the other. The world, the temporal process of history, human society—all are constituted by the ec-static activity proper to the existent self. The movement of transcendence is not confined, however, to enlarging the individual's perspective beyond the present bodily limits, the present moment of time, and the presently possessed private good. The world of utensils, other men, and history is insufficient to satisfy the expansive urge of the self for a perfective union with the other in being. The attitude of transcending is ultimately founded on a nisus to reach beyond the world as a whole. Augustine's saying about the inquietude of the human heart, until it comes to rest in God, is recognized by the existentialists as a religious witness to the final intention of transcendence. Man moves forward and outward not only towards the future and the world at hand but also toward God. As Kierkegaard shrewdly observed, eternity assumes the form of the future in the perspective of temporal existence.

Sartre's atheism is not irreligious in the sense of denying the radical centering of transcendence upon God. But his entire phenomenological ontology is a convoluted expansion of the proposition that the object of transcendence is a contradictory phantom, which can be neither realized nor exorcized. Instead of following the lead of Feuerbach and Marx in draining off the religious motivation to a struggle for humanity or the triumph of the proletariat, Sartre takes complacence in describing our human lot as a stark quest after that which can never be realized in itself or in its finite surrogates. His approach to the characteristic existential situations of dread, freedom, moral choice, and death is a sustained homily on the wisdom of disillusioned atheism. We should always conduct our affairs with the memento that the world is all in all and that nevertheless men are eternally attempting to flee from it in order to secure a divine foundation. Sartre's descriptive elaborations of this underlying theme provide the counterpoint to the theistic exegesis of transcendence.

Jaspers and Marcel face this situation frankly and hence refuse to make an exception in their own favor to their doctrine on freedom. For Jaspers, the signs pointing to the absolute are essentially ambiguous and hooded, so that a universally accepted reading of them cannot be expected or desired. A man must first endure the experience of having his certitudes about God contradicted and shattered, before he can make a personally valid decision about transcendence. Philosophy of existence gives him assurance not about his definite convictions concerning the transcendent being but only about the impossibility of finding assurance one way or the other in the commitments made by other people. Jaspers testifies that his own conception of existence requires him to accept the existence of the one God, but he deliberately repels the inclination of others to let the matter be settled upon his word. His word remains ineffably his own, as far as its truth is concerned. Each man must win his own vision of philosophical faith.

Marcel wants to retain the metaphysical option, without espousing philosophical agnosticism. A definite choice, though not an arbitrary one, is called for by the very conditions of our existence. Its temporal and global aspects both invite the denial of God and at the same time offer a gateway to the transcendent. But that gateway cannot be entered without undergoing a trial of freedom. One must have felt course through his soul the full attractiveness of a doctrine of total immanence, before earning the right to affirm God's existence and our hope of union with Him. A moral scrutiny of the exercise of one's freedom lies at the threshold of metaphysics, if for no other reason than that the acceptance or rejection of being as participation is a human act anterior to every philosophy. Unlike Jaspers, however, Marcel locates the fundamental option at the beginning of philosophizing rather than at its end, so that thought does not culminate in a doubt about the entire process of speculation. Moreover, this option has its origin in the moral factors involved in the appraisal of being, rather than in any radical incapacity of finite existence to manifest something definite, though woefully faint, about the being of the transcendent. Hence for Marcel the typical virtue conditioning all philosophizing is humility in the presence of the utter givenness of being, whereas for Jaspers it is fortitude to stand erect amidst the ruins of existence.

Heidegger allows that, at least in a negative way, the particular beings in the world can convey something about that which transcends the totality of beings. This possibility engages our freedom, however, since we may deliberately turn our attention from the significance of being as such. Heidegger's gradual unfolding of his own position enables him to serve as a bridge between the extremes of atheism and theism. His finite analytic of human existence provided a paradigm for Sartre, who went on the assumption that it represented an adequate statement of the human condition. Thus it is understandable both why the atheistic version of existentialism arose and also why it contains within itself the seeds of its own destruction. Heidegger's later account of how the finite analytic is to be fitted into the context of being removes one major pillar from the edifice of atheistic existentialism. Furthermore, Heidegger questions the sufficiency of the phenomenological method and thus reopens the discussion about Sartre's starting point. Once the contingent world is placed within brackets, all attempts of man to reach the transcendent do end in contradiction and frustration. But it is not evident that an existential philosophy must begin with this bracketing and with the further operation of reducing all data to the sphere of transcendental consciousness, the prereflective Cogito.

Whether Heidegger's own restriction of analysis to a finite view of being is warranted, belongs among the problems still to be debated. He has not taken a stand on whether the religious attitude represents a *sui generis* act of transcendence, aiming at surpassing the limits assigned by him to general ontology. There are methodological obstacles hindering a thorough consideration of this question. For it would be difficult to propose a solution without implying that philosophy can establish something meaningful and certain about the infinite being, God, as the goal of religious transcendence. If this were admitted, then existential philosophy would have to distinguish between God as a religious reality and being as such. In actual fact, Heidegger has only said that being as such cannot be confounded with that notion of God which is modeled after the particular modes of being. He cannot say more without criticizing his own attack on metaphysics and his own theory of being as such.

One critic of existentialism, Leo Gabriel, has stated that the discourse on man's nondivinity is the prelude to a further discourse on the reality of the transcendent God. If existentialism is ever to acquire more than problematic unity, these two phases in the dialectic of existence must be rendered continuous. Only the actual attempt to carry out this program will show whether or not this viewpoint has the internal resources to attain a mature synthesis. The open, progressive character of existential philosophizing is a pledge that such an effort will be made, always respecting the rightful bounds of a philosophical pluralism. It is rash to make further predictions with respect to a tradition which has by no means hardened its categories or foresworn the ways of venturesome exploration. Either under their own power or in alliance with an existential metaphysics of the infinite and the finite modes of being, the existentialists will have to reconsider their major themes, now that the first outlines have been sketched.

NOTES

NOTES

(Complete bibliographical information is given in the notes only for
those references that are not also included in the Bibliography.)

NOTES TO CHAPTER I. EXISTENTIAL BACKGROUNDS.

1. Princeton, N. J., Princeton University Press, 1946; a more explicit
social diagnosis is made in *The Present Age*. New York, Oxford University Press, 1940. See my article, "Three Kierkegaardian Problems, III: The
Nature of the Human Individual." *The New Scholasticism*, Vol. 23, 1949.
2. A concise outline is provided in *Concluding Unscientific Postscript*.
Princeton University Press, 1941, pp. 261-65. A more elaborate and
poetic presentation of this triadic schema is the theme of *Stages on Life's
Way*. Princeton, Princeton University Press, 1940.
3. The classical text is found in *Concluding Unscientific Postscript*, pp.
99-133.
4. *Training in Christianity* (New York, Oxford University Press, 1941)
is a positive presentation of Kierkegaard's religious position; the more polemical side is stressed in *Attack upon Christendom*. Princeton, Princeton
University Press, 1944.
5. All page references to Nietzsche are to the convenient collection:
The Philosophy of Nietzsche. New York, Modern Library edition. It contains *Thus Spake Zarathustra, Beyond Good and Evil, The Genealogy of
Morals, Ecce Homo*, and *The Birth of Tragedy from the Spirit of Music;*
separate pagination for each work. On the criticism and revaluation of
morals, see *Zarathustra*, pp. 126-27; *Good and Evil*, pp. 114-18, 135-36,
200-204; *Ecce Homo*, pp. 133 ff.
6. The announcement of God's death and the collapse of transcendent
values are set forth in *Zarathustra*, pp. 26-28, 97-100, 259-63 (Zarathustra's
meeting with "the last pope"), p. 186. W. Kaufmann, in *Nietzsche: Philosopher, Psychologist, Antichrist*, pp. 77-79, has recently maintained that
Nietzsche is not an atheist but an agnostic and that his verdict of God's
death is a factual cultural report of our loss of belief rather than a metaphysical denial. The existentialists seem closer to the spirit of Nietzsche
when they hold that his cultural pronouncement is itself founded upon a
metaphysical and moral view, in which there is no room for a transcendent, creative God.
7. For the assault upon the ideal of objective, scientific truth, see *Good
and Evil*, pp. 1-10; *Genealogy*, pp. 160-66.

8. *L'Imagination*, p. 139.

9. Husserl's own summary remains unsurpassed: "Philosophie als strenge Wissenschaft." *Logos*, Vol. 1, 1911. The best English summary of Husserl's scientific ideal is M. Farber's *The Foundation of Phenomenology: Edmund Husserl and the Quest for a Rigorous Science of Philosophy*.

10. On the conjunction, in existentialism, between Kierkegaard's existential content and Husserl's structural universality, see A. De Waelhens, "Les constantes de l'existentialisme," *Revue internationale de philosophie*, Vol. 3, pp. 256, 263, 1949.

11. Cf. Husserl's own sketch of his final tendency: "Die Krisis der europäischen Wissenschaften und die transzendentale Phänomenologie." *Philosophia*, Vol. 1, 1936. This phase of his thought is by no means known in detail, since thousands of manuscript pages are only now being prepared for publication by the Husserl Archives at Louvain. For a brief account of his transcendental idealism, consult Husserl's article on phenomenology in the fourteenth edition of *Encyclopaedia Britannica* (1929), and Husserl's Preface to the English edition of *Ideas*. Translated by W. Gibson. New York, Macmillan Company, 1931.

12. There is an extended treatment of this problem in the fifth of Husserl's *Méditations cartésiennes*. Translated by G. Peiffer and E. Levinas. Paris, Joseph Vrin, 1931; the German original has only recently been issued: *Cartesianische Meditationen und Pariser Vorträge*. The Hague, Martinus Nijhoff, 1950.

NOTES TO CHAPTER II. SARTRE.

1. Sartre gives brief sketches of the views of Husserl and Heidegger on intentionality: *L'Imagination*, chap. 4; *The Emotions*, pp. 11-15; *Situations*, I, 31-35.

2. *L'Imagination*, pp. 1-2.

3. *L'Etre et le néant*, pp. 713-14 (henceforth cited as *Etre*). "Ontology seems to us capable of being defined as the explanation of the structures of the being of the existent, taken as a totality, and we will define metaphysics rather as the interrogation of the existence of the existent" (*Etre*, pp. 358-59). Strictly speaking, Sartre's philosophy is an ontology of essential structures rather than a metaphysics of existence in its contingent actuality.

4. *Existentialism*, p. 15.

5. *Etre*, p. 11.

6. *Ibid.*, p. 16.

7. Sartre's most trenchant criticism of Descartes and Husserl is contained in "La Transcendance de l'ego: Esquisse d'une description phé-

noménologique." *Recherches philosophiques*, Vol. 6, 1936-37. The results are incorporated into *Etre* (pp. 18-20) where he proposes to call the primitive state of consciousness "conscience [de] soi," lest it be taken for the derivative case where the self is an object *of* consciousness. For Sartre's relations with Descartes, Husserl, and Heidegger, cf. G. Varet, *L'Ontologie de Sartre*, chap. 5; F. Jeanson, *Le Problème morale et la pensée de Sartre*, part I, chap. 4.

8. Perhaps it is this practical, even moral, interpretation of phenomenological method which leaves Sartre open to the charge that he really abandons Husserl's path by failing to make a complete reduction of the natural attitudes found generally among men. This is the criticism offered by M. Natanson in *A Critique of Jean-Paul Sartre's Ontology*, pp. 104-5. Actually, there is an unresolved tension in Sartre's thought between an effort to make an even more radical and "purified" analysis of consciousness than did Husserl and an equally strong desire to take immediate advantage of ordinary perspectives. Natanson quite rightly points to Hegel's notion of phenomenology as a forerunner of Sartre's approach; the psychological method of Nietzsche leads in the same direction.

9. *Etre*, pp. 27-29. It is in making this return to the testimony of ordinary attitudes that Sartre leaves unclarified exactly how far his phenomenological reduction reaches. In establishing his realistic conclusion, he treats the intentionality of consciousness in a psychological way. But this may be a proof *ambulando* that no strict derivation of a rational sort is possible for the In-itself.

10. *Ibid.*, p. 29.

11. The relevant section has been separately translated: "The Root of the Chestnut Tree." *Partisan Review*, Vol. 13, 1946.

12. See the evaluation by S. Vanni Rovighi, " 'L'Essere e il nulla' di J.-P. Sartre." *Rivista di filosofia neoscolastica*, Vol. 40, 1948.

13. *Etre*, pp. 37 ff.

14. *Ibid.*, p. 57.

15. *De Anima*, 417a 12-20, 429b 22 to 430a 15; *The Basic Works of Aristotle*. Ed. R. McKeon. New York, Random House, 1941, pp. 565, 591-92. For a comparative analysis, cf. C. Fabro, "Il significato dell'esistenzialismo." *Esistenzialismo* (See Bibliography, number 23), p. 21.

16. "A propos de l'existentialisme: Mise au point," *Action*, Dec. 29, 1944; *Existentialism*, pp. 15 ff. A comparison between Sartre and Aquinas concerning the relation between essence and existence is made by B. Pruche in *Existentialisme et acte d'être*, pp. 52-63; G. Phelan, "The Existentialism of Saint Thomas," *Proceedings of the American Catholic Philosophical Association*, Vol. 21, 1946.

17. *Existentialism*, pp. 45-47; cf. Marcel, *Being and Having*, p. 106.

18. Sartre admits (*Etre*, p. 715) that his ontology contains a great contra-

diction in regard to the origin of consciousness. All the evidence points to a state of affairs in which the *en-soi* tries to found itself. But to do this, it would already have to enjoy a certain self-presence, that is, it would have to be endowed with consciousness as a condition for producing consciousness. Hence Sartre abandons the problem to a hypothetical metaphysics.

19. "Existentialism is nothing else than an attempt to draw all the consequences of a coherent atheistic position" (*Existentialism*, pp. 60-61). For his remarks on atheism as a counterpostulation to theism, cf. the discussion following his conference on *Existentialism Is a Humanism*, as reported by P. Descoqs in "L'Athéisme de Jean-Paul Sartre." *Revue de philosophie*, p. 57, note 13, 1946. This pervasive atheism is verified, at the personal plane, by M. Beigbeder in *L'Homme Sartre*, pp. 27 ff., 136

20. *Etre*, pp. 123-24, 133.

21. "The being toward which human reality surpasses itself is not a transcendent God: it is at the heart of human reality and is only this reality as a totality. . . . When this totality of being and absolute absence is hypostasized as transcedence beyond the world, by a further movement of meditation, it receives the name of God" (*Etre*, p. 133).

22. *Ibid.*, pp. 32, 287, 299.

23. Sartre writes that since the existent is a being which has to "exist its being," there can be no divorce of ontology and ethics, and no difference between a man's moral attitude and what the Germans call his *Weltanschauung* (Preface to Jeanson, *Le Problème morale et la pensée de Sartre*, p. 14). *Etre* concludes with a brief section on "moral perspectives" (pp. 720-22). For Beauvoir's remark, see *The Ethics of Ambiguity*. Translated by B. Frechtman. New York, Philosophical Library, 1948, pp. 10-11.

24. "Every human reality is a passion, in that its project is to lose itself so as to found being and constitute, at the same stroke, the In-itself which escapes contingency in being its own foundation: the *Ens causa sui*, which the religions call God. Thus man's passion is the opposite of Christ's, for man loses himself *qua* man so that God may be born. But the idea of God is contradictory, and we lose ourselves in vain. Man is a useless passion" (*Etre*, p. 708). Human reality, therefore, can never extricate itself from its unhappy state (*ibid.*, p. 134).

25. *Etre*, pp. 653-54.

26. *Existentialism*, p. 61.

27. T. Wilder, *The Ides of March*. New York, Harper & Brothers, 1948, p. 37. For Marcel's observation, see *The Philosophy of Existence*, p. 60.

28. *Etre*, p. 521. Sartre gives an ontological justification for these views. "The freedom of the For-itself thus appears as its *being*. But since this freedom is not a given, nor a property, it can be only as choosing itself. The freedom of consciousness is always *engaged;* there is no question here

of a freedom which would be an indeterminate power and which would pre-exist its choice" (*Etre*, p. 558). Those who refuse to acknowledge this situation are guilty of the most deforming mode of bad faith: *l'esprit de sérieux*, the hypocritical pretense that they take their standards from a transcendent source rather than that they are necessarily creative of these standards. But M. Merleau-Ponty, *Phénoménologie de la perception*, pp. 501-2, notes that a certain mountain will be steep for me, regardless of whether or not I entertain the project of climbing it. The relation of my body to the incline of the mountain imposes a value of steepness and difficulty upon me in any case, and my recognition of this objective relation (or even my resolve to climb) does not create the relation itself. There is no bad faith in acknowledging that my projects must be carried out within situations, physical or moral, that already specify at least some of the relations which the intention must respect.

29. *Etre*, p. 515.

30. See above, note 28. In pre-reflective consciousness, there is no distinction between action and passion, what one wills and what one submits to, voluntary action and involuntary spontaneity. Here, there is no room for autonomy of will as an escape from determinism. "La Transcendance de l'ego," pp. 120-21.

31. *Existentialism*, pp. 52-55. Sartre speaks of these normative statements as nonvaluational, logical judgments, but they derive an obligatory force from a primary will-to-freedom. There is an implicit moral norm contained in the resolve to seek freedom as such. In order to function practically, however, certain particular criteria are introduced, with only the blanket approval of the basic search for freedom.

32. Marcel, *Being and Having*, p. 232. See Sartre's *Existentialism*, pp. 20-21.

33. "Hell is—other people!" *No Exit*. Translated by S. Gilbert. New York, Alfred A. Knopf, Inc., 1948, p. 61.

34. *Etre*, p. 717. Italics mine.

NOTES TO CHAPTER III. JASPERS.

1. *Vernunft und Existenz*. Third edition. Bremen, Johannes Storm, 1949, pp. 108-9 (henceforth cited as *Vernunft*); *Existenzphilosophie*, p. 79; *The Perennial Scope of Philosophy*, pp. 20-22 (henceforth cited as *Scope*).

2. "The Rededication of German Scholarship," *The American Scholar*, Vol. 15, 1946.

3. *Philosophie*. Second edition in one volume. Berlin, Springer-Verlag, 1948, pp. 1-3; 56-60.

4. Dewey frames his basic definition of scientific inquiry in terms of

indeterminate and determinate situations; cf. *Logic, The Theory of Inquiry*. New York, Henry Holt & Company, 1938, pp. 66-67, 104-5; *Problems of Men*. New York, Philosophical Library, 1946, part III, chap. 9.

5. *The Modern Age*, p. 104. Jaspers refers to the condition of mass man as *Massendasein*, a term that corresponds to Heidegger's "unauthentic *Dasein*." But Jaspers reserves the term *Dasein* exclusively for unauthentic, nonexistential conditions, whereas Heidegger allows an undifferentiated structure of *Dasein* and locates existence in an authentic attitude of *Dasein*. See below, note 18.

6. The scientific and existential approaches to man are discussed in part IV of *The Modern Age* and in the first book of *Philosophie;* see also the address on *Philosophie und Wissenschaft*.

7. A critique of naturalistic positivism and idealism is given in *Philosophie*, pp. 182-205. For an authoritative statement of the "antireductionist" platform of recent American naturalism, cf. *Naturalism and the Human Spirit*. Ed. Y. Krikorian. New York, Columbia University Press, 1944. Critics of the latter volume have argued, from the most diverse standpoints, that naturalism is attempting an untenable compromise and must either frankly declare its materialism or acknowledge that reductionism can be avoided only by repudiating the materialist view of mind.

8. Dufrenne and Ricoeur (*Karl Jaspers et la philosophie de l'existence*, p. 355) hazard the guess that Husserl's influence upon Jaspers is very slight because of the adaptation of the theory of intentionality to a sphere of immanence and objectivity, whereas existence moves in the region of transcendence and subjectivity. Yet A. De Waelhens, "Les constantes de l'existentialisme," pp. 259-62, points out the *de facto* similarity between the two approaches, in respect to universality of structure. In *Rechenschaft und Ausblick* (pp. 327-28), Jaspers criticizes Husserl for reducing philosophy to science and scientific universality. A similar criticism is made by Heidegger.

9. Yet Husserl (and in this respect he is followed by all the existentialists) takes Descartes to task for reserving the thinking self from rigorous doubt and thus for retaining the notion of a thinking substance (*Méditations cartésiennes*, pp. 20-21). Jaspers broadens out this charge to include other privileged areas, in addition to the ego.

10. On the Cartesian universalizing of the mathematical method and the ideal of a universal mathematics, see *Descartes und die Philosophie*. Second edition. Berlin, Walter de Gruyter & Co., 1948, pp. 33-49 (henceforth cited as *Descartes*).

11. *Ibid.*, pp. 14-15, 23-30. When Jaspers observes that Descartes' doubt is "a methodic doubt of the understanding, not an existential doubt of faith," p. 16, he is repeating, almost verbatim, Kierkegaard's criticism (*Either/Or*, Vol. 2. Translated by W. Lowrie [Princeton, Princeton University Press, 1944], pp. 178-79).

12. *Descartes*, pp. 68-78, on reason and authority. Jaspers is not opposed to faith and authority but only to their theological modes. His own theory of adhesion to being as the comprehensive entails an authoritative, *philosophical* faith.

13. The most succinct comparison is made in *Vernunft*, lectures 1 and 5.

14. For a psychological comparison between the outlooks of Kierkegaard and Hegel, cf. *Psychologie der Weltanschauungen*. Third edition, 1925, pp. 372, 419-32; Nietzsche's assault on the ideal of absolute truth as a survival of Christianity is examined in *Nietzsche*, pp. 147-204.

15. *Vernunft*, pp. 29-30. Here, as well as in *Nietzsche und das Christentum*, pp. 81-82, Jaspers underlines the fact that both Kierkegaard and Nietzsche regarded themselves as exceptions and did not expect us to follow them directly.

16. *Nietzsche*, pp. 379-92; *Scope*, pp. 171-72.

17. This division corresponds to the subtitles of the three volumes of the original edition of Jaspers' *Philosophie: Weltorientierung, Existenzerhellung* and *Metaphysik*. In his *Einführung in die Philosophie*, p. 159 (henceforth cited as *Einführung*), Jaspers agrees with the old adage that a study of Plato and Kant equips one with all the essentials of philosophizing. He applies to Kant alone the same technical terms that describe his own system. *Einführung*, p. 154; *Von der Wahrheit*, p. 17 (henceforth cited as *Wahrheit*).

18. See the communications sent independently by Heidegger and Jaspers to the French Society of Philosophy, when it held a meeting on "Subjectivité et transcendance." *Bulletin de la Société française de philosophie*, Vol. 37, 1937, pp. 193, 198. On the contrast between *Dasein* and *Existenz*, cf. above, note 5; *Philosophie*, pp. 15-23, 33-38, 295-97; *Wahrheit*, pp. 77-79.

19. For Jaspers' notion of ontology, cf. *Philosophie*, pp. 662 ff.; *Scope*, pp. 26-27, 148-49; *Wahrheit*, pp. 158-61. In the last text cited, he draws up a table of eleven major points of difference between ontology and his own "periechontology" or theory of being as the comprehensive (*das Umgreifende, to periechon*).

20. *Wahrheit*, pp. 841, 844, 859. The main targets here are Aristotle, Aquinas, and Hegel, between whose conceptions of a philosophical system Jaspers uncritically supposes there to be a basic identity. He correlates his attack upon "ontology" with one on "catholicity" or the pretense to give an exclusive and complete account of the truth, whether as Thomistic realism and Catholicism or as Hegelian idealism and Protestantism.

21. The contrast between Thomistic metaphysics and Wolffian ontology is highlighted by E. Gilson, *Being and Some Philosophers*. Toronto, Pontifical Institute of Mediaeval Studies, 1949, pp. 112 ff.

22. *Philosophie*, pp. 12-13, 277-81, 298-99; *Vernunft*, pp. 44-45; *Scope*, pp. 27, 34-35 (where the influence of Kant is acknowledged). "Immediate-

ly experienced being is appearance, which refers to something else; mediately known being cannot be experienced in its own nature. Being which simply is being itself cannot be given as an object either immediately or mediately. It cannot be grasped objectively. . . . The being that I know is not being as such and not the being which I myself am." *Wahrheit*, p. 37.

23. On knowledge and awareness, cf. *Existenzphilosophie*, pp. 14-15. On the limitation of philosophical thought to existential possibility, see *Philosophie*, pp. 302, 471-73. Jaspers shows that even practical thinking falls short of actual deeds, but he does not prove (except through Kantian definitions) that there can be no speculative knowledge of existential actuality and deeds.

24. Concerning the strict limitations placed by St. Thomas upon existential knowledge, see J. Maritain, *Existence and the Existent*. Translated by L. Galantière and G. Phelan. New York, Pantheon Books, 1948, pp. 66-67. If "actual being is the existential actualization of an objective essence, knowledge not only can, but must, be at one and the same time both objective and existential. It is directly objective through abstract concepts; it is directly existential through a certain class of judgments," namely, the judgment of existence. E. Gilson, *Being and Some Philosophers*, p. 188. It is clear that "objective" is not taken here in the Kantian sense but as signifying that which exercises its own act of existing independently of the mental act of judging about that existent.

25. The most elaborate treatment of *Das Umgreifende* is found in part I of *Wahrheit;* see also, *Vernunft*, lecture 2; *Einführung*, chap. 3; *Scope*, pp. 9-21.

26. *Philosophie*, pp. 35-39 (where Kant's notion of a *limit* is accepted, with the proviso that we include a material examination of the actual limits as well as a formal principle), pp. 304-5, 467-512. Jaspers devotes separate sections to the analysis of the limit-situations of death, suffering, conflict, guilt, and the ultimate situation of finite historicity. The full play of Jaspers' psychological and psychiatric training is brought to bear in describing these predicaments of human life.

27. *Philosophie*, pp. 28-31, 42-45, and the entire third book.

28. E. Stein, "Ways to Know God," *The Thomist*, Vol. 9, 1946.

29. The peak of metaphysical ambition is attained in the *Lesen der Chiffreschrift*, the project of reading the code message furnished by human existence and the world concerning transcendence. *Philosophie*, pp. 785 ff. But this plan is futile, since it is an attempt "to decipher without a key" (to use a phrase from the Introduction to Hobbes' *Leviathan*).

30. "The manifesting of transcendence is bound to its appearance in empirical being (*an ihre Erscheinung im Dasein*), in which being itself remains torn asunder." *Philosophie*, p. 42. *Dasein* itself is not authentic existence or being as such, and yet it is only in reference to the sphere of *Dasein* that being itself achieves reality for us and that existence can exer-

cise its freedom. But the empirical context prevents any adequate manifestation of being and any successful project of transcendence, until one is reconciled to the situation.

31. The concluding pages of *Philosophie*, pp. 863-79, are devoted to the ultimate cipher of *Scheitern*, the stranding or failure of all metaphysical efforts. We cannot plan this failure, however, and must do all in our power to avoid it and to persevere in our labors. Thus Jaspers, like Sartre, advocates a heroic effort in the face of inevitable defeat and finds in this Promethean activism a lasting consolation.

32. J. Hersch, *L' Illusion philosophique*, pp. 184-85.

33. For comparative studies along these lines, cf. J. Lotz, "Analogie und Chiffre: Zur Transzendenz in der Scholastik und bei Jaspers." *Scholastik*, Vol. 15, 1940; *ibid.*, "Die Transzendenz bei Jaspers und im Christentum," *Stimmen der Zeit*, Vol. 137, 1939-40.

34. Jaspers never tires of repeating the historical verdict that "since Kant, all ontology is condemned." *Existenzphilosophie*, pp. 17-18. Hence he regards the phenomenon/noumenon distinction as inevitable. But, as M. Geiger pointed out ("An Introduction to Existential Philosophy," *Philosophy and Phenomenological Research*, Vol. 3 [1942-43], p. 276), this assumption is the weakest point in Jaspers' philosophy and the reason why reality and ontological questions tend to disappear.

35. No explanation is given of why the various interpretations of metaphysical failure proposed by Jaspers say nothing and yet all say: *Being*. *Philosophie*, p. 876. Actually, this paradoxical language is forced upon Jaspers, because the only determinate content of the concept of being refers to the free decisions of man. Hence he substitutes a study of our consciousness of God for a knowledge of God. *Einführung*, p. 45. See the following note.

36. Chapter 4 of *Einführung* summarizes Jaspers' Kantian criticisms of these proofs; cf. *Philosophie*, pp. 847-50. Following Kant, Jaspers reduces all such proofs to variations of the so-called ontological argument. As demonstrations, they are purely formal and conceptual statements, lacking in content (a similar view is held by Marcel). Their genuine content or "filling" comes from the human existent's consciousness of being. But this makes the demonstrations to be clarifications of one's own awareness rather than proofs of God's existence, ciphers rather than knowledge-yielding inferences. This is another reason why we cannot make a genuine act of transcendence, such as would place our intelligence and will in relation to the transcendent being.

37. For Jaspers, to know being as being means to know the transcendent in its own reality, apart from all reference to empirical modes of being. Hence the failure of the proofs of God's existence is one with the failure of the science of being as being (ontology) to establish its proper object. *Philosophie*, p. 859.

38. See C. Hartshorne, *The Divine Relativity*. New Haven, Yale University Press, 1948, pp. xii, 1. Hartshorne, too, identifies God in His absolute nature with pure being in general, as abstracting from all particular determinations of being; only in His surrelative nature (in reference to *Dasein*, in Jaspers' language) is God concretely actual, pp. 89-90.

39. J. De Tonquédec (*Une Philosophie existentielle*, p. 127), calls attention to this classical description of God. St. Thomas, *Summa Theologiae*, I. q. 13, a. 11, c.

40. *Philosophie*, p. 732.

41. *Being and Some Philosophers*, p. 28. In *God and Philosophy* (New Haven, Yale University Press, 1941, p. 42) Gilson recalls that the third-century Christian *Hortatory Address to the Greeks* made a similar comparison between Moses and Plato, and concluded that both the personal and the impersonal expressions refer to the one, existing God. For Gilson, however, the difference represents "the dividing line between Greek thought and Christian thought," since the personal designation of God follows from an appreciation of existence as His supreme perfection.

42. In *Existenzphilosophie*, pp. 71-85, and *Vernunft*, pp. 109-15, philosophy of existence is located midway between revealed religion and godlessness; it rests on a faith of its own—philosophical faith. These texts summarize the more involved discussions in *Philosophie*, pp. 211-20, 252-72, 666-72, on finding a mean between the extremes of rationalistic unbelief and theological belief. The comparison with Hegel and Goethe is suggested by A. Brunner, "Philosophie oder Religion?" *Stimmen der Zeit*, Vol. 143, 1949.

43. *Scope*, p. 108.

44. *Existenzphilosophie*, pp. 70-71. Jaspers develops the antithesis in terms of three major problems: actuality and possibility, eternity and historicity, unity and multiplicity. Elsewhere ("Philosophy of Existence and Positive Religion," *The Modern Schoolman*, Vol. 23, 1946), I have tried to examine these three issues in detail, on the basis on Jaspers' prewar writings. For a criticism that has the benefit of the more recent texts, cf. H. Fries, *Ist der Glaube ein Verrat am Menschen?* On the mythical nature of the Christian doctrine on the God-Man, as viewed by Jaspers, cf. *Wahrheit*, p. 1052; *Scope*, p. 106. These two latter works contain long polemics against the "Catholic exclusivity" of orthodox Christianity. *Scope*, pp. 89-96; *Wahrheit*, pp. 834-68. The ultimate choice facing thinking men is one between *reason* (as directed to the ambiguous signs of the comprehensive) and "*Catholicity*" (with its antihumanistic claims to exclusive and adequate revelation). This alternative could easily be rephrased in terms of the naturalistic polemic in America against "supernaturalism and the failure of nerve." Only a thoroughly subordinated, and hence denatured, "Catholicity" is compatible with an absolutely autonomous reason.

Wahrheit, pp. 866-67; cf. *Einführung*, chap. 10, on "The Independence of the Philosophizing Man."

45. *Scope*, p. 82. In *Philosophie*, pp. 818-19, 847-48, Jaspers explains that the endowing of God with personality is a mythological function of prayer, which transfers one's inner awareness of personal self-reality to the godhead, addressing it as a specifically religious *Thou* or personal God. This is not nearly so radical a doctrine as Sartre's, since it allows the possibility of a godhead that is not merely a projection of human consciousness. But it raises a challenge for Marcel, who accepts Husserl's insight that "consciousness is above all consciousness *of* something which is other than itself, what we call self-consciousness being on the contrary a derivative act whose essential nature is, indeed, rather uncertain." *Reflection and Mystery*, p. 52. This general principle of intentionality militates against Jaspers' interpretation of the religious experience, supplying another reason why he steers clear of phenomenology, including the reflections on religion made by Max Scheler which run counter to Jaspers' notion of prayer.

46. *Karl Jaspers et la philosophie de l'existence*, pp. 389-93. The enigmatic and polyvalent character of Jaspers' philosophy is preserved to the end, since the *via media* of philosophical faith is deliberately suspended between Nietzsche and Kierkegaard, on both historical and theoretical grounds. But for a sympathetic attempt to reconcile Jaspers with a Thomism developed along the lines of J. Maréchal's cognitional dynamism, cf. B. Welte, "Der philosophische Glaube bei K. Jaspers und die Möglichkeit seiner Deutung durch die thomistische Philosophie," *Symposion*, Vol. 2, 1949.

Notes to Chapter IV. Marcel.

1. See H. Kuhn, *Encounter with Nothingness*, p. 95; M. Grene, *Dreadful Freedom*, p. 132; G. De Ruggiero, *Existentialism*, pp. 73 ff.

2. *Philosophy of Existence*, p. vii (henceforth cited as *Existence*).

3. *Being and Having*, pp. 82, 137, 148 (henceforth cited as *Being*); *Du Refus à l' invocation*, p. 137 (henceforth cited as *Refus*). For a study of the theory of an absurd universe, defiantly advocated by Georges Bataille and Camus, cf. *Homo Viator*. French edition, pp. 259-93.

4. *Being*, pp. 138, 200-201.

5. See the Foreword to Marcel's play, *Le Monde cassé*. Paris, Desclée, De Brouwer et Cie, 1933, pp. 7-8; *Existence*, pp. 15, 78-79. For a convenient collection of Marcel's scattered remarks on the interplay between thought and drama, cf. G. Fessard's *Théâtre et mystère: Le Sens de l'oeuvre dramatique de Gabriel Marcel*, which precedes Marcel's play, *La Soif*.

6. *Refus*, pp. 22-24, 83-85. I approach being in terms of "my system," when I treat it primarily as a technical problem; but when I recognize being as an inexhaustible mystery, I relinquish all claims to make being a province "of mine." *Being*, pp. 127-28. At the same time, philosophical research must always be a personal task. *Reflection and Mystery*, chap. I (cited henceforth as *Reflection*).

7. "Les Conditions dialectique de la philosophie de l'intuition." *Revue de métaphysique et de morale*, Vol. 20, 1912; "Existence et objectivité." *Ibid.*, Vol. 32, 1925. The latter essay is reprinted as an appendix to *Journal métaphysique*, pp. 309-29 (henceforth cited as *Journal*), and references will be to this appendix.

8. "Les Conditions," pp. 638-40.

9. *Refus*, pp. 21-22.

10. "Les Conditions," pp. 648-50.

11. The imbeddedness of thought in being and its ordination to being are among the major themes in N. Hartmann's *Metaphysik der Erkenntnis*. Second edition, Berlin, Walter de Gruyter, 1925, pp. 43 ff. Similar affirmations are made by Marcel, *Being*, p. 36.

12. *Refus*, pp. 7-9. Nevertheless, Lavelle also subordinates the Cartesian Cogito to the self as a participation in being, maintains that intellect is imbedded or inglobed in being, and emphasizes the importance of "my body" as a criterion of the real. See my article, "Louis Lavelle on Human Participation," *The Philosophical Review*, Vol. 56, 1947, esp. pp. 166-70.

13. *Journal*, pp. 43-45, 315-16; *Existence*, pp. 6-7. Marcel's critical attitude toward Descartes (closely resembling Heidegger's reaction) is emphasized by J. Delhomme, "La Philosophie de M. Gabriel Marcel," *Revue thomiste*, Vol. 44, 1938.

14. *Journal*, pp. 317-22. This passage synthesizes a long series of detached reflections (pp. 235 ff., 250 ff.), which began with the view that the senses are not merely, or even primarily, to be regarded as conveyors of a message about an external world (the notion so dear to empiricism). In uncovering the function of the senses as providing an immediate participation in existence, however, Marcel was also confronted with the problem of interpretation and error in regard to sense deliverances. The instrumental and participative aspects of sensation correspond to the dual treatment of the body as both an object and a part of the human subject. *Refus*, p. 39. Cf. M. Merleau-Ponty, *Phénoménologie de la perception*, pp. 405-8, on how the reality of other selves only becomes a problem when sensation is regarded as an unknown message that needs to be decoded.

15. *Being*, p. 108. Marcel seeks to surmount the alternative of choosing either the Cartesian Cogito or the empirical bundle of perceptions, since the former involves a reduction of contingent reality to rational necessity and the latter a reduction of rational truth to atomic fact. *Journal*, pp. 43-

45. The truths contained in these extreme positions can be appropriated only on condition that the mind admits a prior adhesion to the existent universe in both its individual and its pervasive traits.

16. "When I affirm that something exists, I always mean that I consider this something as connected with my body, as able to be put in contact with it, however indirect this contact may be." *Being*, p. 10; cf. *Reflection*, pp. 88-92. Whether the indirectness of this contact permits the predication of existence to nonincarnated modes of being remains an outstanding question. Cf. below, note 30.

17. "At the starting point of this investigation, we must place an indubitable factor, not logical or rational but existential; if existence is not at the beginning, it will be nowhere. I believe that there is no passage to existence which is not sleight of hand or trickery." *Refus*, p. 25.

18. *Journal*, p. 313.

19. M. De Corte, *La Philosophie de Gabriel Marcel*, chap. 2; J. Maritain, *A Preface to Metaphysics*. New York, Sheed and Ward, 1939, pp. 50-53, 60 (following De Corte). More recently, in a long Introduction to a separate edition of Marcel's *Positions et approches concrètes du mystère ontologique*, De Corte completely revised his opinion, holding now that Marcel has made a successful transition from idealism to realism, indeed, to a Christian Aristotelianism, with assimilated Platonic elements, pp. 14, 39-43. Marcel himself regards his thought as being situated at a juncture of Aristotle and Plato (according to a letter quoted by De Corte, p. 39, note 2). It is doubtful, however, whether Marcel's standpoint can be characterized as Aristotelian, let alone Thomistic. Beyond a broad acceptance of the realistic stress upon the primacy of being, he has always experienced difficulties with the detailed epistemological explanations offered by Maritain and Garrigou-Lagrange, the leading Thomists whom he consulted at the time of his conversion to Catholicism. See *Being*, pp. 30, 38, 98, 121.

20. *Ibid.*, p. 37. The second chapter of *Faith and Reality* studies existence and being, in reference to Gilson's view of existence as the act of being. Marcel thinks that this would make being a genus, of which existence is one mode. His difficulty arises from an attempt to grasp the Thomistic doctrine on existence and being, apart from the theory of essence and existence as constitutive potential and actual co-principles of being. Essence is that subject or potential principle of being, of which existence is the *ultimate* act or perfection. The mutual proportion among the principles constituting any instance of being requires an analogical predication of both being and existence, rather than a relation of genus and mode.

21. *Being*, p. 38. De Corte in *La Philosophie de Gabriel Marcel*, p. 15, quotes this text as proof that Marcel's intended realism is not based upon being as such but upon physical existence (Maritain follows this interpretation). But Marcel is, in fact, wrestling with the peculiar difficulty that

existence has no adequate expression in an idea, but is rather the referent of the judgment of existence.

22. *Being*, p. 122; cf. p. 140, on the two primary affirmations (*this is* and *I affirm it because it is*), both of which presuppose the self-presentation of being to us as the condition for pronouncing the existential judgment.

23. *Refus*, p. 89; *Being*, p. 100.

24. Man so regarded is a member of "a broken world." *Reflection*, pp. 27 ff.

25. Cf. two essays in *Refus*: "Phenomenological Aperçus on Being-in-situation" and "Fundamental Situations and Limit-situations according to Karl Jaspers." Also see, *Being*, pp. 112-13, 122-23; *Reflection*, chap. 7 (where Marcel refers more to "situation" than to "condition").

26. *Existence*, pp. 6-7; *Being*, pp. 109-11. Marcel's question: "What am I, I who ask questions about being?" should be compared with Heidegger, *Sein und Zeit*, pp. 7, 13, 15, on the privileged position of one instance of that-which-is, human *Dasein*, which can inquire about the nature of being as such by asking about its own peculiar mode of being.

27. For the clearest expositions of this distinction, see *Existence*, pp. 8-12; *Being*, pp. 100-101, 114-18, 171; *Reflection*, pp. 211-16.

28. *Refus*, p. 154.

29. *Being*, p. 118. Cf. p. 13, notes 2, 3; *Reflection*, pp. 46-48.

30. In his *Journal*, pp. 33-36, Marcel sought to settle the relation of essence and existence to God. Defining the existent as an empirical reality serving as an object of consciousness, he was compelled to deny existence of God and to refuse Him a corresponding objective nature or essence. But instead of accepting a wholly indeterminate Plotinian One, Marcel declared that God is a definite, transcendent reality and a free power, but not an objective cause. Later on (*Being*, pp. 21-22), he noted that experience of the presence of God makes it repugnant to posit Him as lying beyond truth. In some way, there is "a possibility of having an experience *of* the transcendent as such" (*Reflection*, p. 46), and yet the transcendent still lies beyond existence as an incarnate mode of being.

31. *Being*, pp. 113-18; *Existence*, pp. 12-14; *Reflection*, pp. 83 ff.

32. Marcel's notion of a blindfold intuition and the clarifying task of metaphysics approximates Jaspers' doctrine on the clarification of the modes of encompassing being.

33. Marcel praises the nonsubjective aspect of phenomenological meaning (*Being*, pp. 36, 151, 158) but also claims that a hyperphenomenological sort of reflection is required, if philosophy is to pass beyond the essentialism and "as if" attitude of phenomenology toward the existent world. *Refus*, pp. 106-7. This further reflection provides the proper method of an existential metaphysics. Marcel senses the presence of a contradiction between the self-creative marks of the pure, transcendental ego of phenom-

enology and the participated character of the self as grasped in the metaphysics of existence. He himself tries to show how phenomenology can be subordinated to such a metaphysics in his "Sketch of a Phenomenology and a Metaphysic of Hope." *Homo Viator*, pp. 29 ff.

34. *Being*, pp. 17, 20-21; *Existence*, pp. 12-13; *Refus*, p. 80.

35. "Outlines of a Phenomenology of Having," *Being*, pp. 154 ff.

36. *Journal*, pp. 236-41, 252-53; *Being*, pp. 82-84; *Refus*, pp. 28-31; *Reflection*, pp. 92-102.

37. Marcel's earlier doctrine on the global experience of the existent-in-the-world is now expressed in terms of the self as incarnate and therefore as participating in a world not entirely of its own making. *Refus*, pp. 32-33, 44. From this standpoint, my body manifests the nexus of my presence to the world. I am present to the world not in so far as it is my representation (Schopenhauer) but in so far as it is *not* myself and yet *does* inform me.

38. Cf. above, note 3. The comparison between martyr and suicide is now presented as that between the witness to transcendence and one who refuses to bear such testimony (a return to the literal meaning of "martyr"); cf. the essay, "Testimony and Existentialism," *Existence*, pp. 67 ff.

39. *Journal*, pp. 281-82; *Being*, pp. 40, 70, 75, 89; *Refus*, p. 100. This comes close to the resolute intellectual courage demanded by both Jaspers and Heidegger, in the face of the breakdown of conventional views of man. Marcel contrasts it with the secure block universe of Spinoza and Hegel, thus approaching the standpoint of William James on the actual hazards of our universe.

40. E. Gilson, *L'Etre et l'essence*. Paris, Joseph Vrin, 1948, pp. 307, 319-22; Marcel, *Journal*, pp. 179, 197-98; *Being*, p. 74; *Refus*, pp. 100-102.

41. See the essay, "Creative Fidelity," *Refus*, pp. 192 ff.; *Being*, pp. 41 ff., 95-96, 120; *Existence*, pp. 21-24; *Homo Viator*, pp. 160-66, 177-85.

42. See the analysis of Sartre's *L'Etre et la néant*, in *Homo Viator*, pp. 233 ff.; "Existence and Human Freedom," *Existence*, pp. 32 ff. There is also a valuable earlier note on the Bergsonian view of freedom, which is criticized for not subordinating becoming to being. *Being*, pp. 52-53.

43. L. Lavelle, *De l'Acte*. Paris, Fernand Aubier et Cie, 1946, chap. 11. "Participation and Freedom"; *Being*, pp. 130-35, 173-74; *Existence*, p. 73.

44. Throughout his *Journal*, Marcel scrutinized the proofs of God's existence offered by the Cartesians; in *Being and Having*, he turned to an analysis of the Thomistic proofs or, at least, the formulations of R. Garrigou-Lagrange, *God: His Existence and His Nature*. Translated by B. Rose, 2 vols. St. Louis, B. Herder Book Company, 1934-36. Cf. *Being*, pp. 98, 121; "Meditation on the Idea of a Proof of God's Existence," *Refus*, pp. 226-36, for the difficulties Marcel experienced with this treatment, which did not seem sufficiently existential to him. Another indication of

Marcel's non-existential notion of proof is his remark about "the exemplary character of mathematical demonstration" (*Faith and Reality*, p. 174).

45. *Refus*, pp. 108-10; *Existence*, pp. 29-31. The relations between Christian faith and Marcel's existentialism are explored, although not always with due caution, by P. Colin, "Existentialisme chrétien," in *Existentialisme chrétien: Gabriel Marcel*. Cf. Bibliography, number 138.

46. "Is this non-recognition [of revelation] implied in the very notion of philosophy? What is really being done here is to refuse to allow an intrusion to take place in a system *regarded as* closed." *Being*, p. 133. Italics mine. For a comparative study of this issue between Marcel and Jaspers, cf. P. Ricoeur, *Gabriel Marcel et Karl Jaspers*, part III, chap. 1: "Philosophical Faith and Religious Faith."

NOTES TO CHAPTER V. HEIDEGGER.

1. K. Löwith, "Les Implications politiques de la philosophie de l'existence chez Heidegger," in Sartre's journal, *Temps modernes*, Vol. 2, November 14, 1946, and the critical discussion in the July 1947 issue. Professor Löwith, who was a student and friend of Heidegger, kindly permitted me to examine the German original of this article, which contains important excerpts from letters of Heidegger to the author.

2. For a typical wartime utterance, cf. J. Kraft, "The Philosophy of Existence: Its Structure and Significance," *Philosophy and Phenomenological Research*, Vol. 1, 1941.

3. See the critical reviews of this book by E. Cassirer, *Kantstudien*, Vol. 36, 1931, and H. Levy, *Logos*, Vol. 21, 1932.

4. For analyses of these newer currents, cf. N. Picard, "Nuovi orrizonti dell'ontologia di Martino Heidegger," *Esistenzialismo*, pp. 65-84. See Bibliography, number 23; M. Müller, *Existenzphilosophie im geistigen Leben der Gegenwart*.

5. *Was ist Metaphysik?* Fifth edition, p. 17 (henceforth cited as *Metaphysik*). The Introduction is cited according to this German edition, whereas the main text and Postscript are usually cited in the English translation, *Existence and Being*.

6. R. Carnap, "Überwindung der Metaphysik durch logische Analyse der Sprache," *Erkenntnis*, Vol. 2, 1931; cf. *Philosophy and Logical Syntax*. London, George Routledge & Sons, Ltd., 1935, chap. 1. See the similar positivistic attack upon Sartre made by A. Ayer, "Novelist-Philosophers, V: Jean-Paul Sartre," *Horizon*, Vol. 12, 1945.

7. See above, chap. 3, note 18.

8. *Platons Lehre von der Wahrheit, mit einem Brief über den 'Humanismus'*, p. 54 (henceforth cited as *Brief*; the *Letter* occupies pp. 53-119).

9. A. Delp, *Tragische Existenz, passim;* A. De Waelhens, *La Philoso-phie de Martin Heidegger,* pp. 245-46, 265, 315; M. Beck, "Heidegger: 'Sein und Zeit.' Referat und Kritik." *Philosophische Hefte,* Vol. 1, 1928.

10. In *Scholastik,* Vol. 19, 1944; see also, Lotz's review of Heidegger's recent writings. *Ibid.,* Vols. 20-24, 1949.

11. *Sein und Zeit* closes with the question (pp. 436-38): Can the study of human *Dasein* and temporality serve as an approach to the understand-ing of being as such?

12. *Brief,* p. 72. Heidegger refers to the passage from *Being and Time* to *Time and Being* as a *Kehre,* a reversal or about-face, in order to make explicit the embracing context of being itself and the orientation of time to being.

13. *Sein und Zeit,* pp. 39-40, where the problem of time is characterized as a clue to the apprehension of both human *Dasein* and the history of ontology.

14. *Metaphysik,* p. 7. Cf. Descartes, "Letter to the Translator," *Prin-ciples of Philosophy,* in the English translation of *The Philosophical Works of Descartes* by E. Haldane and G. Ross. 2 vols.; Cambridge, Cam-bridge University Press, 1931, Vol. 1, p. 211.

15. *Sein und Zeit,* pp. 25-26, 421-27; *Metaphysik,* p. 16. The Greek and Patristic views on time are proof that "*Dasein* comprehends itself and being as such from the standpoint of the 'world' and that the ontology de-veloped in this manner corrupts the tradition, which it permits to degen-erate into obviousness and (as with Hegel) into mere matter for rehash-ing." *Sein und Zeit,* p. 22.

16. I *Corinthians* 1 : 20, cited by Heidegger, *Metaphysik,* p. 18. On the internal conflict in the Aristotelian notion of metaphysics, cf. J. Owens, *The Doctrine of Being in the Aristotelian Metaphysics.* Toronto, Pontif-ical Institute of Mediaeval Studies, 1951.

17. *Brief,* pp. 99-101. Heidegger gives only a bare mention (*Sein und Zeit,* p. 93) to the Scholastic theory of the analogical predication of the concept of being. He fails to see the connection established by Aquinas between the meaning of being and the need for analogical predication. Furthermore, he does not observe that the distinction between the pri-mary and secondary analogates in such predication is intended as a safe-guard against merely patterning the meaning of being as such after the being of the material world. For the Thomistic doctrine, cf. J. Anderson, *The Bond of Being.* Saint Louis, B. Herder Book Company, 1949.

18. *Sein und Zeit,* pp. 24-25, 89-101 (this analysis of *res extensa* pre-pares for the criticism of *res cogitans* or mind as a substance); *Holzwege,* p. 220. Chapter 4 of W. Biemel's *Le Concept du monde chez Heidegger,* gives a detailed account of the Heideggerian view of Descartes' construc-tion of the world.

19. *Kant und das Problem der Metaphysik.* Second edition, pp. 127 ff., 186-88, 204 ff. (henceforth cited as *Kant*).

20. *Brief*, p. 82; *Metaphysik*, p. 39 (the English translation, *Existence and Being*, p. 382, fails to bring out the reference to Hegel implied in the phrase "*zum Begriff bringt*"); *Holzwege*, pp. 183-91.

21. *Sein und Zeit*, pp. 11-13; *Kant*, pp. 13-14, 208 ff.; *Vom Wesen des Grundes.* Third edition, 1949, pp. 13-15; *Metaphysik*, p. 19.

22. *Existence and Being*, p. 379; *Metaphysik*, p. 9. In the Introduction to *Kant*, p. 13, he refers to his fundamental ontology as a "metaphysics of human *Dasein*" that is required for making intrinsically possible metaphysics itself (as a study of the things-that-are).

23. *Brief*, pp. 82, 87-88.

24. It is entitled: "Nietzsche's Saying: 'God is dead'." Cf. esp. *Holzwege*, pp. 243-45; *Brief*, p. 85.

25. *Existence and Being*, p. 383. The other two major misinterpretations are that his philosophy paralyzes resolute action by dwelling on morbid and debilitating moods, and that it is an antilogical exaltation of feeling. *Ibid.*, pp. 383-84.

26. These lines are from the "Patmos Hymn" and "The Poet's Vocation," English translation in *Existence and Being*, pp. 275, 286. For a philosophical analysis of each of Hölderlin's poems, see Erich Przywara, *Hölderlin.* Nürnberg, Glock und Lutz, 1949.

27. *Existence and Being*, pp. 391-92. The fact that this comparison appears in the Postscript to *What Is Metaphysics?* rather than in the essays on Hölderlin indicates the close bond between Heidegger's poetical and philosophical studies.

28. *Ibid.*, pp. 285-86. The poet (foreshadowing the philosopher) must not be afraid of the imputation of godlessness, when he declares the withdrawal of the divine. For this declaration is motivated by a strong opposition to idolatry and religious formalism, both of which seek to break down the difference (or, at least, gloss over the importance of the difference) between things in the world and the holy. Kierkegaard's attack upon Christendom is thus re-expressed in terms of fundamental ontology and its poetic analogue.

29. *Existence and Being*, pp. 268-69. Hölderlin's provocative question: "Of what use are poets in a time of need?" is used by Heidegger as the title of an essay on Rilke's *Duino Elegies* and *Sonnets to Orpheus. Holzwege*, pp. 248 ff. The office of poets and philosophers of the naught is to make us aware of the overwhelming neediness and godforsakenness of our time and the ground thereof. Marcel has also written a study on "Rilke, Witness of the Spiritual," *Homo Viator* pp. 297 ff. Relying heavily upon Romano Guardini's exegesis of the *Duino Elegies*, Marcel warns that Rilke's "angels" (whether natural manifestations or poets) are not messengers of the Chris-

tian God. The same qualification must be placed upon the use of this term by Hölderlin and Heidegger. Nevertheless, Marcel recognizes in Rilke a powerful witness to a divine principle, a transcendent reality to which man is summoned.

30. *Brief*, p. 90.

31. In the German, this involves a play on words. "Das Denken ist zugleich Denken des Seins, insofern das Denken, dem Sein *gehörend*, auf das Sein *hört*." *Brief*, p. 57. Italics mine; cf. *Metaphysik*, p. 12.

32. *Brief*, pp. 54-56, 111; *Existence and Being*, pp. 387-89. Cf. p. 356. Heidegger distinguishes between strictness or rigor *(Strenge)* and technical exactness *(Exaktheit)*. Essential thought is rigorous, since it attends to the demands of being, but it does not aim at the exactness of the calculative-technical sciences. Husserl's ideal of a rigorous science can only be fulfilled by fundamental ontology.

33. *Sein und Zeit*, pp. 38, 212. These are related propositions, since they refer to the peculiar capacity of human reality for comprehending being and freely determining its own self-reality. In his explanation of comprehension *(ibid.*, pp. 143-44), Heidegger carefully notes that he is treating possibility as an existential trait rather than as a category of objective being. In the latter sense, it is true that the merely possible "is ontologically lower than actuality and necessity." *Ibid.*, p. 143; the Hegelian categories are in question. A cognate proposition to the ones under fire is the remark that "*the 'essence' of Dasein lies in its existence*." *Ibid.*, p. 42. For a typical Scholastic commentary on these theses, cf. C. Nink, "Grundbegriffe der Philosophie Martin Heideggers," *Philosophisches Jahrbuch*, vol. 45, 1932.

34. Both Heidegger's *das Vermögend-Mögend* (*Brief*, p. 57) and St. Thomas's *potentia activa* are hindered by the ambivalent meaning of "power" (pointed out by Aristotle, in the philosophical lexicon to his *Metaphysics*, 1019a 15-1020a 6; *The Basic Works of Aristotle*, pp. 765-66).

35. *Brief*, p. 80. It is noteworthy that Heidegger formulates the metaphysical problem of the naught in a similar way: "Gibt es das Nichts . . . ?" *Metaphysik*, p. 26.

36. *Brief*, pp. 117-18. In *Sein und Zeit* (pp. 297-301), Heidegger explains that existential resoluteness differentiates authentic from unauthentic existence, since it is one with our grasp upon our true situation in the world and our freedom of self-realization. In *On the Essence of Truth* (*Existence and Being*, p. 342), it is pointed out that resolute freedom is an open resolve, directed to the reception of being rather than to introversion. The readiness to respond to the strenuous demands of being involves danger and willingness to make sacrifices. Cf. Marcel, *Reflection and Mystery*, pp. 15-16, on philosophical freedom and courage. These observations are open, unfortunately, to quite divergent practical interpretations concerning specific lines of action.

37. On the "voice of conscience" as man's self-recall from the unexamined life, cf. *Sein und Zeit*, pp. 268 ff. This is comparable with Heidegger's later remarks on homelessness and homecoming. The man of conscience is later spoken of as a "wanderer in the neighborhood of being." *Brief*, p. 93.

38. *Sein und Zeit*, pp. 153, 313-15; *Metaphysik*, p. 15; *Brief*, pp. 98-99. Cf. W. Biemel, "Husserls Encyclopaedia-Britannica Artikel und Heideggers Anmerkungen dazu," *Tijdschrift voor Philosophie*, vol. 12, 1950, for some comments by Heidegger on the need to go behind the transcendental ego or epistemological subject to a view of man in the light of being. These notes date from 1927.

39. If reason cannot be wholly autonomous in the inquiry into the naught and being, then "the very idea of 'logic' disintegrates in the vortex of a more original questioning." *Existence and Being*, p. 372.

40. *Brief*, pp. 110, 116; *Existence and Being*, p. 388.

41. *Ibid.*, p. 386; cf. Marcel, *Being and Having*, p. 190.

42. On *die Welt des Man*, cf. *Sein und Zeit*, paragraphs 27, 35-38, 51-52; *Brief*, p. 59.

43. *Metaphysik*, p. 15 (commenting on *Sein und Zeit*, paragraphs 63-64, on care and self-being).

44. *Existence and Being*, pp. 332-38.

45. Reflection on the projected nature of human reality (*Sein und Zeit*, pp. 145-46, 260-66) leads one to death and dread, because only in this way is one confronted with the naught in its full significance as the sign of being, which is other than human reality. Cf. A. Schopenhauer, *The World As Will and Idea*. English translation by R. Haldane and J. Kemp, 3 vols., London; Kegan Paul, 1906, Vol. 2, pp. 359-60; *Existence and Being*, p. 385. Being retains its power and primacy over human reality, since the relation of being to the world of that-which-is constitutes the essential condition for all human relations to being and the world. *Brief*, pp. 77-78. Heidegger never questions the full mutuality of the relations between being and that-which-is. In any case, "man is not the essential, but being as the dimension of the ec-static aspect of ex-sistence." *Ibid.*, p. 79.

46. *Metaphysik*, pp. 13-14; *Brief*, pp. 68-69; *Existence and Being*, pp. 335-36, 370-74. Actually, the ontological (and not merely anthropological) interpretation of *Dasein* and other basic notions of *Sein und Zeit* was started in section 43 of *Kant*, pp. 211 ff.; *Vom Wesen des Grundes*, p. 39, note 59.

47. *Brief*, pp. 63 ff., 75, 94.

48. *Ibid.*, p. 84.

49. The second section of part I of *Sein und Zeit* concerns *Dasein* and temporality; cf. paragraph 65, for a sketch of the three modalities of time, especially the future as the primary phenomenon of temporality, as that kind of anticipation of self and death whereby human reality exists finitely. p. 329. This attitude constituting the future is now seen to be also a stand-

ing-open to being as a fullness yet to be achieved. *Metaphysik*, pp. 14-16; *Brief*, pp. 70-71; *Existence and Being*, pp. 334 ff. Once again, an ontological meaning is attached to Kierkegaard's observation that eternity stands in the relation of the future to man.

50. R. Scherer, "Besuch bei Heidegger," *Wort und Wahrheit*, Vol. 2, 1947; *Brief*, pp. 85-86, 101-3.

51. *Existence and Being*, p. 377; cf. *Kant*, pp. 206-7, 221-22.

52. *Brief*, p. 80; *Metaphysik*, p. 21.

53. For the position of these theologians toward philosophy, see L. De-Wolf, *The Religious Revolt Against Reason*. New York, Harper & Brothers, 1949, pp. 23-27, and chap. 2.

NOTES TO CHAPTER VI. EXISTENTIAL THEMES.

1. *Process and Reality*. New York, Macmillan Company, 1929, chap. 1, sections 1-2.

2. A good explanation of the Thomistic view of abstraction in the metaphysical order is given by L. Geiger, "Abstraction et séparation d'après S. Thomas," *Revue des sciences philosophiques et théologiques*, Vol. 31, 1947.

3. See the introductory essay on "An Absurd Line of Reasoning," in Camus's *Le Mythe de Sisyphe*. Paris, Librarie Gallimard, 1942.

4. The historical comparison has been worked out by H. Spiegelberg, "Der Begriff der Intentionalität in der Scholastik, bei Brentano und bei Husserl," *Philosophische Hefte*, Vol. 5, 1936.

5. The latest expression of Lewis's adherence to analytic, a priori truths is made in his Carus Lectures, *An Analysis of Knowledge and Valuation*. Lasalle, Illinois, Open Court, 1946, Book I.

6. Lavelle gives an extensive explanation of the moral interpretation of space and time in *Du Temps et de l'eternité*. Paris, Fernand Aubier et Cie, 1945.

7. *Etre*, part III, chaps. 1, 3.

8. *Being and Having*, pp. 104-7; *Homo Viator*, essay on "Myself and an Other."

9. *Philosophie*, pp. 338 ff., 622 ff.

10. *Sein und Zeit*, pp. 117 ff.

11. *Brief*, pp. 81-82; he speaks here of "history" rather than of "historicity," because he is dealing concretely with Hegel and Sartre, and in order to facilitate the transition from "Geschichte" to "Geschick des Seins."

SELECTED BIBLIOGRAPHY

SELECTED BIBLIOGRAPHY OF EXISTENTIALISM

THIS list includes only a fraction of the vast literature on existentialism. Its purpose is to aid further study in the field and hence it emphasizes works of general orientation, especially in Sections II and III. No primary sources are given in Section III, since it would be misleading to name one or two titles and it would be unbalancing to make a complete catalogue of the writings of Kierkegaard, Nietzsche, and Husserl. Only those later editions of books are mentioned in which there are revisions or additions of some significance. No attempt is made to cover periodical literature. Articles can be tracked down in *Bibliographie de la philosophie* (Paris, Joseph Vrin, 1937 ff.) or in *Revue Philosophique de Louvain, Supplément: Répertoire bibliographique* (Louvain, Institut Supérieur, 1934 ff.).

I. BIBLIOGRAPHIES

1. Douglas, K. *A Critical Bibliography of Existentialism (The French School)*. New Haven, Yale French Studies, 1950.
2. Gérard, J., A. De Waelhens, and J. Lemeere. "Bibliographie sur l'existentialisme," *Revue internationale de philosophie*, 3:343-59, July 1949.
3. Jolivet, R. *Französische Existenzphilosophie (Bibliographische Einführungen in das Studium der Philosophie*, number 9). Bern, A. Francke Ag., 1948.
4. Yanitelli, V. "A Bibliographical Introduction to Existentialism," *The Modern Schoolman*, 26:345-63, May 1949.

II. GENERAL SURVEYS

5. Barrett, W. *What Is Existentialism?* New York, Partisan Review, 1947.
6. Benda, J. *Tradition de l'existentialisme ou les philosophies de la vie.* Paris, Editions Bernard Grasset, 1947.
6a. Blackham, H. *Six Existentialist Thinkers.* London, Macmillan Company, 1951.
7. Bobbio, N. *The Philosophy of Decadentism: A Study in Existentialism.* Translated by D. Moore. Oxford, Basil Blackwell, 1948.
8. Bollnow, O. *Existenzphilosophie.* Second edition. Stuttgart. W. Kohlhammer Verlag, 1947. (Originally, a section in N. Hartmann: *Systematische Philosophie*, 1942.)
9. Fabro, C. *Introduzione all'esistenzialismo.* Milano, Società Editrice "Vita e Pensiero," 1943.
10. Foulquié, P. *Existentialism.* Translated by K. Raine. London, D. Dobson, 1948.

10a. Gabriel, L. *Existenzphilosophie. Von Kierkegaard bis Sartre.* Wien, Herold, 1951.

11. Grene, M. *Dreadful Freedom: A Critique of Existentialism.* Chicago, University of Chicago Press, 1948.

12. Harper, R. *Existentialism, a Theory of Man.* Cambridge, Harvard University Press, 1948.

13. Hessen, J. *Existenz-Philosophie.* Basel, Morus-Verlag, 1948.

14. Jolivet, R. *Les Doctrines existentialistes de Kierkegaard à Sartre.* Abbaye St Wandrille, Editions de Fontenelle, 1948.

15. Kuhn, H. *Encounter with Nothingness: An Essay on Existentialism.* Chicago, Henry Regnery Company, 1949.

16. Lukács, G. *Existentialisme ou marxisme?* Translated by E. Kelemen. Paris, Editions Nagel, 1948.

17. Mounier, E. *Existentialist Philosophies, an Introduction.* Translated by E. Blow. London, Rockliff Publishing Corp., 1948.

18. Pareyson, L. *Studi sull'esistenzialismo.* Firenze, G. C. Sansoni, 1943.

19. Ruggiero, G. de. *Existentialism, Disintegration of Man's Soul.* Translated by E. Cocks, with Introduction by R. Heppenstall. New York, Social Sciences Publishers, 1948.

20. Troisfontaines, R. *Existentialism and Christian Thought.* Translated by M. Jarrett-Kerr. London, A. & C. Black, 1950.

21. Verneaux, R. *Leçons sur l'existentialisme et ses formes principales.* Paris, Pierre Téqui, *s.d.*

22. Wahl, J. *A Short History of Existentialism.* Translated by F. Williams and S. Maron. New York, Philosophical Library, 1949.

23. *Acta Pontificiae Academiae Romanae Sancti Thomae Aquinatis,* new series, Vol. 13: *Esistenzialismo.* Torino, Mario E. Marietti, 1947.

24. *Archivio di filosofia,* anno 15, Vols. 1-2, 1946: *Esistenzialismo.*

25. *Atti del Congresso Internazionale di Filosofia,* Vol. 2: *L'Esistenzialismo.* Edited by E. Castelli. Milano, Castellani & C., 1948.

26. "L'Existentialisme devant l'opinion philosophique," *Revue internationale de philosophie,* Tome 3, July 1949.

III. KIERKEGAARD, NIETZSCHE, HUSSERL

A. *Sören Kierkegaard.*

27. Bohlin, T. *Sören Kierkegaard, l'homme et l'oeuvre.* Translated by P. Tisseau. Bazoges-en-Pareds, Chez le traducteur, 1941.

28. Chaning-Pearce, M. *The Terrible Crystal: Studies in Kierkegaard and Modern Christianity.* New York, Oxford University Press, 1941.

29. Jolivet, R. *Introduction to Kierkegaard.* Translated by W. Barber. New York. E. P. Dutton & Company, 1951.

30. Lowrie, W. *Kierkegaard*. New York, Oxford University Press, 1938.

31. Mesnard, P. *Le Vrai visage de Kierkegaard*. Paris, Gabriel Beauchesne et ses Fils, 1948.

32. Ruttenbeck, W. *Sören Kierkegaard: Der christliche Denker und sein Werk*. Berlin, Trowitzsch & Sohn, 1929.

33. Swenson, D. *Something about Kierkegaard*. Minneapolis, Augsburg Publishing House, 1941.

34. Thomte, R. *Kierkegaard's Philosophy of Religion*. Princeton, N. J., Princeton University Press, 1948.

35. Wahl, J. *Etudes Kierkegaardiennes*. Paris, Fernand Aubier et Cie, 1938.

B. *Friedrich Nietzsche*. (See also numbers 89, 92.)

36. Copleston, F. *Friedrich Nietzsche, Philosopher of Culture*. London, Burns, Oates and Washbourne, 1942.

37. Kaufmann, W. *Nietzsche: Philosopher, Psychologist, Antichrist*. Princeton, Princeton University Press, 1950.

38. Löwith, K. *Kierkegaard und Nietzsche, oder philosophische und theologische Überwindung des Nihilismus*. Frankfurt, Vittorio Klostermann, 1933.

39. ———. *Von Hegel bis Nietzsche*. Zürich, Europa Verlag, 1941.

40. Lubac, H. de. *The Drama of Atheist Humanism*. Translated by E. Riley. London, Sheed and Ward, 1949.

41. Morgan, G. *What Nietzsche Means*. Cambridge, Harvard University Press, 1941.

42. Reyburn, H., with H. Hinderks and J. Taylor. *Nietzsche, the Story of a Human Philosopher*. London, Macmillan Company, 1948.

C. *Edmund Husserl*.

43. Berger, G. *Le Cogito dans la philosophie de Husserl*. Paris, Fernand Aubier et Cie, 1941.

44. Brunner, A. *La Personne incarnée: Etude sur la phénoménologie et la philosophie existentialiste*. Paris, Gabriel Beauchesne et ses Fils, 1947.

45. Farber, M., editor. *Philosophical Essays in Memory of Edmund Husserl*. Cambridge, Harvard University Press, 1940.

46. ———, author. *The Foundation of Phenomenology: Edmund Husserl and the Quest for a Rigorous Science of Philosophy*. Cambridge, Harvard University Press, 1943.

47. Folwart, H. *Kant, Husserl, Heidegger: Kritizismus, Phänomenologie, Existenzialontologie*. Ohlau, Verlag Eschenhagen, 1936.

48. Landgrebe, L. *Phänomenologie und Metaphysik*. Hamburg, Marion von Schröder Verlag, 1949.

49. Levinas, E. *En Découvrant l'existence avec Husserl et Heidegger.* Paris, Joseph Vrin, 1949.

50. Merleau-Ponty, M. *Phénoménologie de la perception.* Paris, Librairie Gallimard, 1945.

50a. De Waelhens, A. *Une Philosophie de l'ambiguïté: L'Existentialisme de Maurice Merleau-Ponty.* Louvain, Publications Universitaires, 1951.

51. Vanni Rovighi, S. *La Filosofia di Edmund Husserl.* Milano, Società Editrice "Vita e Pensiero," 1939.

52. Welch, E. *The Philosophy of Edmund Husserl: The Origin and Development of his Phenomenology.* New York, Columbia University Press, 1941.

IV. JEAN-PAUL SARTRE

A. *Sources.*

53. *L'Imagination.* Paris, Presses Universitaires de France, 1936.

54. *Esquisse d'une théorie des émotions.* Paris, Hermann et Cie, Editeurs, 1939.

55. *L'Imaginaire: Psychologie phénoménologique de l'imagination.* Paris, Librairie Gallimard, 1940.

56. *L'Etre et le néant: Essai d'ontologie phénoménologique.* Paris, Librairie Gallimard, 1943.

57. *L'Existentialisme est un humanisme.* Paris, Editions Nagel, 1946.

58. *Situations, I, II et III.* Paris, Librairie Gallimard, 1947, 1948, 1949.

59. Sartre's literary works include: a) Novels: *La Nausée, Les Chemins de la liberté* [*L'Age de raison, Le Sursis, La Mort dans l'âme, La Dernière chance*]; b) Plays: *Théâtre, I* [*Les Mouches, Huis clos, Morts sans sépulture, La Putain respectueuse*], *Les Jeux sont faits, Le Mains sales*; c) Short stories: *Le Mur;* d) Criticism: *Baudelaire,* and some of the essays in number 58.

B. *English Translations.*

60. *Existentialism.* Translated by B. Frechtman. New York, Philosophical Library, 1947. (Translation of work listed in number 57.)

61. *The Psychology of Imagination.* New York, Philosophical Library, 1948. (Translation of work listed in number 55.)

62. *The Emotions: Outline of a Theory.* Translated by B. Frechtman. New York, Philosophical Library, 1948. (Translation of work listed in number 54.)

63. *Anti-Semite and Jew.* Translated by G. Becker. New York, Schocken, 1948. (Translated from *Réflexions sur la Question Juive.* Paris, Paul Morihien, 1946.)

64. N. B., Most of Sartre's literary works, listed in number 59, have been translated into English.

C. *Studies* (See also numbers 44, 50.)

65. Beigbeder, M. *L'Homme Sartre: Essai de dévoilement préexistentiel.* Paris, Pierre Bordas, 1947.

66. Campbell, R. *Jean-Paul Sartre ou une littérature philosophique.* Paris, Editions Pierre Ardent, 1945.

67. Dempsey, P. *The Psychology of Sartre.* Westminster, Md., Newman Press, 1950.

68. Farber, M., editor. *Philosophic Thought in France and the United States.* Buffalo, University of Buffalo Press, 1950.

69. Jeanson, F. *Le Problème morale et la pensée de Sartre.* Paris, Editions du Myrte, 1947.

70. Jolivet, R. *Le Problème de la mort chez M. Heidegger et J.-P. Sartre.* Abbaye St Wandrille, Editions de Fontenelle, 1950.

70a. Natanson, M. *A Critique of Jean-Paul Sartre's Ontology.* Lincoln, University of Nebraska Press, 1951.

71. Pruche, B. *Existentialisme et acte d'être.* Paris, B. Arthaud, 1947.

72. ———. *L'Homme de Sartre.* Paris, B. Arthaud, 1949.

73. Quiles, I. *El existencialismo del absurdo.* Buenos Aires, Espasa Calpe Argentina, 1949.

74. Sánchez Villaseñor, J. *Introduccion al pensamiento de Jean-Paul Sartre.* Mexico City, Editorial Jus, 1950.

75. Stefani, M. *La libertà esistenziale in J.-P. Sartre.* Milano, Società Editrice "Vita e Pensiero," 1950.

76. Troisfontaines, R. *Le Choix de Jean-Paul Sartre: Exposé et critique de 'L'Etre et le néant.'* Second edition, revised and enlarged. Paris, Fernand Aubier et Cie, 1946.

77. Varet, G. *L'Ontologie de Sartre.* Paris, Presses Universitaires de France, 1948.

78. Vietta, E. *Versuch über die menschliche Existenz in der modernen französischen Philosophie: Zum philosophischen Werk von Jean-Paul Sartre.* Hamburg, Hauswedel Verlag, 1948. Revised and enlarged edition of *Theologie ohne Gott.* Zürich, Artemis Verlag, 1946.

79. *Revue de philosophie*, année 1946: *L'Existentialisme.* Paris, Pierre Téqui, 1947.

V. KARL JASPERS

A. *Sources.*

80. *Allgemeine Psychopathologie.* Fifth edition, completely re-written. Berlin, Springer-Verlag, 1946. (First edition, 1913; revised second edition, 1919.)

81. *Psychologie der Weltanschauungen.* Second edition, slightly revised. Berlin, Springer-Verlag, 1922. (First edition, 1919.)

82. *Max Weber.* Tübingen, J. L. B. Mohr, 1921.

83. *Strindberg und van Gogh.* Second edition, enlarged. Berlin, Springer-Verlag, 1926. (First edition; Bern, E. Bircher, 1922.)

84. *Die Idee der Universität.* Berlin, Springer-Verlag, 1923.

85. *Die geistige Situation der Zeit (1931).* Fifth edition, revised. Berlin, Walter de Gruyter & Co., 1932. (First edition, 1931.)

86. *Max Weber: Deutsches Wesen im politischen Denken, im Forschen und Philosophieren.* Oldenburg, G. Stalling, 1932.

87. *Philosophie.* 3 vols. Berlin, Springer-Verlag, 1932.

88. *Vernunft und Existenz.* Groningen, Batavia, J. B. Wolters, 1935.

89. *Nietzsche: Einführung in das Verständnis seines Philosophierens.* Berlin, Walter de Gruyter & Co., 1936.

90. *Descartes und die Philosophie.* Berlin, Walter de Gruyter & Co., 1937.

91. *Existenzphilosophie.* Berlin, Walter de Gruyter & Co., 1938.

92. *Nietzsche und das Christentum.* Hamelin, Verlag der Bücherstube Fritz Seifert, 1946.

93. *Die Schuldfrage.* Heidelberg, Verlag Lambert Schneider, 1946.

94. *Vom lebendigen Geist der Universität.* Heidelberg, Verlag Lambert Schneider, 1946.

95. *Die Idee der Universität.* Berlin, Springer-Verlag, 1946. (Entirely different book from that listed in number 84.)

96. *Vom europaischen Geist.* München, R. Piper & Co. Verlag, 1947.

97. *Philosophische Logik, Band I: Von der Wahrheit.* München, R. Piper & Co. Verlag, 1947.

98. *Die Antwort an Sigred Undset, mit Beiträgen über die Wissenschaft im Hitlerstaat und den neuen Geist der Universität.* Konstanz, Südverlag, 1947.

99. *Unsere Zukunft und Goethe.* Zürich, Artemis Verlag, 1948.

100. *Der philosophische Glaube.* München, R. Piper & Co. Verlag, 1948.

101. *Philosophie und Wissenschaft.* Zürich, Artemis Verlag, 1949.

102. *Vom Ursprung und Ziel der Geschichte.* Zürich, Artemis Verlag, 1949.

103. *Einführung in die Philosophie.* Zürich, Artemis Verlag, 1950.

104. *Vernunft und Unvernunft in unserer Zeit.* München, R. Piper & Co. Verlag, 1950.

104a. *Rechenschaft und Ausblick.* München, R. Piper & Co. Verlag, 1951. (Includes numbers 82, 94, 96, 98, 99, 101.)

B. *English Translations.*

105. *Man in the Modern Age.* Translated by E. Paul. London, George Routledge & Sons, 1933. (Translation of work listed in number 85.)

106. *The European Spirit.* Translated by R. Smith. London, Student Christian Movement Press, 1948. (Translation of work listed in number 96.)

107. *The Perennial Scope of Philosophy.* Translated by R. Manheim. New York, Philosophical Library, 1949. (Translation of work listed in number 100.)

107a. *Way to Wisdom.* Translated by R. Manheim. New Haven, Yale University Press, 1951. (Translation of work listed in number 103.)

C. *Studies* (See also number 35.)

108. Allen, E. *The Self and Its Hazards: A Guide to the Thought of Karl Jaspers.* New York, Philosophical Library, 1951.

109. Brock, W. *An Introduction to Contemporary German Philosophy.* Cambridge, Cambridge University Press, 1935.

110. Dufrenne, M. and P. Ricoeur. *Karl Jaspers et la philosophie de l'existence.* Paris, Editions du Seuil, 1947.

111. Feith, R. *Psychologismus und Transzendentalismus bei Karl Jaspers.* Bern, Buchdrückerei K. Naumann, 1945.

112. Fries, H. *Ist der Glaube ein Verrat am Menschen? Eine Begegnung mit Karl Jaspers.* Stuttgart, Schwaben Verlag, 1948.

113. Hersch, J. *L'Illusion philosophique.* Paris, Félix Alcan, 1936.

114. Jaspers, L. *Der Begriff der menschlichen Situation in der Existenzphilosophie von Karl Jaspers.* Würzburg, Universitätsdrückerei, 1936.

115. Lehmann, K. *Der Tod bei Heidegger und Jaspers, Ein Beitrag zur Frage: Existenzialphilosophie, Existenzphilosophie und protestantische Theologie.* Heidelberg, Evangelischer Verlag Jakob Comtesse, 1938.

116. Paci, E. *Pensiero, esistenza e valore.* Milano, Principato, 1940.

117. Pareyson, L. *La filosofia dell'esistenza e Carlo Jaspers.* Napoli, Loffredo, 1940.

118. Pfeiffer, J. *Existenzphilosophie: Eine Einführung in Heidegger und Jaspers.* Second edition, revised. Hamburg, Felix Meiner, 1949. (First edition, Leipzig, 1933.)

119. Ramming, G. *Karl Jaspers und Heinrich Rickert: Existenzialismus und Wertphilosophie.* Bern, A. Francke Ag., 1948.

120. Ricoeur, P. *Gabriel Marcel et Karl Jaspers: Philosophie du mystère et philosophie du paradoxe.* Paris, Editions du Temps présent, 1947.

121. Tonquédec. J. de. *Une Philosophie Existientielle: L'Existence d'après Karl Jaspers.* Paris, Gabriel Beauchesne et ses Fils, 1945.

V. GABRIEL MARCEL

A. *Sources.*

122. *La Métaphysique de Royce.* Paris, Fernand Aubier et Cie, 1945. (Reprint of four articles originally published in *Revue de métaphysique et de morale,* vols. 25-26, 1918-1919.)

123. *Journal métaphysique, 1913-1923.* Paris, Librairie Gallimard, 1927.
124. *Positions et approches concrètes du mystère ontologique,* preceded by Marcel's play, *Le Monde cassé.* Paris, Desclée, De Brouwer et Cie, 1933. Also issued separately, with an Introduction by M. De Corte. Paris, Joseph Vrin, 1949.
125. *Etre et avoir.* Paris, Fernand Aubier et Cie, 1935.
126. *Du Refus à l'invocation.* Paris, Librairie Gallimard, 1940.
127. *Homo Viator: Prolégomènes à une métaphysique de l'espérance.* Paris, Fernand Aubier et Cie, 1944.
128. *Le Mystère de l'être.* Tome 1: *Réflexion et mystère.* Tome 2: *Foi et Réalité.* Paris, Fernand Aubier et Cie, 1951.
128a. *Les hommes contre l'humain.* Paris, Fernand Aubier et Cie, 1951.
129. Marcel's dramatic works include: *Le Seuil invisible* [*La Grâce, Le Palais de sable*], *Le Coeur des autres, Le Quatuor en fa dièse, Un Homme de Dieu, L'Iconoclaste, Trois pièces* [*Le Regard neuf, Le Mort de demain, La Chapelle ardente*], *Le Chemin de Crête, Le Dard, Le Fanal, La Soif, La Grille, Pièces comiques.*

B. *English Translations.*

130. *The Philosophy of Existence.* Translated by M. Harari. New York, Philosophical Library, 1949. (Translation of the work listed in number 124, together with two articles published in 1946 in *Nouvelle revue théologique,* tome 68, and *Temps présent.* Also included is the concluding autobiographical essay contributed to the work listed in number 138.)
131. *Being and Having.* Translated by K. Farrer. Boston, The Beacon Press, 1951. (Translation of the work listed in number 125.)
131a. *Homo Viator: Introduction to a Metaphysic of Hope.* Translated by Emma Craufurd. Chicago, Henry Regnery Company, 1951. (Translation of the work listed in number 127.)
132. *The Mystery of Being.* Vol. 1: *Reflection and Mystery.* Translated by G. Fraser. Vol. 2: *Faith and Reality.* Translated by R. Hague. Chicago, Henry Regnery Company, 1951. (Translation of the work listed in number 128.)
133. *A Metaphysical Journal.* Translated by B. Wall. Chicago, Henry Regnery Company, (to be published in 1952). (Translation of the work listed in number 123.)

C. *Studies.*

134. Bespaloff, R. *Cheminements et carrefours.* Paris, Joseph Vrin, 1938.
135. De Corte, M. *Introduction* to the work listed in number 124, as reissued. Paris, Joseph Vrin, 1949.
136. ———. *La Philosophie de Gabriel Marcel.* Paris, Pierre Téqui, *s.d.*
137. Fessard, G. *Théâtre et mystère: Le Sens de l'oeuvre dramatique de*

Gabriel Marcel. Paris, Desclée, De Brouwer et Cie, 1938. (Printed with Marcel's play, *La Soif.*)
138. Gilson, E., *et al. Existentialisme chrétienne: Gabriel Marcel.* Paris, Librairie Plon, 1947.
139 Prini, P. *Gabriel Marcel e la metodologia dell'inverificabile.* Roma, Editrice Studium Christi, 1950.
140. Vassalo, A. *Nuevos prolegómenos a la metafísica.* Buenos Aires, Editorial Losada, 1938.
141. Wahl, J. *Vers le concrèt: Etudes d'histoire de la philosophie contemporaine.* Paris, Joseph Vrin, 1932.
142. Zoccoletti, M. *La filosofia dell'esistenza secondo Gabriel Marcel.* Padova, CEDAM, 1942.

VII. MARTIN HEIDEGGER

A. Sources.

143. *Die Lehre vom Urteil im Psychologismus: Ein kritisch-positiver Beitrag zur Logik.* Leipzig, Johann Ambrosius Barth, 1914.
144. *Die Kategorien— und Bedeutungslehre des Duns Scotus.* Tübingen, Verlag von J. C. B. Mohr, 1916.
145. *Sein und Zeit, Erste Hälfte.* Halle, Max Niemeyer Verlag, 1927. (Offprint from *Jahrbuch für Philosophie und phänomenologische Forschung,* Vol. 8, 1927.)
146. *Kant und das Problem der Metaphysik.* Bonn, Verlag Friedrich Cohen, 1929.
147. *Vom Wesen des Grundes.* Third edition, with Foreword added. Frankfurt, Vittorio Klostermann, 1949. (First edition, Halle, Max Niemeyer Verlag, 1929; offprint from *Jahrbuch für Phil. u. phän. Forschung, Ergänzungsband: Festschrift E. Husserl,* 1929.)
148. *Was ist Metaphysik?* Fifth edition, with Introduction and Afterword added. Frankfurt, Vittorio Klostermann, 1949. (First edition, Bonn, Verlag Friedrich Cohen, 1930; the Afterword was added to the fourth edition, 1943, and was retained thereafter; the Introduction was added to the fifth edition.)
149. *Die Selbstbehauptung der deutschen Universität.* Breslau, Verlag Korn, 1933.
150. *Platons Lehre von der Wahrheit, mit einem Brief über den 'Humanismus.'* Bern, A. Francke Ag., 1947. (*Platons Lehre* first published in Vol. 2 of E. Grassi's *Geistige Überlieferung,* 1942; the *Brief,* a reply to questions sent by Jean Beaufret in 1946.)
151. *Vom Wesen der Wahrheit.* Second edition, with slight addition. Frankfurt, Vittorio Klostermann, 1949. (First edition, 1943.)
152. *Erläuterungen zu Hölderlins Dichtung.* Frankfurt-am-Main, Vit-

torio Klostermann, 1944. (Contains third edition of *Hölderlin und das Wesen der Dichtung* [first published separately at München, Albert Langen and Georg Müller, 1937], with Foreword added; also contains *Andenken an den Dichter: 'Heimkunft–An die Verwandten.'*)

153. In 1951, there was published a "second, unchanged" edition of *Erläuterungen zu Hölderlins Dichtung.* But it also contains: *Hölderlins Hymne: 'Wie wenn am Feiertage . . .'* [first published, Halle, Max Niemeyer Verlag, 1941] and *Hölderlins Gedicht: 'Andenken'* [first published in the collective volume, *Hölderlin-Gedenkschrift.* Tübingen, J. C. B. Mohr, 1943].

154. *Holzwege.* Frankfurt, Vittorio Klostermann, 1950.

B. *English Translation.*

155. *Existence and Being.* Translated by D. Scott, R. Hull, and A. Crick. With Introduction by W. Brock. Chicago, Henry Regnery Company, 1949. (Translation of the work listed in numbers 148 [the fourth edition], 151, 152.)

C. *Studies* (See numbers 47, 49, 109, 115, 118.)

156. Astrada, C., *et al. Martin Heideggers Einfluss auf die Wissenschaften.* Bern, A. Francke Ag., 1949.

157. Biemel, W. *Le concept de monde chez Heidegger.* Louvain, E. Nauwelaerts, 1951.

158. Brock, W. Introduction to work listed in number 155.

159. Chiodi, P. *L'esistenzialismo di Heidegger.* Torino, Taylor, 1947.

160. Delp, A. *Tragische Existenz: Zur Philosophie Martin Heideggers.* Freiburg, Herder Verlag, 1935.

161. De Waelhens, A. *La Philosophie de Martin Heidegger.* Louvain, E. Nauwelaerts, 1942.

162. De Waelhens, A., and W. Biemel. Introduction to their French translation of the work listed in number 151: *De l'Essence de la verité.* Paris, Joseph Vrin, 1948.

163. Fischer, A. *Die Existenzphilosophie Martin Heideggers.* Leipzig, Felix Meiner, 1935.

164. Heinemann, F. *Neue Wege der Philosophie: Geist, Leben, Existenz.* Leipzig, Verlag Quelle und Meyer, 1929.

165. Hoberg, C. *Das Dasein des Menschen: Die Grundfrage der Heideggerschen Philosophie.* Zeulenroda, Sporn, 1937.

166. Marcic, R. *Martin Heidegger und die Existenzphilosophie.* Bad Ischl, Philosophische Gesellschaft, 1949.

167. Müller, M. *Existenzphilosophie im geistigen Leben der Gegenwart.* Heidelberg, F. H. Kerle-Verlag, 1949.

168. Sternberger, A. *Der verstandene Tod: Eine Untersuchung zu Martin Heideggers Existenzialontologie.* Leipzig, S. Hirzel, 1934.
169. Vanni Rovighi, S. *Heidegger.* Brescia, Ed. La Scuola, 1945.
170. Vietta, E. [pseudonym for Egon Fritz]. *Die Seinsfrage bei Heidegger.* Stuttgart, C. E. Schwab, 1950.
171. Wagner de Reyna, A. *La ontologia fundamental de Heidegger.* Buenos Aires, Editorial Losada, 1939.
172. *Anteile: Martin Heidegger zum 60. Geburtstag.* Frankfurt, Vittorio Klostermann, 1950.

INDEX

INDEX

(This Index is intended primarily as an aid to the inductive study of existentialist themes in their several developments. Page numbers in **boldface type** indicate key references.)